LANGUAGE,

THOUGHT,

and REALITY

LANGUAGE,
THOUGHT,
and REALITY

SELECTED WRITINGS OF BENJAMIN LEE WHORF

Edited and with an introduction by
JOHN B. CARROLL

Foreword by STUART CHASE

THE M.I.T. PRESS
Massachusetts Institute of Technology
Cambridge, Massachusetts

Second printing, August 1962
Third printing, first MIT Press paperback printing, December 1963
Fourth printing, December 1965
Fifth printing, April 1967
Sixth printing, April 1969
Seventh printing, December 1970
Eighth printing, August 1971
Ninth printing, August 1972
Tenth printing, October 1973
Eleventh printing, June 1974
Twelfth printing, January 1976
Thirteenth printing, January 1978

ISBN 0 262 23003 8 (hardcover)
ISBN 0 262 73006 5 (paperback)

Library of Congress catalog card number: 56-5367
Printed in the United States of America

FOREWORD

Once in a blue moon a man comes along who grasps the relationship between events which have hitherto seemed quite separate, and gives mankind a new dimension of knowledge. Einstein, demonstrating the relativity of space and time, was such a man. In another field and on a less cosmic level, Benjamin Lee Whorf was one, to rank some day perhaps with such great social scientists as Franz Boas and William James.

He grasped the relationship between human language and human thinking, how language indeed can shape our innermost thoughts.

We are thus introduced to a new principle of relativity, which holds that all observers are not led by the same physical evidence to the same picture of the universe, unless their linguistic backgrounds are similar, or can in some way be calibrated.

Indo-European languages can be roughly calibrated—English, French, German, Russian, Latin, Greek, and the rest; but when it comes to Chinese, Maya, and Hopi, calibration, says Whorf, is structurally difficult if not impossible. Speakers of Chinese dissect nature and the universe differently from Western speakers. A still different dissection is made by various groups of American Indians, Africans, and the speakers of many other tongues.

Whorf was a profound scholar in the comparatively new science of linguistics. One reason why he casts so long a shadow, I believe, is that he did not train for it. He trained for chemical engineering at M.I.T., and thus acquired a laboratory approach and frame of reference. The work in linguistics was literally wrung out of him. Some driving inner compulsion forced him to the study of words and language—not, if you please, the mastery of foreign languages, but the why and how of language, any language, and its competence as a vehicle for meaning.

As a writer, I have long been interested in semantics, sometimes defined as "the systematic study of meaning." It does a writer no harm, I hold, to know what he is talking about. Whorf, using linguistics as a tool for the analysis of meaning, has made an important contribution to semantics. No careful student of communication and meaning can afford to neglect him. One might add that no philosophical scientist or scientific philosopher can afford to neglect him. Linguistics, he boldly proclaims, "is fundamental to the theory of thinking, and in the last analysis to all human sciences." He is probably right. Every considerable advance in science, such as quantum theory, involves a crisis in communication. The discoverers have to explain first to themselves, and then to the scientific world, what has been found.

Whorf as I read him makes two cardinal hypotheses:

First, that all higher levels of thinking are dependent on language.

Second, that the structure of the language one habitually uses influences the manner in which one understands his environment. The picture of the universe shifts from tongue to tongue.

II

There is a good deal of competent scientific support for the first hypothesis. The biologist, Julian Huxley, for instance, declares that "the evolution of verbal concepts opened the door to all further achievements of man's thought." Language, observes Whorf, is the best show man puts on. Other creatures have developed rough communication systems, but no true language. Language is cardinal in rearing human young, in organizing human communities, in handing down the culture from generation to generation. Huxley goes so far as to venture that adaptation through the culture, depending, of course, on language, may be displacing the biological processes of evolution. When the next Ice Age moves down, for instance, instead of growing more fur, *homo sapiens* may step up the production of air-conditioning units.

The power to reason constitutes the "uniqueness of man," to philosophers as well as biologists. Unprotected by claws, teeth, thick hide, fleetness of foot, or sheer strength, *homo sapiens* has to think his way out of tight places. It has been his chief weapon for survival.

Probably everyone experiences brainstorms too fast to be verbal. In writing, I frequently have them. But before I can handle such bolts from the blue, I must verbalize them, put them into words for sober reflection, or discussion. Unverbalized brainstorms do not get any-where on paper.

Perhaps driving a car furnishes a good analogy for Whorf's initial hypothesis. Light waves and sound waves are enough to guide the driver's hand on the wheel along straight roads. But threading his way through a cloverleaf intersection, or reading a road map, will require a good deal more than reflex action. The first, a very clever chimpanzee might learn to do; the second is forever beyond it.

III

The Greeks, so active mentally, and so reluctant to exert themselves in observation post and laboratory,[1] were the first to inquire into logic and reason. The Sophists were apparently the Madison Avenue boys of the Aegean, teaching young men how to capsize an opponent in de-bate or legal case, and to choose the most effective slogans in political campaigns. Aristotle invented the syllogism, and fashioned his Three Laws of Thought, beginning with the Law of Identity, A is A, now and forever—against which we semanticists sometimes protest.

The Greeks took it for granted that back of language was a universal, uncontaminated essence of reason, shared by all men, at least by all thinkers. Words, they believed, were but the medium in which this deeper effulgence found expression. It followed that a line of thought expressed in any language could be translated without loss of meaning into any other language.

This view has persisted for 2500 years, especially in academic groves. Whorf flatly challenges it in his second major hypothesis. "A change in language," he says, "can transform our appreciation of the Cosmos."

The day-by-day experience of skilled translators at the United Na-tions goes a long way to support him. Edmund S. Glenn of the State Department, for instance, aided by a grant from the Rockefeller Foun-dation, has waded through masses of U.N. transcriptions, looking for differences in concepts due to language.[2] An English speaker in one of Mr. Glenn's cases says "I assume"; the French interpreter renders it "I

[1] James Harvey Robinson, the historian, lays it to the large number of slaves.
[2] Peter T. White, "The Interpreter: Linguist Plus Diplomat." New York *Times* Magazine, November 6, 1955.

deduce"; and the Russian interpreter "I consider"— By that time the
assumption idea is gone with the wind!

After isolating twenty similar instances, Mr. Glenn concludes that,
while the translation technique was smooth enough on the surface,
"the degree of communication between the Russian and English-speaking delegates appears to be nil" in these cases.

If there is thus some difficulty among Western peoples, all speaking
varieties of Indo-European, it is not surprising that a much wider chasm
yawns between languages from wholly different stocks—between the
language of Hopi Indians, say, and English. This is the field which
Whorf cultivated intensively, and on which he largely bases his concept
of linguistic relativity.

In English we say "Look at that wave." But a wave in nature never
occurs as a single phenomenon. A Hopi says "Look at that slosh."
The Hopi word, whose nearest equivalent in English is "slosh," gives
a closer fit to the physics of wave motion, connoting movement in a
mass.

"The light flashed," we say in English. Something has to be there
to make the flash; "light" is the subject, "flash" the predicate. The
trend of modern physics, however, with its emphasis on the *field*, is
away from subject-predicate propositions. Thus a Hopi Indian is the
better physicist when he says *Reh-pi*—"flash"—one word for the whole
performance, no subject, no predicate, no time element. We frequently
read into nature ghostly entities which flash and perform other miracles.
Do we supply them because some of our verbs require substantives in
front of them?

The thoughts of a Hopi about events always include *both* space and
time, for neither is found alone in his world view. Thus his language
gets along adequately without tenses for its verbs, and permits him to
think habitually in terms of space-time. Properly to understand Einstein's relativity a Westerner must abandon his spoken tongue and take
to the language of calculus. But a Hopi, Whorf implies, has a sort of
calculus built into him.

"The formal systematization of ideas in English, German, French,
or Italian seems poor and jejune"—in dealing with certain classes of
phenomena, when contrasted with the flexibility and directness of
Amerindian languages. Whorf demonstrates the trouble we Westerners

have with masculine and feminine genders, and with our built-in, two-valued, either-or logic.

> Does the Hopi language show here a higher plane of thinking, a more rational analysis of situations than our vaunted English? Of course it does. In this field and in various others, English compared to Hopi is like a bludgeon compared to a rapier.

For other classes of phenomena English might be the rapier and Hopi the bludgeon. Both languages have been developed over the ages, largely unconsciously, to meet the experiences and problems of their speakers, and we cannot call one higher or more mature than the other. For, while human societies vary widely in their supply and consumption of artifacts, the human mind, reflected in language, shows no examples of primitive functioning. . . . "American Indian and African languages abound in finely wrought, beautifully logical discriminations about causation, action, result, dynamic or energic quality, directness of experience, all matters of the function of thinking, indeed the quintessence of the rational."

As you will see in Mr. Carroll's excellent biography, Whorf early in his Indian language studies noted similarities between certain Mayan inscriptions and that on an Aztec temple in Tepoztlan. I climbed to that rocky shrine in the same year, 1930, though not to study the hieroglyphics. With Aztec he combined studies in Maya and then in Hopi. He found the last the most subtle and expressive of the three, and compiled a Hopi dictionary, as yet unpublished. If he seems sometimes more affectionate than coldly scientific about his Indian tongues, it is easy to forgive him.

IV

Most of the above quotations I have taken from a monograph, also hitherto unpublished, which Whorf wrote in 1936. You will find it at page 65, and it deals with the thought processes of primitive peoples. He had planned to send it to H. G. Wells and H. L. Mencken, as well as to various distinguished linguists like Sapir. I wish that he might have done so, for it brings together all his remarkable qualities: his learning, his creative imagination, his idea of linguistic relativity, and his hopes for the future. What the essay says to me, a layman, is in essence this:

There is no one metaphysical pool of universal human thought.

Speakers of different languages see the Cosmos differently, evaluate it differently, sometimes not by much, sometimes widely. Thinking is relative to the language learned. There are no primitive languages.

Research is needed to discover the world view of many unexplored languages, some now in danger of extinction.

Somewhere along the line it may be possible to develop a real international language. Some day all peoples will use language at capacity, and so think much straighter than we now do.

Theoretically this might mean the end of linguistic relativity, but it would not mean the mountain had been climbed. The next great task would be to devise new forms of speech to bring us ever closer to reality, to move capacity on and up. "So far as we can envision the future, we must envision it in terms of mental growth."

It is tragic for us all that the mental growth of Benjamin Lee Whorf was so prematurely interrupted.

STUART CHASE

Georgetown, Connecticut
November 23, 1955

CONTENTS

[1] Dates in parentheses are dates of composition.

INTRODUCTION

1

The career of Benjamin Lee Whorf might, on the one hand, be described as that of a businessman of specialized talents—one of those individuals who by the application of out-of-the-ordinary training and knowledge together with devotion and insight can be so useful to any kind of business organization. On the other hand, his career could be described as that of an unusually competent and diligent research worker in several otherwise almost completely neglected fields of inquiry—the study of the lost writing system of the Mayas and the study of the languages of the Aztecs of Mexico and the Hopis of Arizona. Neither description, of itself, would mark him as a particularly engaging subject for biographical treatment. When it is realized, however, that he combined both these careers, achieving recognition in his business activities at the very same time that he advanced to high eminence in scholarly work—without even having undergone the usual preliminaries of formal academic study signalized by an advanced degree—and in addition injected into contemporary discussions on the study of man and his culture a challenging set of hypotheses concerning the relation of language to thinking and cognition, his biography becomes a matter of more than passing interest.

He was born in Winthrop, Massachusetts, on April 24, 1897, the son of Harry Church and Sarah Edna (Lee) Whorf. He was a scion of an old American stock, his ancestors having come from England to settle in

Provincetown and other parts of the Bay Colony soon after the landing of the Pilgrims. In England, the Whorf name had been found most frequently in West Riding, in Yorkshire, and there may be some obscure connection with the name of the Wharfe River in that locality.

Benjamin was very much the child of his father, as were also his two younger brothers, each in his own way. Benjamin was the "intellectual," the more bookish and idea-centered. John, born in 1903, became a well-known artist, particularly noted for his watercolors. Richard, born in 1906, has distinguished himself as an actor and director on the legitimate stage and in motion pictures.

Intellectual, artist, dramatist—the father was all three. After a brief career as a rather indifferent student at Massachusetts Institute of Technology (it is said that he did not care to apply himself to his engineering studies), Harry Church Whorf drifted into commercial art, or what he liked to call "designing," an occupation which drew upon his talents in draftsmanship as well as his fertile imagination. In this work he was very successful. Among his productions which survive even today is the chain of little Dutch girls which encircles each tin of a well-known brand of cleansing powder. He made himself a master of the then rapidly developing art of photolithography. But he was not content to remain within the confines of his occupation. He lent his artistic talents to numerous enterprises, stage designing being the foremost of these. He also wrote and directed plays for church groups and charitable organizations, and he wrote the libretto for *Bobby Shaftoe*, a musical comedy which was once given a performance in Boston. He enjoyed giving illustrated lectures on various subjects, and apparently had a knack of pleasing an audience. At the time of his death in 1934, he was at work on a manuscript concerning the Massachusetts littoral—its geology, history, fauna and flora, and so forth.

Even before the birth of their first child, Harry Whorf and his wife had taken up residence in a modest house in Winthrop, a residential suburb situated on a peninsula which flanks Boston harbor on the north. With the collections of drawings, books, manuscripts, chemicals, photographic equipment, and odds and ends which the father had accumulated, the house provided a stimulating environment for three abnormally curious and inquisitive boys, all endowed with talents with which to take advantage of it. Like his brothers after him, Benjamin early acquired some considerable skill in drawing, but the chemicals, dyes, and photographic apparatus intrigued him most. He loved to perform such experiments as the one in which liquids of various colors are made to form different layers in a single vessel. It may have been his early experiences with chemicals which led Benjamin later to choose to study chemical engineering at the Massachusetts Institute of Technology.

He went to the public schools of Winthrop, through the high school, where we are told he did well. We are further told that he developed his powers of concentration at this time—even to the extent of apparent absentmindedness. Once, on being sent to the cellar to fill the coal hod, he brought it, filled, all the way back to his room rather than to its place beside the kitchen stove. (Later in his life, friends occasionally complained that he passed them on the street without even a sign of recognition.) While not especially strong, he had sufficient confidence in his physical prowess to protect his younger brothers from neighborhood bullies. Particularly with John, who was six years his junior, he liked to play intellectual games. A favorite was the game of secret codes; Benjamin could nearly always solve even the most complex ciphers his brother could devise. In the meantime, while alone, Benjamin read voraciously and amused himself with composing humorous verse.

After graduation from Winthrop High School in 1914, he entered the Massachusetts Institute of Technology, majoring in chemical engineering (Course X). His academic performance there appears to have been of only average quality; his record shows no marks in the highest category (H, corresponding to what is now ordinarily called A), even in English composition or in French. This is, of course, a commentary on the precarious relationship which exists between performance rated in college and performance in later life. In the fall term of his senior year, a mysterious illness acquired in an ROTC summer camp forced Whorf to be absent from classes; the necessity of making up deficiencies the following summer delayed his obtaining the degree of Bachelor of Science in Chemical Engineering until October 1918.

We do not know what sort of professional career Whorf planned for himself while a student at M.I.T. Most probably, he hoped to find employment as an engineer in some type of chemical production plant or factory. His professional career was to prove most unusual, for he emerged as a specialist in a line of work which, as he once complained in a letter to his M.I.T. alumni organization, was at the time hardly recognized as a distinct field of engineering even by his alma mater. In

1919, not long after his graduation from M.I.T., he was selected as a trainee in fire prevention engineering by the company which employed him for twenty-two years, up to the time of his death. According to an account prepared by C. S. Kremer, Chairman of the Board, Hartford Fire Insurance Company, "he was selected by an officer of the company, Mr. F. C. Moore, who was himself an M.I.T. graduate and had charge of the underwriting and handling of the insurance on buildings equipped with automatic sprinklers." After graduating from the company school which Mr. Moore conducted for fire prevention engineers, Whorf was assigned to the home office of the company, in Hartford, to assist in fire prevention inspection of properties insured by the company in the northeastern part of the country. The company was starting to develop what was then a new idea in the business, namely, fire-prevention engineering inspections as a service to the property owner and policy holder. In this work, which necessitated constant travel, he became extremely skillful. "In no time at all," writes Kremer, "he became in my opinion as thorough and fast a fire prevention inspector as there ever has been. . . . He was intensely practical and taught what he knew as facts to engineers and skillful men in various manufacturing businesses." He specialized more and more in the inspection of plants which utilized chemical processes in manufacturing.

On one occasion while inspecting a chemical plant he was refused admission to a certain building on the ground that it housed a secret process. Even the head of the plant, to whom he was referred, insisted that no outsider could inspect this building. Whorf said, "You are making such-and-such a product?" The answer was "Yes," whereupon Whorf picked up a pad, quickly wrote down a chemical formula, and handed it to the head of the plant, saying, "I think this is what you are doing." The surprised manufacturer replied, "How in the world did you know, Mr. Whorf?", to which Whorf answered calmly, "You couldn't do it in any other way." Needless to say, he was admitted to the building which contained the secret process.

He was so much respected among chemical manufacturers that his advice was eagerly sought. In an inspection of a very complicated chemical plant in Connecticut, he suggested to the management that a certain process be abandoned until it could be made safer, and indicated how this could be done. Some time later, after the suggested improvements had been made, the management delayed starting the process for several days until Whorf could return to the plant and approve going ahead.

He was admired not only for his technical skill but also, strange as it may seem to anyone who may know only Whorf's linguistic work, for his ability to attract business for his company. He was once asked to make a fire prevention inspection of some public schools on which the company had only a trifling amount of business. The recommendations which he submitted so impressed the school board that they decided to appoint Whorf's company as the manager of their insurance account, quite to the surprise of the local agent, who had found this particular school board difficult to approach.

The value put on Whorf's services by his employer was signalized by his appointment in 1928 as Special Agent, and by his election in 1940 as Assistant Secretary of his company. It may have been that the company was proud of his accomplishments in linguistics and anthropology, and we know that it was liberal in granting him occasional leaves to carry on these activities,[1] but he was valued primarily for his actual services to his employer, which must have been of a high order, far beyond the ordinary. It is truly remarkable that he was able to achieve distinction in two entirely separate kinds of work. During certain periods of his life, his scholarly output was enough to equal that of many a full-time research professor; yet he must have been at the same time spending some eight hours every working day in his business pursuits. His friends often speculated on why he chose to remain in his occupation. Although several offers of academic or scholarly research positions were made to him during the latter years of his life, he consistently refused them, saying that his business situation afforded him a more comfortable living and a freer opportunity to develop his intellectual interests in his own way.

As if his insurance work, his linguistic studies, and his extensive reading were not enough to occupy him, he found time for certain community activities, such as serving on a fire prevention committee of the Hartford Chamber of Commerce. From about 1928 on, he became

[1] Nevertheless, Whorf often combined business with science on these trips. In the course of the field trip to Mexico in 1930, he inspected the Mexico City agency of the company and wrote a comprehensive report of his findings and recommendations.

increasingly popular as a lecturer before men's clubs, historical societies, and the like.[2]

In 1920 he married Celia Inez Peckham, by whom he had three children, Raymond Ben, Robert Peckham, and Celia Lee. In somewhat the same way that his father had done for him, he was able to arouse in his children, as if by magnetic induction, something like his delightful curiosity and his unhesitating imagination.

By his own account, Whorf did not become interested in linguistics until 1924, but one can trace a distinct succession of intellectual enthusiasms which led him to this. Even as a boy, along with his preoccupation with chemistry experiments, he was an avid reader. He became interested in Middle American prehistory through reading (several times, we are told) Prescott's *Conquest of Mexico*. On one occasion his father was engaged in doing the stage designs for a play which he had written about a Maya princess, and in this connection assembled all manner of books about Maya archaeology. Young Ben was intrigued with the resulting display of stage designs, which doubtless portrayed ornate façades of Maya temples, and he may have begun to wonder about the meaning of Maya hieroglyphs. The interest in secret ciphers, mentioned earlier, may have reinforced this curiosity, but, if so, it lay dormant until a somewhat later period. Instead, he began to spend a good deal of time on a variety of scientific topics. He became interested in botany, and learned the English and Latin names for thousands of plants and trees. (This was a lasting interest; on his trip to Mexico in 1930 he took copious notes on Mexican flora, and as late as 1936 we find him filling several pages of one of his linguistic notebooks with a "quiz" on botanical terminology and curiosities.) As if to contrast with this, he was for a time intensely interested in astrology and amused himself with casting horoscopes for his friends. At some time in his adolescence he began to manifest what might seem an almost pathological graphomania, for at the age of 17 he began to keep a diary, a practice which he continued throughout his life. He contrived some sort of secret writing which he occasionally used to conceal some of the

[2] My own acquaintance with Whorf developed as a consequence of my attending a lecture he gave at the Children's Museum of Hartford, December 1, 1929. The title of the lecture, announced as a "chalk talk," was "The Aztec and Maya Indians of Mexico."

contents of his diaries, and which he also used to record his dreams in a series of "dreambooks."

Shortly after settling in Hartford, Whorf became increasingly concerned about the supposed conflict between science and religion. It seems that he had been deeply impressed by the fundamentalist shadings of his Methodist Episcopal religious background, which at times seemed to controvert the current doctrines in science. He became so deeply preoccupied with this issue that he wrote a 130,000-word manuscript on the subject, described as a book of religious philosophy in the form of a novel. This manuscript, completed in 1925, was submitted to several publishers and as promptly rejected by them, even over his protests. Another, briefer manuscript prepared about this time was entitled "Why I have discarded evolution." An eminent geneticist to whom it was submitted for comment made a very courteous reply, starting with the admission that, although the manuscript at first appeared to be the work of a crank, its skill and perceptiveness soon marked it as otherwise, but continuing with a point-by-point rebuttal of Whorf's arguments.

In the meantime, Whorf's reading led him to believe that the key to the apparent discrepancy between the Biblical and the scientific accounts of cosmogony and evolution might lie in a penetrating linguistic exegesis of the Old Testament. For this reason, in 1924 he turned his mind to the study of Hebrew.

It may come as a surprise to some that Whorf's interest in linguistics stemmed from one in religion. The reader may incidentally be reminded of the considerable connection which has long existed between linguistic and religious enterprises—the philological work represented in the Séptuagint, in Ulfilas's creation of the written Gothic into which he could translate the Bible, in the study of hundreds of non-European languages by missionaries in the seventeenth and eighteenth centuries, and in the thoroughly scientific investigations being carried out by contemporary linguistic missionaries. Whorf, however, was not interested in any translation of the Bible, at least not in any ordinary sense; he seriously believed that fundamental human and philosophical problems could be solved by taking a new sounding of the semantics of the Bible. Whether this conviction was independently reached by him we do not know. We do know that sometime during 1924 there came to his attention a book which could have buttressed his beliefs, and which at

any rate drew him closer to linguistics. He himself gives testimony of
this in a hitherto unpublished paper which appears in the present collection. This book, hardly known to contemporary scholars, was by a
French dramatist, philologist, and mystic of the early nineteenth century, Antoine Fabre d'Olivet (1768–1825). It was entitled *La langue
hébraïque restituée*, and was published in two volumes in Paris in
1815–16. Whorf most probably read an English translation of this
scarce work published in 1921, for the name of the translator, Nayán
Louise Redfield, appears in his notes.[3]

According to the *Grand dictionnaire universel du XIXᵉ siècle*, Fabre
d'Olivet died "avec le reputation d'un fou ou d'un visionnaire." A
rather indifferent dramatist, he retired in his later life to extensive philological lucubrations. In *La langue hébraïque*, his major work in this
field, he attempted to show that the hidden meanings of the Book of
Genesis could be elucidated by an analysis *au fond* of the structure of
the triliteral Hebrew root. Each letter of the Hebrew alphabet, according to him, contained an inherent meaning; for example, the letter
Aleph was to him "the sign of the power and stability of ideas, of unity
and the principle which determines it." The letter Yodh was a sign of
"manifestation"; thus the partial root Aleph-Yodh "designates," wrote
Fabre d'Olivet, "the center towards which the will tends, the place
where it enfixes itself, the sphere of activity in which it operates." Since
he concluded that the letter Tsadhe denoted "termination," he was not
surprised to find that the triliteral root Aleph-Yodh(or Waw)-Tsadhe
meant "any desire tending toward an end." The principle of the root-
sign was applied to all parts of Hebrew grammar, and to the interpretation of several hundred Hebrew roots. The whole was offered as
partly a linguistic study to illuminate the principles of language (he
claimed having been hard put to choose whether Chinese, Sanskrit, or
Hebrew would be the basis for his project), and partly as the fulfilment
of his desire to discover the secret meaning of the cosmogony of Moses.
In the English translation which Fabre d'Olivet himself obligingly provided, the first verse of the Bible comes out as follows: 'At-FIRST-IN-
PRINCIPLE, he-created, Ælohim (he caused to be, he brought forth
in principle, HE-the-Gods, the-Being-of-Beings), the-selfsameness-of-
heavens, and-the-selfsameness-of-earth.' He tosses off the comment that

---

[3] Miss Redfield, for some years a resident of Hartford, also translated several
other works by Fabre d'Olivet.

this is not a mere result of some system he has established on the basis of "more or less happy conjectures or probabilities," but "the very language of Moses which I have interpreted according to its structural principles, which I have taken pains to develop to a satisfactory point."

Despite the dubiety of Fabre d'Olivet's startling results, his book seems to have made a strong impression on Whorf, who later characterized him as having been "one of the most powerful linguistic intellects of any age." Whorf maintained that, while the Biblical exegesis attempted by Fabre d'Olivet could not be taken seriously, his "root-sign" was really a foreshadowing of what is nowadays called the phoneme. What intrigued Whorf was Fabre d'Olivet's method. For example, in arriving at his "meanings" of the letters of the Hebrew alphabet, Fabre d'Olivet had systematically compared and contrasted a wide variety of roots in which they occurred, much as one might attempt to obtain a "meaning" for the letter M in English by educing the common meaning in all English words beginning in M. We may permit ourselves to imagine that Fabre d'Olivet could have found a common element even in such opposite words as 'mother' and 'murder'! There are limits to which such a method can be pushed, which Fabre d'Olivet far exceeded; nevertheless, it remains true that such a technique of identifying isolates is in essence similar to the procedures of contemporary linguistics in identifying phonemes and morphemes. As we shall see, however, Whorf's methods in certain spheres of his work closely paralleled those of Fabre d'Olivet. This is illustrated in his early efforts to read Maya hieroglyphs, as well as in some of his unpublished work on the structure of Aztec. Another and perhaps a more profound way in which his methods resembled Fabre d'Olivet's is represented in his always bold and penetrating search for inner meanings. Just as Fabre d'Olivet pushed imagination to the limit in looking for an underlying significance in a segment of a Hebrew root, so Whorf persisted in the struggle to wrest from the bare linguistic fact its ultimate purport.

The discovery of the work by Fabre d'Olivet stimulated Whorf to read more widely and deeply on the subject of language. He made use of the rich collections of the Watkinson Library, a scholarly research library in Hartford founded in 1857 under the provisions of the will of a wealthy English-born Hartford merchant who wanted the city to have a general library of reference. Visited chiefly by an occasional genealogist or art historian who sought access to its hundred-thousand-odd dusty volumes, the library was housed in the upper reaches of a fortress-like building known as the Wadsworth Atheneum, which also contained the Hartford Public Library and the collections of the Connecticut Historical Society.[4] At least during the period that Whorf was in the habit of frequenting it after his business hours, its extreme stillness and bookish odor were conducive to deep concentration. Its first librarian had been James Hammond Trumbull, who was among other things a scholar in American Indian lore. During his service as librarian from 1863 to 1893, Trumbull had built up the library's collections in American Indian ethnology, folklore, and language to an extent that would be considered unusual except for a large university library. This collection reawakened Whorf's interest in Mexican antiquities and lore, and directed his attention especially to the Aztec (Nahuatl) language and, later, to Maya hieroglyphs. Just what prompted Whorf to study Aztec, in particular, we do not know. Conceivably he chanced upon an account of Nahuatl which reminded him of the ideas he had found in *La langue hébraïque*. Be that as it may, Whorf began studying Aztec in 1926; he probably did not work seriously on Maya until 1928. He worked not only at the Watkinson Library, but also at any library he could profitably visit on his numerous business trips away from Hartford. He made rapid progress, and began corresponding with various scholars in Mexican archaeology and linguistics, including Herbert J. Spinden of the Brooklyn Museum and Alfred M. Tozzer of Harvard University. At Dr. Spinden's suggestion he addressed himself to an attempt to work out a translation of a page of an old Mexican manuscript, a photographic reproduction of which was to be found in the Peabody Museum of Harvard University. The result was a paper read before the Twenty-Third International Congress of Americanists in September 1928 and a corresponding first scholarly publication, "An Aztec account of the period of the Toltec decline" (1928),[5] which shows an antiquarian's interest in the details of Toltec history and chronology as well as a linguist's pride in forcing a cranky Aztec word "to yield up its secret," as Whorf himself put it. This paper, as read before the Congress, attracted a considerable amount of attention and publicity for the young insurance agent, who was hailed

[4] In 1952 the Watkinson Library was removed to spacious and modern quarters at Trinity College in Hartford.

[5] See the bibliography of Whorf's writings, pp. 271–276; this is followed by a short list of related writings to which references are made.

in newspaper reports for his having "unlocked mysteries" which had "baffled" other scholars. About the same time there was completed another Aztec translation, published in 1929 under the title "The reign of Huemac."

These publications were, however, only the first and easy fruits of a period of study in which Whorf was also delving into comparative linguistics, presumably without any tutoring other than the necessarily brief contacts he may have had with such men as Spinden and Tozzer, and, in addition, J. Alden Mason of the University of Pennsylvania, whom he met during a visit to the first Linguistic Institute, held in the summer of 1928. At the International Congress of Americanists, Whorf had read another paper besides the one on Toltec history. It attracted much less attention, but was closer to his true interests; entitled simply "Aztec linguistics," it reported his assertion that Aztec was what he called an oligosynthetic language, that is, that all its words were built up out of a relatively few elements, perhaps as few as fifty basic monosyllabic roots, "each conveying a general notion capable of wide modulation without loss of the basic sense" (or so he wrote in the published abstract of the paper). On looking into whether the same roots he found in Aztec would show up also in languages related to Aztec, he was immediately gratified by the results. Toward the end of 1928 the work he had done on the familial relationships among Tepecano, Piman, and Aztec—all Mexican languages—appeared so promising to Tozzer and Spinden that they advised him to seek a research fellowship from the Social Science Research Council to enable him to obtain needed materials and work more intensively. Whorf countered with the proposal that he use such a fellowship to make a field trip to Mexico to locate old Aztec manuscripts for the Watkinson Library, one of the trustees of that library having expressed a desire to build up its collection of Aztec materials. Tozzer opined, however, that if he wanted to go to Mexico he would be better advised to investigate modern Nahuatl, a suggestion to which Whorf readily assented. In a letter to Mason dated December 6, 1928, Whorf commented, in reference to the fellowship for which he was applying, "It is a question whether I get it, because these Fellowships are supposed to be for men with Ph.D. degrees, and while they sometimes make exceptions, these exceptions are rare and hard to get, requiring very good recommendations." His application to the Social Science Research Council was accompanied, first, by a general statement of his scholarly plans, and second, by a nearly completed article entitled "Notes on the oligosynthetic comparison of Nahuatl and Piman, with special reference to Tepecano." In the first of these documents, Whorf revealed himself as avowedly visionary, but he may have felt its content necessary to win the interest of the committee which reviewed his fellowship application:

> With the aid of this Research Fellowship if possible I plan to do and publish sufficient work on Mexican linguistics to make the principle of oligosynthesis a live topic and to interest other investigators in the basic substratum of language to which it belongs.
>
> After I have become better known in this way the next step will be to arouse interest in the phenomenon that I call BINARY GROUPING in Hebrew and the Semitic languages. I am of course still working on this and will continue right along to bring it to the attention of Semitic researchers.
>
> After binary grouping has also become a live topic I will begin to make a union between this principle and that of oligosynthesis and thereby reach the still deeper principle underlying the Hebrew and Semitic languages.
>
> The next step will be to use these principles in working out the primitive underlying basis of all speech behavior. This will amount to laying the foundations of a new science, and although this consummation lies some little time in the future I feel that it is quite distinctly in sight. Still further ahead are the possible applications of such a science restoring a possible original common language of the human race or in perfecting an ideal natural tongue constructed of the original psychological significance of sounds, perhaps a future common speech into which all our varied languages may be assimilated, or, putting it differently, to whose terms they may all be reduced. This may seem at the present time very visionary, but it would be no more remarkable than what science has already done in other fields when it has got hold of sound principles to point the way, and I believe my work is tending to unfold such principles. And with the ultimate development of these researches will come manifestation of the deeper psychological, symbolic, and philosophical sense contained in the cosmology of the Bible, the starting point and original inspiration of these studies.

Oligosynthesis is explained further in the first few paragraphs of the second document which accompanied Whorf's fellowship application:

> Oligosynthesis is a name for that type of language structure in which all or nearly all of the vocabulary may be reduced to a very small number of roots or significant elements, irrespective of whether these roots or elements are to be regarded as original, standing anterior to the language as we know it, or as never having had independent existence, theirs being an implicit existence as parts in words that were always undissociated wholes.

Such a structure was recognized by the writer in the Nahuatl or Aztec language of Mexico, in which he has made numerous studies and the term oligosynthesis was thereupon proposed by him. . . . Briefly, the conclusions are that nearly all and probably quite all the present known native vocabulary of Nahuatl is derived from the varied combination and varied semantic development of NO MORE THAN THIRTY-FIVE ROOTS, for which the writer prefers the name of "elements," each of which elements stands for a certain general idea, including something of the surrounding field of related ideas into which this central idea insensibly shades off. These thirty-five elements (it now begins to seem very unlikely that their number will be increased) have been obtained by extensive stem-analysis and are listed . . . in the appendix of the present article. They explain the meaning of thousands of Nahuatl words, including great numbers of words learned recently, which have had the meaning that would be expected from their elements. Furthermore, it is becoming increasingly evident to me that these elements are to be regarded as original roots anterior and ancestral to the present language, and my previous view that they might be the result of assimilative back-formation is becoming less and less of a serious claimant for consideration. Obviously we have here a structure, a point-to-point correspondence between the path of ideation and the successions of lip, tongue, and glottal activities (i.e. consonants and vowels) that may be of great linguistic, glottogonic, and psychological significance.

Binary grouping referred to a principle which Whorf believed to inhere in the structure of Hebrew roots, as may be seen in the following quotation from an unpublished manuscript: "A binary group is a group of Semitic roots having in common a certain sequence of two consonants, containing all the roots with this sequence in one language, and having these roots with but few exceptions allocated to a FEW CERTAIN KINDS OF MEANING."

These quotations are of special interest when viewed in the light of Whorf's early enthusiasm for Fabre d'Olivet. As a further note, it should be added that Whorf started to extend the application of the oligosynthetic principle to his first work with Maya, concerning which he read a paper before the Linguistic Society of America (of which he had just become a member) in December 1929, "Stem series in Maya." In the abstract of this paper submitted to the program committee of the Linguistic Society, we find Whorf pointing out that the majority of Maya stems beginning *QE*- bear the meaning 'turn.' He writes further: "So other series, e.g. *QI*-, radiate, glow, burn, scatter; *QO*-, *QU*-, inward; *BI*-, move; *TA*-, connect; *TZA*-, come or bring together; *MA*-, pass. In other words, 'ideology follows phoneticism.' "

The response of the SSRC to his application for a research fellowship being favorable, Whorf set about making arrangements for his field trip to Mexico. He obtained a few weeks' leave from his company and left for Mexico City with Mrs. Whorf and her mother in January 1930. En route he spent a few days researching in the library of the Department of Middle American Research at Tulane University of Louisiana. On arrival in Mexico City, he sought the assistance of several Mexican specialists in Aztec, especially Professor Mariano Rojas of the National Museum of Mexico. Partly with their aid, he gained access to several excellent informants who spoke a form of Aztec which was believed to approximate, as closely as one could expect over the years, the classical dialect of Aztec once spoken in Tenochtitlan (now Mexico City) at the time of Montezuma. These individuals lived in an outlying suburb in the Federal District, known as Milpa Alta, and it is their dialect of which Whorf made a detailed linguistic analysis, published posthumously in 1946 in Hoijer's *Linguistic structures of native America*. In the meantime, Whorf poked around the Mexican countryside in search of suggestive archaeological material. In a ruined temple overlooking the village of Tepoztlan, where he conducted further linguistic studies, he came upon, apparently quite by chance, a band of sculptured figures which had previously escaped the close attention of scholars. His sharp observation and close familiarity with both Aztec and Maya graphic art enabled him to recognize almost immediately that these figures deviated from their usual forms as "day signs" of the Aztec calendar and showed certain resemblances to Mayan characters. This discovery of "a definite, clearly demonstrable rapport between Nahuatl hieroglyphs and early Maya ones," as Whorf regarded it, was the basis of one of the papers reprinted in the present collection, "A central Mexican inscription combining Mexican and Maya day signs." It furnishes an excellent example of Whorf's methods of work, and is also his earliest publication pointing toward his later researches into Maya hieroglyphs.

For several years after his return from Mexico, Whorf occupied himself with working up the data amassed during the Mexican sojourn. Not only was it necessary to sketch out the linguistic analysis of the Milpa Alta Nahuatl; it was also urgent to follow up the leads provided by the discoveries concerning Mexican and Maya day signs, which had had the effect of confirming or modifying certain hunches he had developed previously. A major series of publications concerning Maya hieroglyphs started about this time, first with a monograph published by the Peabody Museum of Harvard, "The phonetic value of certain characters in Maya writing" (1933) and later with an article, "Maya writing and its decipherment" (1935). In the earlier publication, which Professor Tozzer of Harvard urged him to prepare, he set forth in detail and with his evidence his thesis that Maya writing was at least partly phonetic, and he offered a specimen translation of a simple Maya text from one of the codices. Since the hypothesis of phoneticism in Maya writing had been all but abandoned by Maya scholars at least fifty years previously, Whorf's materials must have been exceedingly impressive, at least at the time, to have gotten published at all. The later publication, "Maya writing and its decipherment," was a reply to a critique published by Richard C. E. Long in the journal *Maya Research*. Besides taking issue with many points of detail raised by Mr. Long, Whorf attempted to explain why he regarded Long's approach as fundamentally mistaken; he also offered another specimen translation of a Maya text. In this article, furthermore, he mentioned that he had been working on a manuscript, "First steps in the decipherment of Maya writing," which he then hoped to publish within a short time. This manuscript, found among Whorf's papers, has thus far remained unfinished and unpublished, though some parts of it are reflected in a paper which Whorf read before a scientific congress in 1940 and which is reprinted in the present collection, "Decipherment of the linguistic portion of the Maya hieroglyphs." Whorf was bitterly disappointed by the rather cool reception generally accorded his work by Maya scholars after 1933; he was entirely confident that his linguistic approach held the key to the interpretation of Maya hieroglyphs. The paper he read in 1940 was apparently a last-ditch effort to win support for his approach.

Up to the time of the Mexican trip, Whorf seems to have had very little contact, either face-to-face or by correspondence, with any of the persons who were later to be his close colleagues in the field of linguistics. His scholarly relations had been chiefly with a group of specialists in Mexican archaeology, none of whom were particularly well qualified in, or concerned with, general linguistics. In view of this, the competence that Whorf had achieved in general linguistics and linguistic field methods, purely on the strength of his own untutored study, was remarkable. Nevertheless, his talents might never have fully matured if he had not eventually met Edward Sapir (1884–1939), a

foremost authority not only on American Indian languages but also on
the general science of language. Whorf had, of course, been aware of
Sapir's work, and he had doubtless read Sapir's book *Language* (New
York, 1921) with intense interest. He first met Sapir, though only
briefly, at the September 1928 International Congress of Americanists,
and talked with him further at subsequent meetings of scientific societies in 1929 and 1930. He could not, however, make any close contact with Sapir until the latter came from the University of Chicago in
the fall of 1931 to take his post at Yale as Professor of Anthropology to
teach linguistics. Whorf lost no time in enrolling in Sapir's first course
at Yale in American Indian linguistics; among the Whorf papers can be
found a manuscript, entitled "The structure of the Athabaskan languages," a term paper which Sapir awarded a grade of A and much
praise. Although Whorf nominally enrolled for a program of studies
leading to the doctorate, he never sought or obtained any higher degree;
he pursued his studies for pure intellectual ends. The effects of Whorf's
first formal studies in linguistics were noticeable and demonstrable. His
early interests in "oligosynthesis," "binary grouping," and other unusual
linguistic theories became tempered at least to the extent that he was
brought to see them in the light of the accumulated experience of men
like Sapir. (I can find no mention of the idea of oligosynthesis, as such,
in any of Whorf's writings after 1931.) More important, Whorf was
put in close touch with the linguistic theories and techniques which
were most advanced at that time, as well as with the problems which
were currently considered the most essential to solve. Finally, his
studies at Yale brought him into contact with a small but earnest band
of Sapir's students, including such individuals as Morris Swadesh, Stanley Newman, George Trager, Charles Voegelin, Mary Haas, and Walter
Dyk, all of whom have since made important contributions to linguistics
or anthropology. In 1937–38, Whorf was a Lecturer in Anthropology at
Yale.

Whorf's association with Sapir thus served to intensify his desire to
develop further the field of American Indian linguistics. In the monograph about Maya hieroglyphs published in 1933, we find Whorf credit-
ing Sapir with certain suggestions about the interpretation of the zero
sign. Sapir was probably more influential, however, in encouraging
Whorf to expand his work on the Uto-Aztecan languages (a large stock
of languages whose relationships Sapir had established), in particular

to take up the study of the Hopi language, a distant relative of Aztec. In December 1932 Whorf read a paper entitled "The characteristics of the Uto-Aztecan stock" at the meeting of the Linguistic Society of America held at New Haven. His further work on Uto-Aztecan linguistics (exclusive of Hopi) is represented by a review (1935) of Kroeber's *Uto-Aztecan languages of Mexico,* and several articles, "The comparative linguistics of Uto-Aztecan" (1935), "The origin of Aztec TL" (1937), and (with G. L. Trager) "The relationship of Uto-Aztecan and Tanoan" (1937). In these articles, Whorf recognized a superfamily language stock which he proposed to call Macro-Penutian, to include Penutian, Uto-Aztecan, Mayan, and Mixe-Zoque-Huave. Later, he used this structuring in preparing a revision of Sapir's classification of American Indian languages.

In linguistic work as such, Whorf was best known for his studies of Hopi. Perhaps through the good offices of Sapir, he made contact with a native speaker of Hopi, who then lived, conveniently enough, in New York City. Beginning in the spring of 1932 and with the support of a small research subvention obtained for him by Sapir, Whorf worked intensely on developing a linguistic analysis of Hopi, utilizing field research methods in which he had received instruction from Sapir. Whorf and his informant exchanged visits in New York and Wethersfield (where Whorf resided); in 1938 Whorf was able to spend a short time on the Hopi reservation in Arizona. By 1935 he had prepared a tentative grammar and dictionary of Hopi. Except for the brief sketch of Hopi grammar in Hoijer's *Linguistic structures of native America* (1946)—a sketch prepared by Whorf in late 1939—the major outcomes of these studies remain unpublished. Nevertheless, one can be grateful for the two brief but very influential technical articles about Hopi which Whorf published during his lifetime: "The punctual and segmentative aspects of verbs in Hopi" (published in 1936, first read as a paper before the Linguistic Society of America in December 1935), and "Some verbal categories of Hopi" (1938). In these papers one can see how their author was beginning to be fired with the notion, developed more extensively in later popularized papers, that the strange grammar of Hopi might betoken a different mode of perceiving and conceiving things on the part of the native speaker of Hopi. In the first, he asserted that "the Hopi actually have a language better equipped to deal with . . . vibratile phenomena than is our latest scientific terminology." This was followed by "An American Indian model of the universe" (probably written in 1936 but not published until 1950), which explores the implications of the Hopi verb system with regard to the Hopi conception of space and time. The work with Hopi must have also influenced the writing, about this same time, of the paper entitled "A linguistic consideration of thinking in primitive communities" (published in the present collection for the first time). "Some verbal categories of Hopi" (1938) discusses several interesting distinctions which Hopi makes between kinds and modes of happening which English treats as the same, and "Linguistic factors in the terminology of Hopi architecture" (written in early 1940 and not published until 1953) contains the thesis that the Hopi mind automatically separates the "occupancy" or spot of ground or floor on which the occupancy occurs from the use to which the occupancy is put, whereas the speaker of English tends to merge these, as where "school" is thought of as both an institution and a building. (Indeed, do we not almost instinctively feel that an institution must of necessity be housed in some kind of building?) Whorf is probably best known for the article "The relation of habitual thought and behavior to language," written in 1939, and for the three articles which were published in 1940 and 1941 in the *Technology Review*—all based to a considerable extent upon his research in Hopi. What is important to note is that, first, these latter papers were grounded upon a solid foundation of linguistic analysis done much earlier, and, second, that the ideas of linguistic relativity expressed therein were by no means new in Whorf's mind; on the contrary, the seeds of these ideas were already apparent in materials prepared as early as 1935, if not earlier.

The three articles written for the *Technology Review* of M.I.T. and the article entitled "Language, mind, and reality" and published in an Indian journal of theosophy were addressed to lay audiences. Undoubtedly Whorf had it in mind to bring linguistics before the general public in a manner that had scarcely ever been attempted; in fact, he may be credited with being the first popularizer of modern linguistic science. He realized, however, that it would be impossible to popularize linguistics, and there would be little purpose in doing so, unless linguistics held a message of popular appeal. This message, Whorf believed, was that linguistics has much to say about how and what we think.

It may be of interest to recount what led to the writing of the articles for the *Technology Review*. As early as 1932 there was an exchange of correspondence between Whorf and the editor of the *Technology Review*, J. R. Killian Jr. (now president of M.I.T.), to whose attention Whorf's article on the Mexican day signs had come. Killian invited Whorf to write an account of his trip to Mexico, and asked whether he had unearthed any material relating to "the history of engineering, architecture, and the practical sciences." Almost disdainfully Whorf replied that this trip had "no bearing on engineering, architecture, or the practical sciences"—that "the investigation was conducted thoroughly in the spirit of scientific research, but it was in the social sciences, not the physical sciences." Nevertheless, he did eventually agree to prepare an article on his trip, but for some reason such an article does not seem to have been written. The next exchange was between Whorf and President Karl T. Compton, in late 1939. Whorf initiated this correspondence as a result of "a slight difficulty" he had had in filling out some sort of questionnaire sent him by the Register of Former Students—namely, that the questionnaire omitted any mention of insurance, insurance engineering, fire prevention, or the like, fields which Whorf felt ought to receive recognition as engineering professions. He wanted to bring this apparent omission to President Compton's attention, and proceeded to describe in detail the nature of his own work. In this same letter, he took occasion to mention other activities of his which did not quite fit the list of rubrics on the questionnaire, to wit, his research on American Indian languages. President Compton's reply, after explaining that the apparent omission on the questionnaire form was the result of abbreviation rather than deliberate exclusion, expressed interest in Whorf's avocational work and asked permission to submit his letter for publication in the *Technology Review*. Permission was granted, and the letter (in much condensed form) is to be seen in the January 1940 issue of the *Review*. In the course of ensuing correspondence, the editor of the *Review*, then F. G. Fassett, Jr., wrote Whorf on November 14, 1939: "Your linguistic studies offer a very interesting and provocative possibility to anyone responsible for a magazine. 'Inasmuch as the analysis of reality is a matter of language, and the relativity of such analyses can only be appreciated through studies that show the immense range of possible diversity in linguistic expression it will be seen that there is a connection here with the attempts of science to understand the universe and man'—I think it would be very interesting to see the ideas implicit in this statement from your October letter expanded in an article aimed at the *Review* group. Is this prospect of interest?" Evidently it was, for Whorf was able to submit the first article, "Science and linguistics," as early as January 30, 1940, and it was printed in the *Review* shortly thereafter. The exceedingly warm reception this article got, both from regular readers of the *Review* and from the recipients of reprints, pointed to the desirability of further articles. The second article, "Linguistics as an exact science," was submitted on September 16, 1940, and the third and last, "Languages and logic," on February 14, 1941, at a time when Whorf's health was failing and his physical weakness was already apparent in his handwriting.

Even in the year when he was writing these brilliant articles on linguistics and at the same time fighting off ill health, Whorf became consumed with still another interest. On account of a lecture which his oldest son attended and described to him, Whorf became acquainted with Fritz Kunz, a well-known speaker and writer, at present the executive vice-president of the Foundation for Integrated Education, Inc. Kunz and Whorf had many common interests, especially (as Mr. Kunz has written me) in the philosophy and metaphysics of India, and it was this that brought them to work together quite closely. One result of this friendship was Kunz's suggestion that Whorf write an article about linguistics for a theosophical journal published at Madras, India; the article entitled "Language, mind, and reality" was the result. Kunz was on the point of founding a new journal, *Main Currents in Modern Thought*, and Whorf was of great help in putting out the first few issues, in late 1940 and early 1941. The journal (still published today, but in a different format) was of an interesting and unusual character; it was intended as a clearing house of ideas and information in all sorts of fields in natural science, social science, the humanities, mathematics, logic, and philosophy; it was to be written chiefly by its subscribers. Published in those days in mimeographed form, the varied colors of its pages were keyed to subject matter. Whorf wrote literally dozens of pages in the first volume, doing highly creative book reviews and contributing little abstracts on such diverse subjects as "The Hurrians of old Chaldea," "Shrinking glass," and "Notes on the demonstration of 'wetter' water." One of his reviews is based on two books on the economics of primitive societies, and is provocatively titled "We may end the war that is within all wars that are waged to end all war." "These books," Whorf wrote, "are outstanding examples of a type of investigation that is gradually unsettling the old-style materialistic theory of economics. And since both Marxian communism and private capitalism are based on a stereotyped materialistic formulation of economics, such irrefutable scientific expositions of the fact that economic behavior is conditioned by culture, not by mechanistic reactions, may be the forerunner of a NEW ERA." This quotation is only one of many that could be cited to show Whorf's broad humanism and concern for the commonweal. Nor did Whorf neglect to bring the implications of linguistics to the attention of readers of *Main Currents*. Reporting several interesting facts which had appealed to his interest at a scientific meeting, he wrote, in a piece entitled "A brotherhood of thought":

There is no word for 'word' in Chinese. The nearest thing is the element *tsz*, which is translated 'word' but means rather 'syllable' or 'syllabic element.' Many such elements never occur free but only in a few combinations, like the 'pyr-' in 'pyrometer.' Words in the sense of vocabulary units exist as either of one or two syllables, a fact obscured by the traditional Chinese system of writing, which keeps every syllable separate. This was pointed out by Dr. Y. R. Chao of Yale in a paper "Word conceptions in Chinese" at the meeting of the Linguistic Society of America in Providence, R. I., 12/30/40. The nature of Chinese grammar is only just beginning to be understood; Dr. Chao and others have exploded the idea that Chinese is a monosyllabic language. At the same meeting Dr. G. A. Kennedy of Yale, analyzing "Complex attributive expressions in Chinese," showed that Chinese has no relative clauses, and that a different kind of order-system rules the logic of such relationships. If the element *te* used in this logic be translated '-ish,' then "The House that Jack Built" would go in Chinese: 'This is Jack-ish build-ish house; this is Jack-ish build-ish house-ish in-ish lie-ish malt,' etc.

It is not sufficiently realized that the ideal of worldwide fraternity and cooperation fails if it does not include ability to adjust intellectually as well as emotionally to our brethren of other countries. The West has attained some emotional understanding of the East through the esthetic and belles-lettres type of approach, but this has not bridged the intellectual gulf; we are no nearer to understanding the types of logical thinking which are reflected in truly Eastern forms of scientific thought or analysis of nature. This requires linguistic research into the logics of native languages, and realization that they have equal scientific validity with our own thinking habits.

After a long and lingering illness, during which he valiantly struggled to keep up his study and his writing, Whorf succumbed on July 26, 1941, at the age of 44. He had accomplished more than he knew, yet only a small part of what he might have done. His passing was taken notice of by editorial obituaries not only in the local newspapers but also in such papers as the *New York Times*, and later, of course, in several scholarly journals.

I cannot close this biographical memoir without a few remarks about Whorf's personality and habits of work. Above all he was capable of extremely deep and steadfast concentration in everything he did. Nothing was treated lightly or carelessly. His penciled manuscripts, in beautifully neat and always legible handwriting, exemplify his meticulousness; it is also exceedingly rare to find an error in his typescripts (he nearly always did his own typing of scholarly manuscripts and correspondence). He was willing to work almost endlessly; his published writings represent but a small fraction of the manuscript material he produced, and his notebooks are truly voluminous. Without hesitation, he would if necessary go to the trouble of copying out, in longhand or script printing, page after page of detailed linguistic texts. In writing, he was able to express himself artistically, convincingly, and effortlessly; in many cases, his first draft—with a minimum of emendations—was final. Yet, he nearly always made a pencil draft preparatory to typing, even for correspondence. This tireless devotion to scholarship undoubtedly took its toll of Whorf's strength and health, although he never appeared visibly fatigued. He habitually worked late into the night, relaxing himself only by taking short catnaps or by playing a few rolls of classical music on his mechanical grand piano. He was somewhat casual about his hours at the office, being dilatory in both arrival and departure on many occasions, but he accomplished much while there. For exercise, he enjoyed walking, often making the four- or five-mile trip from his office to his home in Wethersfield on foot, with perhaps a stop at the Watkinson Library en route.

Social life held little significance for him except when it involved his linguistic colleagues, to whom he was always a delight. He maintained an air of cheerful curiosity, and continually had interesting and novel things to say. As I have recalled elsewhere, "Whorf was a quiet, contemplative teacher; he would not stop at remaining silent for a seemingly interminable time while searching his mind to recall something or to think through a problem. Yet, when he became prompted to tell me of some new insight he had reached, the smoothness and lucidity of his remarks were little short of awesome. His mode of behavior was that of neither the scholar nor the businessman—he gave only the impression of calm, unhurried, effortless inspiration. Self-seeking was entirely alien to him and it is a tribute to him that he was so generous in sharing his remarkable perspectives with others."

II

The title of this volume, *Language, thought, and reality,* is the title of a book that Whorf hoped to write, and for which a brief outline is to be found among the papers left at his death. The book would have been dedicated to the memory of Edward Sapir and Antoine Fabre d'Olivet, and would have attempted to present the implications of linguistics for the clarification of our thinking about the external world of reality. The notes indicate that the book, designed as a college textbook and provided with suitable chapter-end quizzes, would have included in its appendix language sketches of Latin, Greek, Hebrew, Kota, Aztec, Hopi, Shawnee, Russian, Taos, Chinese, and Japanese. This book, of course, was never written, but I believe its title is a fitting one for the present edition, which includes nearly all of Whorf's writings which are pertinent to what he called the principle of linguistic relativity, which states, at least as a hypothesis, that the structure of a human being's language influences the manner in which he understands reality and behaves with respect to it. This edition also includes what are believed to be the most interesting and useful writings of Whorf in Middle American linguistics and in general linguistics.

A study of the whole procession of Whorf's writings discloses an underlying theme which had its roots in his very early thinking, perhaps concurrently with his first steps in linguistic work. We have already seen how Whorf tried, as early as 1925, to verify the theories of the French mystic and Hebrew scholar, Fabre d'Olivet—theories which proposed that certain Hebrew letters and combinations of letters contained mysterious, fundamental root-ideas. In order to verify these, Whorf found himself playing with subtle, below-the-surface similarities between seemingly unrelated ideas. This was the first step—to penetrate beneath the veneer of dry, brittle, isolated words which might conceal fundamental concepts. We see Whorf's concern with basic mental operations, and his seeming discomfort with the straitjacket represented by language, in a short essay which I have entitled "On the connection of ideas." This essay, printed here for the first time, was written in 1927 as a letter to the psychologist Horace B. English, who had just authored a dictionary of psychological terms; Whorf was appealing to English to supply him with a term for a new kind of association of ideas. Whorf was groping toward concepts or terms of a more general or abstract nature than those provided by any language. None of the psychological schools on the contemporary scene were of any real help, as Whorf complained in a short unpublished note which, supplied with the wholly arbitrary title "On psychology," is also printed here. Yet, much of Whorf's work is extremely close to psychology. The search for root-ideas led Whorf on many a byway, even in his work with Aztec and Maya linguistics. The two papers on Maya hieroglyphs included here give only a glimpse of this fact, but it would have emerged very obviously if it had been thought desirable to print here, for example, the unpublished paper "Stem series in Maya and certain Maya hieroglyphs," to which reference has already been made. Unfortunately, one has the suspicion that Whorf occasionally allowed himself too many liberties in arraying together ideas which to another would appear totally unrelated. For example, at one point in his "Stem series" paper, he cites a series of Maya roots which he believed contained "all sorts of ideas of dispersal: be dispersed, disappear, spread, radiate, shine." Edward Sapir, to whom Whorf at one time submitted the manuscript, pinned this comment to it: "I am sorry, but I cannot honestly say I feel the cohesiveness of the *sa*-set as clearly as you do. 'Sand,' 'white,' 'weave cloth,' 'much,' and 'dislocate,' for instance, on the basis of fundamental 'dispersal' seems to be a purely subjective construction." [6] Whorf became aware of the need for objectifying semantic inferences; there is to be found among his unpublished papers a brief proposal for an experiment in which an individual would be presented with a series of Aztec words, together with their English meanings, all involving the letters ZE-. The subject was to be asked to arrive at some sort of semantic grouping for these words; he was to be told that he might decide (1) that ZE- has a single meaning throughout, or (2) that there are two, three, or more ZE-'s with distinct and quite unconnected mean-

[6] The material on the *sa*- group was considerably reworked before publication in the monograph "The phonetic value of certain characters in Maya writing" (1933), p. 11.

ings, or (3) that ZE- has no connection with the meanings whatsoever. Apparently, Whorf never performed this experiment.

It will also be recalled that Whorf early noticed, or believed he noticed, that Hebrew, Aztec, and Maya seemed to be built on a different plan from that of English and other languages which he later called "SAE" (standard average European) languages. He called them "oligosynthetic" languages, that is, languages whose vocabularies were built up out of a very small number of elements. "Each element," he stated in a paper concerning Aztec linguistics read in 1928, "is, first, a very simple piece of articulation-behavior, and, second, a broad idea or complex of related ideas that goes with this piece of behavior." He thought he had been able to analyze the Aztec vocabulary into no more than thirty-five such roots. "It should now be noted," he continued, "that this oligosynthetic phenomenon opens up certain new territories in the little-explored field of language-psychology. In it we see the whole ideational field of a language partitioned out among or shared between some thirty-five elementary notions, so as to give us for the first time a map or plan of an actual realm of ideas. Previously when ideas have been distributed among a set of categories, those categories have been the result of some philosopher's introspection, but not so this idea-map of a language—we come upon it as we do upon the facts of nature, and its as yet dimly seen configuration challenges us to investigate it by experimental and inductive methods." In these somewhat daring ideas we may see, first, a certain appeal to the notion of phonetic symbolism, the notion that there may be inherent relations (over and above the arbitrary relations established in any given language) between sounds and meanings, and, second, the faint suggestion of a theory of linguistic relativity. The problem of phonetic symbolism has long challenged both linguists and psychologists. Edward Sapir, who was sympathetic to the notion, performed an experiment which pointed in a positive direction,[7] and the problem is still alive among contemporary psychologists. With reference to the theory of linguistic relativity foreshadowed in Whorf's theory of oligosynthesis, the key is the notion of a "broad idea or complex of related ideas" which might be associated with a linguistic element, for from this it is but a short step to the notion that languages with different collocations of semantic ideas might pro-

[7] Edward Sapir, "A study in phonetic symbolism," *J. exp. Psychol.*, 12:225–239 (1929).

vide different "maps" of the realm of possible ideas, or, as Whorf put it much later, that different languages might provide different "segmentations of experience."

The idea of linguistic relativity did not emerge in a full-fledged form until after Whorf had started studying with Sapir. Not until he began to analyze Hopi, a language with a grammar much more complex and subtle than that of Aztec or even that of Maya, did he begin to appreciate that the notion of linguistic relativity could be developed in a much more telling and effective way by noticing differences not only in "lexation" but also in grammatical structure. The various papers on Hopi which are published in this collection will speak for themselves; in them Whorf tells of his provocative discoveries in the tense and aspect systems of the Hopi verb, in the Hopi treatment of noun classes, and so on.

Whorf's whole outlook in linguistics, apart from his early religious concerns, stemmed from his concern with fundamental problems of meaning, or, as I like to think, with fundamental intellectual operations. In the very interesting and revealing paper written about 1936 and printed for the first time in this volume, "A linguistic consideration of thinking in primitive communities," Whorf insists that "linguistics is essentially the quest for MEANING." The "real concern" of linguistics, he writes, "is to light up the thick darkness of the language, and thereby of much of the thought, the culture, and the outlook upon life of a given community with the light of this 'golden something,' as I have heard it called, this transmuting principle of meaning." Whorf was concerned more with substance than with process. That is, he was more interested in what, in some abstract sense, was being thought about than with the mental processes by which one might think, and this outlook led him to linguistics, full of "content," rather than to psychology, relatively "contentless" in its concern with generalized stimulus-response mechanisms. Whorf appeared to believe, indeed, that the content of thought influences the process of thought, or that differing contents produce differing species of process, so that generalization about process becomes impossible without content's being taken into account. It was his belief that differences in thought content and their corresponding effects on thought processes and behavior in general would be spectacularly revealed by comparison of different language structures. He was extremely ingenious in ferreting out both the obvious and the subtle differences in language structures, and fully demonstrable differences they were, at least on the linguistic level. He did not stop there, however; he attempted also to adduce evidence of behavior variations associated with different language phenomena. While this attempt may not have been wholly successful, it was at any rate embodied in the article written in the summer of 1939 for the Sapir volume, "The relation of habitual thought and behavior to language." It was the last article he wrote on the subject which was addressed chiefly to his colleagues. The principle of linguistic relativity was stated in the most appealing terms, however, in the articles which appear as the last four of this collection; they were written primarily for lay audiences.

Whorf's principle of linguistic relativity, or, more strictly, the Sapir–Whorf hypothesis (since Sapir most certainly shared in the development of the idea) has, it goes without saying, attracted a great deal of attention. Through various reprintings of one or the other of the *Technology Review* articles, beginning as early as 1941 (in Hayakawa's *Language in action*, a Book of the Month Club selection), the material has been brought to the notice of a wide public as well as of linguists, anthropologists, and psychologists. One wonders, indeed, what makes the notion of linguistic relativity so fascinating even to the nonspecialist. Perhaps it is the suggestion that all one's life one has been tricked, all unaware, by the structure of language into a certain way of perceiving reality, with the implication that awareness of this trickery will enable one to see the world with fresh insight. Surely, at any rate, it would have been farthest from Whorf's wishes to condone any easy appeal to linguistic relativity as a rationalization for a failure of communication between cultures or between nations. Rather, he would hope that a full awareness of linguistic relativity might lead to humbler attitudes about the supposed superiority of standard average European languages and to a greater disposition to accept a "brotherhood of thought" among men, as he wrote in the short article of that title quoted above. But, even if research in native languages is not for the purpose of helping to bridge intellectual gulfs between cultures, Whorf would nevertheless aver that the investigation of the "logics" of those languages will contribute to our understanding of our own thinking habits.

In truth, the validity of the linguistic relativity principle has thus far not been sufficiently demonstrated; neither has it been flatly refuted. It seems to be agreed that languages differ in many strange and striking ways, but it is a moot point whether such differences in language structure are associated with actual differences in ways of perceiving and conceiving the world. Among the writers who are most impressed with the possibilities of such an association are Kluckhohn and Leighton (1946), Laura Thompson (1950), Hoijer (1953), and Kluckhohn (1954). Kluckhohn and Leighton, for example, state that the Navaho tongue is so radically different from ours that an understanding of Navaho linguistic structure is virtually a prerequisite to understanding the Navaho mind; they cite the tremendous translation difficulties existing between Navaho and English, and imply that the two languages almost literally operate in different worlds. Hoijer claims to have found a suggestion of a correlation between the world view implied by the Navaho verb system (that people only "participate" or "get involved" in acts rather than initiate them) and the passivity and general restlessness or fatefulness of Navaho mythology.

Two sharp critics of Whorf's methodology and conclusions, on the other hand, have been Lenneberg (1953) and Feuer (1953). Lenneberg attacks chiefly the methodology. First, he criticizes on several grounds the technique of translation which Whorf so often employed to demonstrate differences in languages; large differences in the linguistic handling of an event like cleaning of a gun do not necessarily imply corresponding differences in the perception of that event, and may merely result from metaphorical developments in the language, of which the speakers may not ordinarily be aware (just as we do not ordinarily think of "breakfast" as breaking a fast). Second, Lenneberg insists that linguistic and nonlinguistic events must be separately observed and described before they can be correlated, and that the usual canons of evidence must be applied in demonstrating any association between such events. Otherwise, the linguistic relativity principle becomes embarrassingly circular, or at least tautological, in that the only evidence for differences in "world view" turns out to be the linguistic differences. Feuer, a social philosopher, believes that on a priori grounds one would not expect cultures speaking different languages to have different ways of perceiving space, time, causation, and other fundamental elements of the physical world, because a correct perception of these elements is necessary to survival.

Since these and other logical, methodological, and psychological difficulties have recently received a thorough discussion at the hands of a special conference of linguists, anthropologists, psychologists, and philosophers (Hoijer, 1954), it seems pointless to labor them here. It is perhaps desirable to counteract, however, the essentially negative, pessimistic tone which pervaded this conference, by pointing out that extremely little research of an appropriate character has thus far been conducted on the Sapir–Whorf hypothesis. Except for the experiment reported by Brown and Lenneberg (1954), which showed that differences in ability to recognize and remember colors were associated with availability of specific color names, there have been virtually no researches which have adequately tested the existence of correlations between linguistic structure and nonlinguistic behavior. Numerous suggestions pointing toward such research have been made in a monograph edited by Osgood and Sebeok (1954).

There is a further consideration which has not been sufficiently stressed in the various discussions of the Sapir–Whorf hypothesis, namely, that the principle of linguistic relativity may not be so tautological as it has been made to appear. It has been said that one merely states a tautology when one appeals to differences in languages as showing differences in behavior, in "world view." It has also been said that it is necessary to find nonlinguistic behaviors which are correlated with the linguistic differences. This would doubtless be desirable, but there is something to be said for being interested in linguistic differences as such, regardless of nonlinguistic behavioral correlates. If we assume that there is such a thing as covert, implicit behavior, consisting of mental states, sets, attitudes, "mediational processes," and the like, we shall have to grant that such behavior is largely inaccessible to public observation save through the medium of verbal report. Whether or not, in fact, we assume any mental processes standing behind them, we are led to put a high value on verbal responses in their manifold forms as the chief data relating to perception and cognition.

Suppose, now, we found that, by varying certain environmental conditions, we could produce corresponding changes in the verbal reports made by speakers of a given language. For example, we might be able to find that we could in this way control which of several words (each standing for one of several environmental stimuli) was used as the subject of a sentence reporting the situation. Suppose further that, upon experimenting with speakers of another language, we found it impossible to produce changes in sentence structure corresponding to the varying environmental conditions—that all speakers invariably used the linguistic expression for ONE of the several stimuli as the subject of a sentence reporting the situations, and that, upon being questioned, the speakers of this language stated that it would be "unnatural" or "nonsense" to use any other linguistic expression in subject position in the sentence. The difference between the language behaviors would then be of interest in itself; we would have to conclude that we must take language structure into account in describing the verbal behavior of speakers in selecting the subject component of sentences. If, further, we had some fundamental knowledge about the grammatical meaning of sentence subject, we might be able to make some comparisons of the cognitive processes of speakers of the two languages. For example, suppose that the grammatical meaning of sentence subject were to be "entity perceived as a potential agent," then we might be permitted to conclude that the speakers of the second language in our illustration do not readily perceive certain stimuli as "potential agents."

This illustration has had to be somewhat far-fetched in several respects: partly that we do not yet know whether differences of the sort described could be found between speakers of different languages, and partly that we do not know very well how to specify behavioral correlates of grammatical categories. Yet, it is this kind of language difference which Whorf offers on an intuitive basis. He assumes that differences between languages would be found to correspond to differences in ways of reporting events, and that we can feel intuitively the grammatical and behavior forces underlying the linguistic phenomena which he describes. It must be granted that we have only begun to obtain detailed information about language differences and the behavioral pressures exerted by these differences, but, even when we get this information, much of it will be strictly in the realm of verbal behavior and the environmental stimulus complexes which evoke this verbal behavior.

One caution that needs to be stated in connection with the linguistic relativity principle, regardless of whether it is valid or not, is that the interest it has aroused and will continue to arouse should not be allowed to distract attention from the importance of language universals. Language universals, phenomena found in all languages, would be of as much interest psychologically as language differences. Is it true that all languages have subject-predicate construction in sentences? Do all languages have some type of noun-verb contrast? What features of verb-tense system are common to all languages? Answers to such questions would assist in the development of a generalized psychology of cognitive functions.

Because Whorf is chiefly known for his ideas on linguistic relativity, this volume features those of his writings which are most relevant to this problem. His studies in at least two other areas deserve recognition, however.

Whorf's early work in translating obscure Aztec documents was undoubtedly brilliant and made a distinctive contribution to a neglected corner of Middle American research. His interest in translating Aztec shortly gave way, however, to the quest for a means of reading the noncalendrical portions of Maya hieroglyphic writings. Here the validity of Whorf's work is at least highly controversial. There is no gainsaying that his observations in this area were exceedingly acute, and his "detective work" searching and clever. It is not for a nonspecialist to say how much Whorf actually accomplished toward the interpretation of the Maya hieroglyphs. There is certainly a great deal of plausibility in the translation processes which he presents, as in the paper reprinted here ("Decipherment of the linguistic portion of the Maya hieroglyphs"), and Whorf was too objective and intelligent a scholar to present mere ad hoc constructions which could not be tested and generalized. Yet, objections have been raised by several Maya scholars—during Whorf's lifetime by Long (1935, 1936) and Andrews (1938), and, most recently and also most severely, by J. Eric S. Thompson (1950). Nevertheless, the criticisms of Long and Andrews related chiefly to minor points, some of which Whorf was subsequently able to adjust, and Thompson does not seem to have answered fully the deeply rooted complaint of Whorf that the tradition in Maya hieroglyph research has been to ignore linguistic evidence. As late as 1939, Tozzer (1939) was willing to state his belief that there were considerable phonetic components cf Maya hieroglyphs, as Whorf urged, and we are told that the eminent Maya scholar, Herbert J. Spinden, was enthusiastic about the paper which Whorf read at the Eighth American Scientific Congress in May 1940. This paper is included here because so little progress has been made in reading Maya hieroglyphs and because it so well presents Whorf's notions about the problem and about writing systems in general.

Finally, Whorf's contributions to general linguistics should not be underestimated. His early theories of "oligosynthesis" and "binary grouping" were, to be sure, certainly overdrawn, and, except as might be implied by his continued admiration for the work of Fabre d'Olivet, he ceased to appeal to any such theories after he became a student of Sapir. Nevertheless, Whorf developed his theory of oligosynthesis with characteristic originality and acumen, and it is perhaps unfortunate that he never was able to bring himself to publish any full and mature description of the theory, for it is at least conceivable that there are languages, of which Aztec and Maya are possible examples, in which submorphemic elements are more productive throughout the whole of the vocabulary than the occasional "phonesthemes" which have been noted in English (such as the *sp* in 'spit, splash, spray, spout, sputter, splatter,' etc., which has seemed, to some, to carry the notion of "forceful outward motion").

Whorf was, at any rate, a master of straight linguistic description. His sketches of Milpa Alta Aztec and Mishongnovi Hopi as published by Hoijer (1946) are exemplary; they are characterized not only by the customary minute phonological and morphological descriptions but also by an unusual emphasis on seeking to find the meaning of grammatical categories. Some of this sort of approach can be seen in papers published in the present volume; for Hopi, in the paper "Some verbal categories of Hopi," and for English, or for languages in general, in the paper "Grammatical categories," in which he introduced a distinction between overt and covert grammatical categories, and first applied the term "cryptotype." I believe it can fairly be said that contemporary linguists have only begun to explore the full implications of Whorf's concept of cryptotype.

Even when Whorf worked on purely phonetic and phonemic problems, he was highly original. He was apparently the first to propose the term "allophone," now in common use among linguistic scientists. His model of the English monosyllable, as presented in his paper "Linguistics as an exact science," was at the time an original synthesis of facts about English sound clusters. He wrote an interesting paper on the phonemics of his own (Boston) dialect of English, published posthumously in 1943.

Whorf was everywhere an exceedingly acute observer of interesting and subtle phenomena in language structures. For example, in his hands a massive compilation of information about Shawnee, a language which he had not previously studied, was able to suggest several novel perspectives on figure-ground relationships as exemplified in Shawnee word formation; the reader is referred to the paper "Gestalt technique of stem composition in Shawnee," printed in this volume. As if to roll up in one package all the bases of his insights into language structure, Whorf once had occasion to prepare an outline which he thought anthropological field workers could use in collecting information about new languages. The outline was referred to in a publication by Murdock, "Outlines of cultural materials" (1938), but it has never before been published. In the belief that it will still be useful, even though its publication is belated, I have included it in the present collection under Whorf's title "Language: plan and conception of arrangement." It will doubtless demand considerable linguistic sophistication on the part of the reader to catch the meanings which are often only vaguely suggested by its outline form and sketchy phraseology, but at least it may serve in this way to stimulate in the reader some of the productive imagination which was characteristic of Whorf in whatever he touched.

* * *

SPECIAL NOTE

The reader is cautioned that the phonetic orthography for Hopi used in this volume varies according to the particular system employed in each individual paper. To have attempted to regularize this orthography would have required a major linguistic investigation, which the editor was not prepared to accomplish.

* * *

ACKNOWLEDGMENTS

Acknowledgment is here made for permission to include in this volume various writings of Whorf previously published elsewhere:

To Dr. Sol Tax, editor, for "A central Mexican inscription combining Mexican and Maya day signs" from the *American Anthropologist*, vol. 34, no. 2.

To Dr. Bernard Bloch, editor, for "The punctual and segmentative aspects of verbs in Hopi," "Some verbal categories of Hopi," and "Grammatical categories" from *Language*, vol. 12, no. 2; vol. 14, no. 4; and vol. 21, no. 1, respectively.

To Dr. C. F. Voegelin, editor, for "An American Indian model of the universe" and "Linguistic factors in the terminology of Hopi architecture" from the *International Journal of American Linguistics*, vol. 16, no. 2, and vol. 19, no. 2.

To Leslie Spier, editor, for "The relation of habitual thought and behavior to language" from *Language, Culture, and Personality*, pp. 75–93 (Menasha, Wis.; Sapir Memorial Publication Fund, 1941).

To Dr. Leonard Carmichael, secretary, Smithsonian Institution, for "Decipherment of the linguistic portion of the Maya hieroglyphs" from *The Smithsonian Report for 1941*, pp. 479–502.

To Dr. N. Sri Ram, president, the Theosophical Society, for "Language, mind, and reality" from *The Theosophist*, January 1942.

The illustrations for several of Whorf's papers in this volume have been specially redrawn by J. Martin Rosse, who prepared illustrations for Whorf's *Technology Review* papers in 1940 and 1941 from rough sketches which Whorf himself had supplied.

I am indebted to several persons for furnishing information and documents which were necessary to the preparation of this edition. Dr. George L. Trager helped me decide which of Whorf's writings should be included. Professor C. F. Voegelin supplied numerous scarce reprints, and a manuscript copy of "Language: plan and conception of arrangement" was lent by Professor Norman McQuown. Professor Herbert Hackett provided several bibliographical items which I might have otherwise missed.

I am particularly grateful to several members of the Whorf family for their kindness in granting me interviews: to Whorf's widow, Mrs. Celia Peckham Whorf, and to his brother, John Whorf of Provincetown, Massachusetts. Special thanks are due to Whorf's son, Robert Peckham Whorf, for allowing me to spend several days at his home examining Whorf's papers and correspondence, and for permitting me to borrow a number of his manuscripts, some of which are printed in this volume for the first time.

JOHN B. CARROLL

Arlington, Massachusetts
June, 1955

ON THE CONNECTION OF IDEAS*

320 Wolcott Hill Road
Wethersfield, Conn.
July 12, 1927

Dear Dr. English:

I have been intending to write you in regard to your little dictionary and especially to ask you for a name by which to denote a certain psychological concept, but I have not found a chance until the present, and I don't know whether this season will find you at your Middletown address. I must say that I appreciate that dictionary; it is not only actually interesting—a rare thing for a dictionary—but valuable as well. But I have not been able to find in it or in any other source a recognized term for one of the phenomena in which I am interested and would like to know if you know of such a term or could suggest one.

I have not been able to find a term that I need to denote a kind of connection or relation, approximation, closeness, allied character, between ideas. The only psychological term I know of that expresses connection between ideas is "association," but this has quite a definite meaning and one that will not do for the meaning I have in mind. The

* This unpublished essay was found by me among Whorf's papers as a partly typewritten, partly handwritten draft of a letter, dated July 12, 1927, to the psychologist Dr. Horace B. English, then of Wesleyan University, who had just published a dictionary of psychological terms. There is some question whether the letter was ever finished and sent, but Dr. English, now at The Ohio State University, has a vague recollection of receiving something like it. I have made minor editorial emendations and alterations where necessary.

"connection" of ideas, as I call it in the absence of any other term, is quite another thing from the "association" of ideas. In making experiments on the connecting of ideas, it is necessary to eliminate the "associations," which have an accidental character not possessed by the "connections." The subject must not jump at the first idea that comes to mind as in a "free association" experiment; hence the experiment might be considered a form of "controlled association"; yet it may be quite "free" in its own sphere, for any connection may be permitted.

"Connection" is important from a linguistic standpoint because it is bound up with the communication of ideas. One of the necessary criteria of a connection is that it be intelligible to others, and therefore the individuality of the subject cannot enter to the extent that it does in free association, while a correspondingly greater part is played by the stock of conceptions common to people. The very existence of such a common stock of conceptions, possibly possessing a yet unstudied arrangement of its own, does not yet seem to be greatly appreciated; yet to me it seems to be a necessary concomitant of the communicability of ideas by language; it holds the principle of this communicability, and is in a sense the universal language, to which the various specific languages give entrance.

For an example of connection, consider first the idea 'down,' and then the following ideas: 'set, sink, drag, drop, fall, hollow, depress, lie.' I will call these group A. It is clear that there is a "connection" between 'down' and each of the ideas in group A. Consider now group C, consisting of the ideas: 'upright, heave, hoist, tall, air, uphold, swell.' There is a "connection" between these ideas and the idea 'up.' Now in a connection experiment the subject, on receiving the idea 'down' would be free to connect with any of the ideas in group A or others like them but could not give any of the ideas in group C or the like. Yet, if it were a question of ASSOCIATIONS only, he might associate an idea in group C with 'down.' He might for instance have had an unpleasant experience in a boat when there was a heavy 'swell' on, from which he retained a vivid impression of continually going DOWN. But this association would not be a connection. It would pertain to his own personal experience rather than to the social or collective experience which is embodied in the common linguistic stock of concepts, and the reason for the association would not be intelligible immediately without explanation; it would require an explanation bringing in his personal experience. In this sense of immediate intelligibility, 'swell' is connected with 'up' or the like, and is distinctly removed from 'down.' So, in further definition of this concept of connection, it may be said that connections must be intelligible without reference to individual experiences and must be immediate in their relationship. Mediate connections, i.e., connections through the medium of other connections, are to be called rather chains or paths of connection, or possibly "communications."

It is possible to formulate another group of ideas, group *B*, which mediate between A and C, so that we can pass, by means of various chains or paths of connective communication, from A to C and hence from 'down' to 'up' entirely in a connective way and without the aid of association. For instance:

A	set	sink	drag	drop	hollow	depress	lie	DOWN
B	stand	heavy	pull	precipice	space	bear	extend	
C	upright	heave	hoist	tall	air	uphold	swell	UP

Subjects feeling their own way through the congeries of ideas between 'down' and 'up' do not always follow these paths but often find others. For instance, subject M. F. went as follows: 'set—heavy—swell—up.' Asked to explain the connection 'set—heavy,' it appeared that 'set' entailed a strong notion of fixation or fixity, and suggested 'rigidification, congelation, stiffening, thickening,' as in the setting of jelly, while 'heavy' implied to the subject not merely 'weight' but 'body, density, viscosity,' an idea closely similar to the preceding 'set.' This is a true connection, although it was not instantly intelligible to the experimenter, but it was quickly understood without reference to any personal experience. The connection 'heavy—swell' also was not instantly perceived, but it developed that 'heavy' conveyed essentially the idea of quantity or mass, including 'massiveness, size, increase': hence 'enlarge, expand, swell.' This again is a true connection. The same subject starting with 'up' traversed the path 'up—hoist—pull—drag—down.' Subject W. W. gave 'down—drop—heavy—hoist—up.' Asked to explain the connection 'heavy—hoist,' it appeared that heavy suggested the feeling or bearing of weight, the 'hefting' of a thing, essentially as lifting action. If the word 'heave' had been more familiar to the subject, he might have chosen it in preference to 'hoist.'

But a different and nonconnective process appeared when a young man having reached an idea 'past' took as the next step 'hiding,' overlooking an obvious 'before' in the same group. This still might be a connection if it yielded a satisfactory explanation, but the best explanation he could give was that one's past was usually unpleasant and so one would prefer not to remember it; hence it was in hiding. This might perhaps be only an awkward way of expressing the connection, but it appeared not. He did not respond to the suggestions that 'past' meant 'receded, withdrawn, retired, concealed,' or that it meant 'gone, vanished, invisible, concealed,' or that it meant 'existent (in memory)' but not 'apparent, stored up, hoarded,' etc., but persisted in this quite extraneous idea of the unpleasantness of the past. Hence I concluded either that an unpleasant past really had colored his way of thinking, or that he wished to pose as somewhat of a misanthrope or cynic, or that he had been reading psychoanalysis: that in any case we had to do here with something personal, which was indeed an ASSOCIATION yet not a CONNECTION. In telling him that I wanted connections that had nothing to do with personal experiences, he admitted that this might not apply to his association, and then chose 'before.'

Sometimes a subject will jump to a true connection by association and then get the connection later; e.g., W. W., a college freshman with intelligence distinctly above the average, said he thought the connection between 'drag' and 'down' was like this: 'drag' meant 'pull' and things went 'down' because PULLED by the ATTRACTION of gravity. He had just taken an examination in physics. I asked him whether he could have recognized a connection if he had never heard of gravity and he supposed not. I suggested that gravity might prove to be a compacting together due to a kind of external pressure, and then what would become of the connection? A mere hint was sufficient to lead him to the true connection, which is simply one of linguistic meaning, i.e., 'drag' = 'trail, dangle'; what is 'dragging' is in general 'down,' not 'up.' This is an interesting commentary on the inability to distinguish theory from fact in what is learned, even in an exceptionally intelligent student. (Or perhaps especially in such a one? That is, if intelligent means quick to learn, perhaps it also means receptive and hence too credulous?)

Can you suggest any better term for this sort of affinity than "connection"? I might say that my mental image of the relation is not at all one of ideas hitched together by bonds of attachment which they possess like miniature hooks and eyes. It is more a concept of continuity, with the ideas as relative locations in a continuous medium. Take an idea like "up," and say it corresponds to a certain location where we are. Now I can conceive that something like motion may happen to us. The idea "up" is a sort of neighborhood, and we are leaving that neighborhood. We cannot tell exactly where any neighborhood leaves off. We know that the idea UP is assuming a different nuance: it is growing to be like the idea RISE. But, after a certain amount of this change or "motion" has taken place, we know that we are in a different spot; the idea is now definitely 'rise,' not 'up.' Motion continues, and 'rise' becomes 'left.' 'Left' insensibly becomes 'carry,' and this becomes 'sustain.' We are now definitely out of the vicinity of 'up.' Any one of these ideas might have become something else by varying the "direction" of motion. 'Sustain' might become 'nourish,' or it might become 'continue.' 'Nourish' might become 'feed,' and 'continue' might become 'long.'

ON PSYCHOLOGY *

Psychology has developed a field of research that may no doubt be useful or valuable in itself, but it throws little or no light on problems of the normal human mind or soul. The person who wishes to understand more fully the laws and, so to speak, topography, of the inner or mental life is as much thrown back on his own difficultly acquired store of wisdom and his native judgments, intuitions, sympathies, and common sense as though the science of psychology did not exist. Such a one, for instance, is the teacher, educator, sociologist, anthropologist, trainer, coach, salesman, preacher, manager, diplomat, executive: anyone who must deal with human intangibles, especially the man concerned in leadership of any sort. If he seeks aid from books, he will get far more information about this field from literature not intended to be scientific, that is, from the best works of the novelists, playwrights, and poets, than he will from any textbook of psychology. There are certain courses that psychology has elected to follow that have estranged it, perhaps permanently, from the truly mental field.

First, the "old school" of experimental laboratory psychology has rather definitely assumed the character of a branch of physiology. Its

* This hitherto unpublished note was found by me among Whorf's papers as a rough handwritten manuscript. The date of its composition is unknown, although I would hazard a guess that it was written about the same time as the letter to English, that is, about 1927. The latter part of the note is extremely sketchy; perhaps this is only the outline of a longer paper which Whorf contemplated writing. I have supplied a title and made extremely minor editorial changes.

findings and their value all redound back to physiology. It is undoubtedly valuable to the student of mental phenomena to know the mechanisms of the body, but rather in the character of auxiliary information than anything else; and knowledge about the oxidation of the blood and the details of brain and nerve responses, sense perceptions, and association times are equally of this character. Moreover, one is impressed (and depressed) by the appalling sterility of the vast mass of minutiae that this science accumulates, and the dearth of integrating principles.

Second, the school of behaviorism has begun to appear in its true character as simply the old experimental psychology over again in a more pick-and-shovel aspect. That it is in many ways an improvement on the old school and has enlarged our understanding in certain fields I personally believe. It has been of service by teaching us to think more in terms of behavior, but, when all is said and done, it can teach us little that is new. It has shown us how behavior may be conditioned by physical means, but along much the same lines that we already knew although they have been more systematically explained. It has become apparent that we may "condition" either with or against the cooperation of truly psychic considerations. This we already knew, but we are particularly interested in "conditioning" WITH the cooperation of and in accordance with the particular laws of the psychic. No doubt the same process of stimulus and response "conditions" a man into being a scientist or a maniac, a leader of men or a nervous wreck, a good workman or one who cannot hold a job, an inspiring helper or a resentful cog in the machine; but behaviorism does not show us which lines to work upon in order to be really in accord with human intangibles, except by way of announcing in behavioristic terms things already obvious to common sense.

Gestalt psychology does seem to me to have discovered an important truth about mind, the importance of configurations in the mental domain. At the same time the Gestalt psychologists have their hands full with the manifold mechanical, experimental, and personal data required to develop this large subject, most of which data are chiefly valid on the animal level. When we attempt to apply the configurative principle to the understanding of human life, we immediately strike the cultural and the linguistic (part of the cultural), especially the latter, as the great field par excellence of the configurative on the human level.

Here the Gestalt psychologists let the matter drop. They have neither the time nor the linguistic training required to penetrate this field; moreover their ideas and terminology inherited from the old laboratory psychology are a liability rather than an asset.

Psychoanalysis is the one school that really deals with mental material, and it sometimes gets results, but it works only in the sphere of the abnormal and the deranged, and it is becoming evident that the abnormal is not the key to the normal. Moreover, it is so resolute in its determination to deal with intangibles that it shows almost a contempt for the external world and strays continually into the realms of phantasm. It is too heavily stamped with the signature of its founder, Freud, an erratic genius with a faculty of apperceiving deep but obscure truths, and is notion-obsessed and cluttered with weird dogma. As an empirical tool for the clinic it may serve for a while, but I do not see how it can possibly be a means for the careful scientific scrutiny of the normal mind.

All the schools then have been surveyed and found wanting, and the seeker for knowledge about the human mind is forced to fall back on the long-collected mass of empirical observations sometimes called "the wisdom of the ages," on the works of keenly intuitive authors, on his own insight, and on what few general truths he can cull here and there from all the above schools.

One fact that stands out to a detached viewpoint, but is not stressed by any of the schools, is the great and perhaps basic importance of the principle we denote by the word "meaning." Meaning will be found to be intimately connected with the linguistic: its principle is symbolism, but language is the great symbolism from which other symbolisms take their cue.

A CENTRAL MEXICAN INSCRIPTION

COMBINING MEXICAN

AND MAYA DAY SIGNS *

When in Mexico during the winter of 1930, engaged in Nahuatl linguistic research, I visited the village of Tepoztlan in the state of Morelos and while there made the accompanying sketch (Figure 1) of a band of sculptured figures in the ruined temple of the Tepoztecatl, the ancient tutelary deity, which stands on a great rock pinnacle overlooking the town.

The temple has been described by Saville,[1] Seler,[2] and Novelo,[3] but nowhere do any of them discuss the figures dealt with herein. The structure bears indications [4] of dating from the reign of the Aztec king Ahuitzotl, who died in 1502; but, as the figures in question show likenesses to forms known to be over a thousand years more ancient than this, it may be that in the building of the temple they were carved in obedience to artistic traditions, or copied from older architectural work of this region. They form a band extending along the top of a much more conspicuous frieze of larger carvings on the inner walls of the inner room or court. My sketch and remarks apply only to a clearly preserved portion of the band in the southern half of the court.

Stylistically and on the basis of general probabilities, the figures would,

* Reprinted from Amer. Anthrop., 34:296–302 (1932).

[1] Bull. Amer. Mus. Nat. Hist. (1896); also Monum. Records, February 1898.

[2] Bull. 28, Bur. Amer. Ethnol., 347; "Die Wandskulpturen im Tempel des Pulque-gottes von Tepoztlan," Gesamm. Abh., 3:487.

[3] "Guia para visitar las principales ruinas arqueologicas del estado de Morelos," Publ. Sec. Educacion, Publica, 3 (1929).

[4] See Seler, Bull. 28, Bur. Amer. Ethnol.

Figure 1.   Inscription in the Temple of the Tepoztecatl, Tepoztlan, Morelos, Mexico.

I think, strike any student as a band of the day signs of the tonalamatl, such as one sees continued interminably along with the successions of pictures in the Mexican codices. But many of the signs bear little resemblance to their Mexican form, the form corresponding to the Aztec names Cipactli, Ehecatl, Calli, etc. Nevertheless, as we shall presently see, the signs Acatl, Malinalli, and Atl are in practically their regular Mexican forms, and to clinch the matter are precisely the correct number of signs apart. But moreover, and here the unusual enters, some of the signs bear an unmistakable likeness to the quite un-Mexican-looking Maya forms, corresponding to the Maya names Imix, Ik, Akbal, etc., and these signs, too, are in exactly their proper places. The ruin is of course far removed from historical Maya territory, being only about forty miles from Mexico City in a region of Toltec and post-Toltec influence.

As I sketched the figures, their general un-Aztec look quickly struck me, but the first clear impression that I was drawing a MAYA HIEROGLYPH came when I began to copy the sign Figure 1, no. 10. Comparison with a very common Maya hieroglyph, whose most usual form is that shown in Figure 2, no. 10, indicates the similarity. The Maya sign is a hand having the distinctive characteristics of a prominent thumb more or less opposed toward the fingers, and having invariably on the wrist a circle usually with a central dot and a small taglike projection from the rim. The fingers are usually bent toward the thumb, but there are forms on the Maya monuments in which they are extended straight as in the Tepoztlan figure. This sign is a hieroglyphic element of wide and varied use, but it is especially a grapheme [5] that stands for the day sign Manik. In the Mexican day-sign system there is no grapheme even remotely resembling a hand. The sign corresponding to Manik is called Mazatl, and its grapheme is a deer's head (Figure 2, no. 9).

Can it be that this Tepoztlan hand figure represents Manik–Mazatl? Do the other signs fall into the proper places required by such an assumption? Let us see. In both day-sign systems the sign before Manik–Mazatl is called by a similar name, Cimi in Maya and Miquiztli in Aztec, both meaning "death." The grapheme in both systems is a death's head

[5] Grapheme is a word formed on the analogy of morpheme, semanteme, to denote any written symbol, especially as a linguistic factor, in place of "ideogram," "pictograph," or the ambiguous "character." In discussing hieroglyphs it is desirable to have a term that does not presuppose anything about the nature of the denotative process employed.

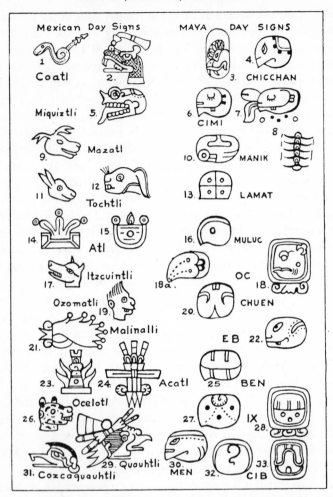

Figure 2. The Mexican and Maya day signs from Coatl–Chicchan to Cozca-quauhtli–Cib in their order. Bibliographic references: 1, 9, 11, 15, 17, 19, 23, and 26 from Sahagun manuscript, 2 and 5 from Zouche Codex; 12 and 31 from Fejervary-Mayer manuscript; 14 from Codex Telleriano–Remensis; 21, 24, and 29 from Seler's *Caractère des inscriptions;* 3, 4, 6, 13, 16, 18, 20, 22, 25, 27, 28, 30, 33 from Morley's *Introduction to Maya hieroglyphs* (3, 18, and 28 inscription forms from p. 38, 33 an inscription form from p. 95, the others codex forms from p. 39); 7, hieroglyph of death god, from Dresden Codex, p. 15; 8, representation of human skeleton from Uxmal, from Spinden's *Maya art,* and 32, Codex Peresianus, from Spinden's *Maya art,* p. 94; 10, from Codex Tro-Cortesianus; 18a, Maya hieroglyph based on dog's head and related to Oc (18), from Dresden Codex.

or head of the death god, stylistically different, however, in the two systems. Figure 2, no. 5 shows the Aztec type of grapheme, a fleshless skull; Figure 2, no. 6, the Maya type; and Figure 2, no. 7, the hieroglyph of the Maya death god as it appears in the Maya codices. Now the direction of Aztec and Maya writing is like our own, from left to right. The figure to the left of the hand (Figure 1, no. 9) bears no resemblance to Miquiztli or Cimi. But the figure to the RIGHT of the hand (Figure 1, no. 11), strange to say, shows a most curious likeness to the hieroglyph of the Maya death god. The two prefixes attached to the head are especially characteristic of this grapheme, indeed are found nowhere else. The Tepoztlan glyph however has a suffix that is not found in the death-god grapheme, but is an element in other Maya hieroglyphs. It is particularly characteristic of the month sign Kankin, and according to Seler represents a human skeleton. It seems to be related to the skeletal representation shown in Figure 2, no. 8, taken from Figure 115, page 86 of Spinden's *Maya Art*, where Spinden treats of the artistic symbolism of bones and death among the Maya.

The fact is, as will soon be proved, that we have here an inscription which for some unknown reason is written in reverse order, from right to left, and this death-god sign stands for Cimi–Miquiztli. Once this is realized, the student of the subject will soon notice another out-and-out Maya sign, namely the ninth figure to the left of the hand, Figure 1, no. 1. In the Mexican system the ninth sign after Mazatl is called Cozcaquauhtli, and its grapheme is the head of a vulture (Figure 2, no. 31) or of an eagle wearing a collar. In the Maya system the ninth sign after Manik is called Cib, and its grapheme (Figure 2, nos. 32 and 33) is a curved line like a question mark or sometimes rather like a letter C turned over or turned backward. This last is the form of the Tepoztlan figure.

The two dots beside the curve are not found in the Maya Cib, but they nevertheless confirm the identification. Seler, from the fact that the sign Cib was often represented on liquor vessels, connected it with a similar sign placed by the Aztec on their drinking vessels and called *ometoch*, from the god of intoxication Ome Tochtli, literally 'Two Rabbit.' This god is often represented (e.g., Sahagun Madrid Manuscript, under his name Totochtin) carrying a shield with a sign very similar to the Tepoztlan figure. An Aztec note on the Sahagun picture says that the god bears an *ometoch-chimalli*, that is, 'shield with the device

Two Rabbit.' In our present case the two dots are merely the usual expression of the number part of such a name as Two Rabbit. Ome Tochtli and Tepoztecatl are considered to be the same or related deities, so that their especial cult in Tepoztlan might perhaps employ their emblem as a day-sign grapheme when it would not be so employed elsewhere. The point is that they should have employed it, not for *Tochtli* or 'Rabbit,' but for *Cozcaquauhtli* or 'Vulture,' of all signs the one corresponding in position to Maya Cib.

Let us check the positions of the other signs proceeding from no. 10, or Manik, toward Cib. Number 9 is too worn to be distinctly recognizable as anything; yet, by comparison with the form of the Mexican sign Tochtli, shown in Figure 2, no. 12, it will be seen to resemble a worn-down carving of this form.

The next sign, no. 8, is crowded against the following sign no. 7 and is placed in an angle where the band turns the corner of the wall. If it is compared with the grapheme of the Aztec sign *Atl* ('Water') shown in Figure 2, no. 14, the likeness will be evident.

Number 7, the next figure, occupies the place of the Aztec *Itzcuintli* ('Dog') and the Maya Oc. It shows a head that looks more like a toucan or some such bird than a dog. It certainly shows little resemblance to the naturalistic dog's head (Figure 2, no. 17), the grapheme for this day sign in the Mexican system. Now a toucan-like conventional head, shown in Figure 2, no. 18*a*, is one of the commonest hieroglyphic elements in the Maya codices, and Beyer [6] has shown that this conventionalized head is derived from that of the dog. The Maya day sign corresponding to Itzcuintli is called Oc, and has two distinct forms of grapheme. The form of the codices has no resemblance to the Tepoztlan. The form of the Maya inscriptions, shown in Figure 2, no. 18, may be compared with the Tepoztlan form. The dog hieroglyph may be further compared in that it always bears a suffix containing a two-lobed figure, while the Tepoztlan glyph shows suffixed to the head a square frame containing a two-lobed figure.

Sign 6 shows a certain resemblance to the Maya Chuen, Figure 2, no. 20, and is quite unlike the naturalistic monkey head of the Aztec Ozomatli (Fig. 2, no. 19).

Sign 5 agrees with the Aztec grapheme for the same position.

[6] *Amer. Anthrop.*, 31 (1929).

Although it is much worn and a cavity in the stone seems to have been scooped out of a part of it, the brush of tonguelike streamers characteristic of Malinalli is recognizable (cf. the form of Malinalli shown in Fig. 2, no. 21). Here there is no trace of the Maya form (Eb, Fig. 2, no. 22).

Sign 4 shows in proper position the distinctive features of certain forms of the Mexican Acatl. (Cf. especially the form shown in Fig. 2, no. 24.) The Maya Ben, Figure 2, no. 25, is quite different.

Sign 3 however is a very strange one. It is certainly nothing like the Mexican Ocelotl, a jaguar head, Figure 2, no. 26. Nor is there any external resemblance to the Maya Ix, Figure 2, nos. 27 and 28. And yet it contains in a curious way two elements of the Ix grapheme. The really essential element of the grapheme is the three dots, and the Tepoztlan figure displays very prominently three large dots on the left and three smaller dots on the right. Distinctive of the codex form of Ix are the two converging dotted lines, and the Tepoztlan sign bears a shield-shaped figure on which are two similarly placed lines.

Sign 2 bears no resemblance to the Maya Men (Fig. 2, no. 30) nor to the ordinary form of the Aztec Quauhtli, an eagle's head. But Seler [7] pictures a form of Quauhtli (Fig. 2, no. 29) in which the eagle wears a headdress that compares interestingly in its main features with the Tepoztlan figure. This brings us to sign 1, or Cib, which we have already discussed. There is a sign beyond this which I have not shown, as it is worn and hard to make out, and I did not secure a good drawing. It shows no likeness to the unmistakable Aztec Olin or to the Maya Caban.

What does the band show to the right of sign 11, or Cimi? A blank space where the stone has been broken away. Beyond this space appears one more sign, no. 12. Of course we do not know whether any signs were inscribed in this space, or if so how many, though I should say the space would contain only two. Allowing two signs for the space would make no. 12 become no. 14, the position of the Aztec Calli or the Maya Akbal, neither of which has any resemblance to it. It is a conventionalized serpent jaw, a common Middle American art motive. Therefore I think that no signs need be allotted to the broken space and that we have here the day sign before Cimi–Miquiztli, which is the Maya Chicchan (Fig. 2, nos. 3 and 4), the Aztec *Coatl* (Serpent) (Fig. 2, nos. 1 and

[7] *Caractère des inscriptions Aztèques et Mayas.*

2). The common Aztec form is not conventionalized to the degree of this figure.

It is perhaps these figures to which Novelo refers in his words:

——hay otros jeroglíficos cuya interpretacion no ha sido posible de hacer, alguno de los cuales tienen cierta semejanza con los mayas.

Moreover he refers to the Maya influence in these terms:

——parece existir en los relieves de origen tlahuica (Tepoztlan y Xochicalco) cierta influencia maya cuya cultura floreció en Mexico, como se sabe, en los primeros siglos de la Era Cristiana.

He also tells us that pilgrims from far-away Chiapas and Guatemala, regions once of Maya culture, were accustomed to visit the sanctuary of Tepoztlan.

Yet it is certainly unexpected to encounter here, not far from Mexico City, definite day signs denoted by graphemes which, like Cib and Manik, were being carved on the structures of the old Maya Empire in distant Central America a millennium and more before the date of the Aztec temple on which they appear interchangeably with ordinary Aztec forms. And why was the sign series recorded backward? Here again the only comparable thing that I can think of is a Maya one, the fact that the Maya inscriptions record a number series in reverse order when it is counting back into the past: that is, when its total is to be subtracted from, and not added to, a beginning date, in order to reach a second date. Does this Tepoztlan inscription seek to show the tonalamatl receding into the past?

We have here for the first time evidence of a definite, clearly demonstrable rapport between Nahuatl hieroglyphs and early Maya ones. The whole subject of the relation of Mexican and Maya graphemes, as it reveals itself in other places, is something of which I hope to treat extensively and from a linguistic viewpoint at another time.

THE PUNCTUAL AND

SEGMENTATIVE ASPECTS OF

VERBS IN HOPI*

Verbs in the Hopi language are noteworthy for their very rich and expressive development of verbal aspects and voices. I shall say nothing in this paper of the nine voices (intransitive, transitive, reflexive, passive, semipassive, resultative, extended passive, possessive, and cessative); and of the nine aspects (punctual, durative, segmentative, punctual–segmentative, inceptive, progressional, spatial, projective, and continuative) I shall deal with only two. It may be noted that there are no perfective and imperfective aspects; in fact Hopi does not in any way formalize as such the contrast between completion and incompletion of action. Its aspects formalize different varieties of the contrast between point-locus and extent-locus of phenomena, indifferently in time or space, or in both. Hopi also has three tenses: factual or present–past, future, and generalized or usitative. Hopi verbs belong to seven classes or conjugations having slightly different inflectional systems. Class 1, the largest and most creative class, contains a few categories not found in the other classes, among them the segmentative aspect.

The simplex of the class-1 verb is a bare root of the form CVCV, and is in the third person singular intransitive voice, punctual aspect, and present–past tense. The segmentative aspect is formed by final reduplication of this root plus the durative suffix -ta, and produces a change in the meaning of the simplex of the following character: the

* Reprinted from *Language* 12:127–131 (1936). The paper was read before the Linguistic Society of America in December 1935.

phenomenon denoted by the root, shown in the punctual aspect as manifested about a point, becomes manifested as a series of repeated interconnected segments of one large phenomenon of a stretched-out segmental character, its extension usually being predominantly in one dimension, indifferently of space or time or both. The nature of the change can best be shown by examples.

ha'ri	it is bent in a rounded angle	*hari'rita*	it lies in a meandering line, making successive rounded angles (applied for instance to meander patterns in decoration)
ho''ci	it forms a sharp acute angle	*hoci'cita*	it is zigzag
pa''ci	it is notched	*paci'cita*	it is serrated
pi'va	it is gullied out	*piva'vata*	it extends in successive gullies and gulches (said of ground)
ca'mi	it is slashed inward from the edge	*cami'mita*	it is fringed, it is slashed into a fringe along the edge

In these and similar examples, the phenomenon is such that it requires a rigid or semirigid substance for its field of manifestation. When this is the case the punctual intransitive has somewhat the character of a passive,[1] and the segmentative shows the phenomenon multiplied along one dimension of space, like a candle flame between mirrors. In both aspects, the phenomenon shows up as an effect established and thereafter retained in the rigid substance, so that we are presented with a static TABLEAU of this effect as it is disposed in space.

Suppose, however, that the phenomenon denoted by the verb root is such as to require a nonrigid or mobile substance for its field of manifestation, for example a liquid or a swarm of mobile particles. In that case a deformation of substance such as is denoted by the root will not be a permanent deformation but will result in a vibrative or pulsative agitation of the substance. The intransitive will no longer seem like a passive from our English-speaking viewpoint but will be decidedly active, and the punctual will denote one pulse of the deformation or disturbance, while the segmentative will refer to the entire train or field of the vibrations, both as extending in space and as continuing in time. Thus, for instance:

---

[1] It is not a true passive because it does not imply any external agent; it is not a static (at least not in the ordinary sense) because it does not imply duration in time; it is not a true active because activity and result are presented as one.

wa'la it (e.g. a liquid) makes one wave, gives a slosh

wala'lata it is tossing in waves, it is kicking up a sea

nö'ya several come out (applied to objects or persons)

nöya'yata it is coming out in successive multitudes, it is gushing or spraying out (applied e.g. to a fountain)

Note that with mobile-substance phenomena the segmentative is both durative in time, in contrast to the momentaneous punctual, and extended in space, in contrast to the definitely "spotted" location of the punctual. Some phenomena are capable of manifestation in both mobile and rigid substances, especially those defined in terms of a certain type of contour; e.g. *ta'ho* 'it exhibits one wavelike curve, or makes one undulation'; *taho'hota* referring to a mobile substance means 'it is undulating' (for example a liquid surface, a snake, a shaken rope), to a nonmobile substance 'it is scalloped' or 'it forms a wave pattern.'

But suppose again that the phenomenon denoted by the stem is one resulting from the type of force known in physics as torque (tendency to produce rotation), which in order for any effect to be apparent requires that the substance be a body with at least a certain degree of rigidity and yet capable of certain degrees of motion relative to other bodies. In this case a single deformation or displacement as denoted by the punctual will be either a single oscillation or a single turning of this body according to the degree of freedom implied in the root-meaning; while, if the effect continues, it will continue as a train of oscillations or a continued rotation and may or may not involve an advance through space at the same time: this, then, will be the meaning of the segmentative. Examples of this type of meaning are:

wa'ya makes a waving shake (like a small tree shaken)
ya'ya makes a sway from one side to the other
pï·'ya makes a flap like a pair of wings
ta'ya makes a racking shake
yö'ya makes a circuit (axial turning combined with advance in an arc)
ro'ya makes a turn or twist
ri'ya makes a quick spin

It is interesting to note that a great many (though not all) of these torque movements are denoted by stems ending in *-ya*. The segmentatives of this type correspond to English durative forms denoting vibrative or rotative motion, e.g.:

waya'yata	it is shaking	*pï·ya'yata*	it is flapping wings
ŋaya'yata	it is swaying	*ŋöya'yata*	it is circling round and round
roya'yata	it is rotating	*riya'yata*	it is spinning, whirling

In the case of *mï'ma* 'rolls over,' where necessarily a lateral motion accompanies the turning, we get this phase of the action necessarily extended in *mïma'mata* 'it is rolling along.'

Another type of this general class of phenomena is one which manifests punctually as a shock, jar, or other sudden disturbance necessarily momentary in nature, and is related to a pulsative phenomenon also occurring in the natural world as a rapid succession of such shocks. Here English generally employs two different stems, but Hopi simply uses the punctual and segmentative of the same stem. An example from inanimate nature is *ti'li* 'it receives a slight jar,' *tili'lita* 'it is vibrating' (like an engine, a wagon, an automobile). But Hopi also discerns a great many such phenomena in the animate world, for example:

ti'ri	he gives a sudden start	*tïrï'rïta*	he is quivering, trembling
wi'wa	he trips over something, or is suddenly caught by the legs, like a lassoed horse	*wiwa'wata*	he is stumbling or hobbling along
ya'ro	his teeth strike on something hard or gritty, e.g. in the food	*yaro'rota*	he is chewing forcibly on something hard
hɛ'ro	he (or it) gives out a sudden hollow gurgle from within	*hɛro'rota*	he is snoring

Often, again, such verb forms are applied to rhythmical movements of the body and limbs:

wï''ki	he takes a step without moving from place	*wikï'kita*	he is doing steps, or dancing in one place
kⁿⁱi'la	he takes a step forward	*kʷila'lata*	he does a walk forward (not 'is walking forward' which English expression is almost a punctual)
yo''ko	he gives one nod of the head	*yoko'kota*	he is nodding

Again, the phenomenon may be one of disturbance at a point in a subtle medium, that is one that would be scientifically classed as gaseous or etheric. Such a medium gives little or no evidence of either motion or extension in space, and the segmentative in these cases denotes only pulsation in time:

rï"pi	it gives a flash	rïpi'pita	it is sparkling
ʔï'wi	it flames up	ʔïwi'wita	it is flaming
ʔï'mï	it explodes, goes off like a gun	ʔïmï'mïta	it is thundering

Finally, there is one class of events to which the segmentative is not applied. It is not applied to "mental," "emotional," or other "inner" or "psychological" experiences. It concerns only the world of external observation.

All this has a wider interest than the mere illustration of an aspect-form. It is an illustration of how language produces an organization of experience. We are inclined to think of language simply as a technique of expression, and not to realize that language first of all is a classification and arrangement of the stream of sensory experience which results in a certain world-order, a certain segment of the world that is easily expressible by the type of symbolic means that language employs. In other words, language does in a cruder but also in a broader and more versatile way the same thing that science does. We have just seen how the Hopi language maps out a certain terrain of what might be termed primitive physics. We have observed how, with very thorough consistency and not a little true scientific precision, all sorts of vibratile phenomena in nature are classified by being referred to various elementary types of deformation process. The analysis of a certain field of nature which results is freely extensible, and all-in-all so harmonious with actual physics that such extension could be made with great appropriateness to a multiplicity of phenomena belonging entirely to the modern scientific and technical world—movements of machinery and mechanism, wave processes and vibrations, electrical and chemical phenomena—things that the Hopi have never known or imagined, and for which we ourselves lack definite names. The Hopi actually have a language better equipped to deal with such vibratile phenomena than is our latest scientific terminology. This is simply because their language establishes a general contrast between two types of experience, which contrast corresponds to a contrast that, as our science has discovered, is all-pervading and fundamental in nature. According to the conceptions of modern physics, the contrast of particle and field of vibrations is more fundamental in the world of nature than such contrasts as space and time, or past, present, and future, which are the sort of contrasts that our own language imposes upon us. The Hopi aspect-contrast which we have observed, being obligatory upon their verb forms, practically forces the Hopi to notice and observe vibratory phenomena, and furthermore encourages them to find names for and to classify such phenomena. As a matter of fact the language is extraordinarily rich in terms for vibratory phenomena and for the punctual events to which they are related.

AN AMERICAN INDIAN MODEL

OF THE UNIVERSE *

I find it gratuitous to assume that a Hopi who knows only the Hopi language and the cultural ideas of his own society has the same notions, often supposed to be intuitions, of time and space that we have, and that are generally assumed to be universal. In particular, he has no general notion or intuition of TIME as a smooth flowing continuum in which everything in the universe proceeds at an equal rate, out of a future, through a present, into a past; or, in which, to reverse the picture, the observer is being carried in the stream of duration continuously away from a past and into a future.

After long and careful study and analysis, the Hopi language is seen to contain no words, grammatical forms, constructions or expressions that refer directly to what we call "time," or to past, present, or future, or to enduring or lasting, or to motion as kinematic rather than dynamic (i.e. as a continuous translation in space and time rather than as an exhibition of dynamic effort in a certain process), or that even refer to space in such a way as to exclude that element of extension or existence that we call "time," and so by implication leave a residue that could be

* The manuscript of this article, together with pertinent linguistic notes, was among the papers left by Whorf at his death and turned over to George L. Trager. Dr. Trager and Dr. E. A. Kennard edited the manuscript for publication, making no substantial changes, and the paper is presented here in the form in which it appeared in the *Int. J. Amer. Linguistics*, 16:67–72 (1950). Internal evidence and certain comments found in Whorf's correspondence suggest that the paper was written in about 1936.

referred to as "time." Hence, the Hopi language contains no reference to "time," either explicit or implicit.

At the same time, the Hopi language is capable of accounting for and describing correctly, in a pragmatic or operational sense, all observable phenomena of the universe. Hence, I find it gratuitous to assume that Hopi thinking contains any such notion as the supposed intuitively felt flowing of "time," or that the intuition of a Hopi gives him this as one of its data. Just as it is possible to have any number of geometries other than the Euclidean which give an equally perfect account of space configurations, so it is possible to have descriptions of the universe, all equally valid, that do not contain our familiar contrasts of time and space. The relativity viewpoint of modern physics is one such view, conceived in mathematical terms, and the Hopi Weltanschauung is another and quite different one, nonmathematical and linguistic.

Thus, the Hopi language and culture conceals a METAPHYSICS, such as our so-called naïve view of space and time does, or as the relativity theory does; yet it is a different metaphysics from either. In order to describe the structure of the universe according to the Hopi, it is necessary to attempt—insofar as it is possible—to make explicit this metaphysics, properly describable only in the Hopi language, by means of an approximation expressed in our own language, somewhat inadequately it is true, yet by availing ourselves of such concepts as we have worked up into relative consonance with the system underlying the Hopi view of the universe.

In this Hopi view, time disappears and space is altered, so that it is no longer the homogeneous and instantaneous timeless space of our supposed intuition or of classical Newtonian mechanics. At the same time, new concepts and abstractions flow into the picture, taking up the task of describing the universe without reference to such time or space—abstractions for which our language lacks adequate terms. These abstractions, by approximations of which we attempt to reconstruct for ourselves the metaphysics of the Hopi, will undoubtedly appear to us as psychological or even mystical in character. They are ideas which we are accustomed to consider as part and parcel either of so-called animistic or vitalistic beliefs, or of those transcendental unifications of experience and intuitions of things unseen that are felt by the consciousness of the mystic, or which are given out in mystical and (or) so-called occult systems of thought. These abstractions are definitely given either explicitly in words—psychological or metaphysical terms—in the Hopi language, or, even more, are implicit in the very structure and grammar of that language, as well as being observable in Hopi culture and behavior. They are not, so far as I can consciously avoid it, projections of other systems upon the Hopi language and culture made by me in my attempt at an objective analysis. Yet, if MYSTICAL be perchance a term of abuse in the eyes of a modern Western scientist, it must be emphasized that these underlying abstractions and postulates of the Hopian metaphysics are, from a detached viewpoint, equally (or to the Hopi, more) justified pragmatically and experientially, as compared to the flowing time and static space of our own metaphysics, which are *au fond* equally mystical. The Hopi postulates equally account for all phenomena and their interrelations, and lend themselves even better to the integration of Hopi culture in all its phases.

The metaphysics underlying our own language, thinking, and modern culture (I speak not of the recent and quite different relativity metaphysics of modern science) imposes upon the universe two grand COSMIC FORMS, space and time; static three-dimensional infinite space, and kinetic one-dimensional uniformly and perpetually flowing time—two utterly separate and unconnected aspects of reality (according to this familiar way of thinking). The flowing realm of time is, in turn, the subject of a threefold division: past, present, and future.

The Hopi metaphysics also has its cosmic forms comparable to these in scale and scope. What are they? It imposes upon the universe two grand cosmic forms, which as a first approximation in terminology we may call MANIFESTED and MANIFESTING (or, UNMANIFEST) or, again, OBJECTIVE and SUBJECTIVE. The objective or manifested comprises all that is or has been accessible to the senses, the historical physical universe, in fact, with no attempt to distinguish between present and past, but excluding everything that we call future. The subjective or manifesting comprises all that we call future, BUT NOT MERELY THIS; it includes equally and indistinguishably all that we call mental—everything that appears or exists in the mind, or, as the Hopi would prefer to say, in the HEART, not only the heart of man, but the heart of animals, plants, and things, and behind and within all the forms and appearances of nature in the heart of nature, and by an implication and extension which has been felt by more than one anthropologist, yet would hardly ever be spoken of by a Hopi himself, so charged is the idea with religious and magical awesomeness, in the very heart of the Cosmos, itself.[1] The subjective realm (subjective from our viewpoint, but intensely real and quivering with life, power, and potency to the Hopi) embraces not only our FUTURE, much of which the Hopi regards as more or less predestined in essence if not in exact form, but also all mentality, intellection, and emotion, the essence and typical form of which is the striving of purposeful desire, intelligent in character, toward manifestation—a manifestation which is much resisted and delayed, but in some form or other is inevitable. It is the realm of expectancy, of desire and purpose, of vitalizing life, of efficient causes, of thought thinking itself out from an inner realm (the Hopian HEART) into manifestation. It is in a dynamic state, yet not a state of motion—it is not advancing toward us out of a future, but ALREADY WITH US in vital and mental form, and its dynamism is at work in the field of eventuating or manifesting, i.e. evolving without motion from the subjective by degrees to a result which is the objective. In translating into English, the Hopi will say that these entities in process of causation 'will come' or that they—the Hopi—'will come to' them, but, in their own language, there are no verbs corresponding to our 'come' and 'go' that mean simple and abstract motion, our purely kinematic concept. The words in this case translated 'come' refer to the process of eventuating without calling it motion—they are 'eventuates to here' (*pew'i*) or 'eventuates from it' (*angqö*) or 'arrived' (*pitu*, pl. *öki*) which refers only to the terminal manifestation, the actual arrival at a given point, not to any motion preceding it.

This realm of the subjective or of the process of manifestation, as distinguished from the objective, the result of this universal process, includes also—on its border but still pertaining to its own realm—an aspect of existence that we include in our present time. It is that which is beginning to emerge into manifestation; that is, something which is beginning to be done, like going to sleep or starting to write, but is not yet in full operation. This can be and usually is referred to by the same verb form (the EXPECTIVE form in my terminology of Hopi grammar) that refers to our future, or to wishing, wanting, intending, etc. Thus, this nearer edge of the subjective cuts across and includes a part of our present time, viz. the moment of inception, but most of our present

---

[1] This idea is sometimes alluded to as the 'spirit of the Breath' (*hikwsu*) and as the 'Mighty Something' (*ʔaʔne himu*), although these terms may have lower and less cosmic though always awesome connotations.

belongs in the Hopi scheme to the objective realm and so is indistinguishable from our past. There is also a verb form, the INCEPTIVE which refers to this EDGE of emergent manifestation in the reverse way—as belonging to the objective, as the edge at which objectivity is attained; this is used to indicate beginning or starting, and in most cases there is no difference apparent in the translation from the similar use of the expective. But, at certain crucial points, significant and fundamental differences appear. The inceptive, referring to the objective and result side, and not like the expective to the subjective and causal side, implies the ending of the work of causation in the same breath that it states the beginning of manifestation. If the verb has a suffix which answers somewhat to our passive, but really means that causation impinges upon a subject to effect a certain result—i.e. 'the food is being eaten,' then addition of the INCEPTIVE suffix in such a way as to refer to the basic action produces a meaning of causal cessation. The basic action is in the inceptive state; hence whatever causation is behind it is ceasing; the causation explicitly referred to by the causal suffix is hence such as WE would call past time, and the verb includes this and the incepting and the decausating of the final state (a state of partial or total eatenness)ᴵ in one statement. The translation is 'it stops getting eaten.' Without knowing the underlying Hopian metaphysics, it would be impossible to understand how the same suffix may denote starting or stopping.

If we were to approximate our metaphysical terminology more closely to Hopian terms, we should probably speak of the subjective realm as the realm of HOPE or HOPING. Every language contains terms that have come to attain cosmic scope of reference, that crystallize in themselves the basic postulates of an unformulated philosophy, in which is couched the thought of a people, a culture, a civilization, even of an era. Such are our words 'reality, substance, matter, cause,' and as we have seen 'space, time, past, present, future.' Such a term in Hopi is the word most often translated 'hope'—*tunátya*—'it is in the action of hoping, it hopes, it is hoped for, it thinks or is thought of with hope,' etc. Most metaphysical words in Hopi are verbs, not nouns as in European languages. The verb *tunátya* contains in its idea of hope something of our words 'thought,' 'desire,' and 'cause,' which sometimes must be used to translate it. The word is really a term which crystallizes the Hopi philosophy of the universe in respect to its grand dualism of objective and subjective; it is the Hopi term for SUBJECTIVE. It refers to the state of the subjective, unmanifest, vital and causal aspect of the Cosmos, and the fermenting activity toward fruition and manifestation with which it seethes—an action of HOPING; i.e. mental-causal activity, which is forever pressing upon and into the manifested realm. As anyone acquainted with Hopi society knows, the Hopi see this burgeoning activity in the growing of plants, the forming of clouds and their condensation in rain, the careful planning out of the communal activities of agriculture and architecture, and in all human hoping, wishing, striving, and taking thought; and as most especially concentrated in prayer, the constant hopeful praying of the Hopi community, assisted by their exoteric communal ceremonies and their secret, esoteric rituals in the underground kivas—prayer which conducts the pressure of the collective Hopi thought and will out of the subjective into the objective. The inceptive form of *tunátya*, which is *tunátyava*, does not mean 'begins to hope,' but rather 'comes true, being hoped for.' Why it must logically have this meaning will be clear from what has already been said. The inceptive denotes the first appearance of the objective, but the basic meaning of *tunátya* is subjective activity or force; the inceptive is then the terminus of such activity. It might then be said that *tunátya* 'coming true' is the Hopi term for objective, as contrasted with subjective, the two terms being simply two different inflectional nuances of the same verbal root, as the two cosmic forms are the two aspects of one reality.

As far as space is concerned, the subjective is a mental realm, a realm of no space in the objective sense, but it seems to be symbolically related to the vertical dimension and its poles the zenith and the underground, as well as to the 'heart' of things, which corresponds to our word 'inner' in the metaphorical sense. Corresponding to each point in the objective world is such a vertical and vitally INNER axis which is what we call the wellspring of the future. But to the Hopi there is no temporal future; there is nothing in the subjective state corresponding to the sequences and successions conjoined with distances and changing physical configurations that we find in the objective state. From each subjective axis, which may be thought of as more or less vertical and like the growth-axis of a plant, extends the objective realm in every physical direction, though these directions are typified more especially by the horizontal plane and its four cardinal points. The objective is the great cosmic form of extension; it takes in all the strictly extensional aspects of existence, and it includes all intervals and distances, all seriations and number. Its DISTANCE includes what we call time in the sense of the temporal relation between events which have already happened. The Hopi conceive time and motion in the objective realm in a purely operational sense—a matter of the complexity and magnitude of operations connecting events—so that the element of time is not separated from whatever element of space enters into the operations. Two events in the past occurred a long 'time' apart (the Hopi language has no word quite equivalent to our 'time') when many periodic physical motions have occurred between them in such a way as to traverse much distance or accumulate magnitude of physical display in other ways. The Hopi metaphysics does not raise the question whether the things in a distant village exist at the same present moment as those in one's own village, for it is frankly pragmatic on this score and says that any 'events' in the distant village can be compared to any events in one's own village only by an interval of magnitude that has both time and space forms in it. Events at a distance from the observer can only be known objectively when they are 'past' (i.e. posited in the objective) and the more distant, the more 'past' (the more worked upon from the subjective side). Hopi, with its preference for verbs, as contrasted to our own liking for nouns, perpetually turns our propositions about things into propositions about events. What happens at a distant village, if actual (objective) and not a conjecture (subjective) can be known 'here' only later. If it does not happen 'at this place,' it does not happen 'at this time'; it happens at 'that' place and at 'that' time. Both the 'here' happening and the 'there' happening are in the objective, corresponding in general to our past, but the 'there' happening is the more objectively distant, meaning, from our standpoint, that it is further away in the past just as it is further away from us in space than the 'here' happening.

As the objective realm displaying its characteristic attribute of extension stretches away from the observer toward that unfathomable remoteness which is both far away in space and long past in time, there comes a point where extension in detail ceases to be knowable and is lost in the vast distance, and where the subjective, creeping behind the scenes as it were, merges into the objective, so that at this inconceivable distance from the observer—from all observers—there is an all-encircling end and beginning of things where it might be said that existence, itself, swallows up the objective and the subjective. The borderland of this realm is as much subjective as objective. It is the abysm of antiquity, the time and place told about in the myths, which is known only subjectively or mentally—the Hopi realize and even express in their grammar that the things told in myths or stories do not have the same kind of reality or validity as things of the present day, the things of practical concern. As for the far distances of the sky and stars, what is known and said about them is supposititious, inferential—hence, in a way subjective—reached more through the inner vertical axis and the pole of the zenith than through the objective distances and the objective processes of vision and locomotion. So the dim past of myths is that corresponding distance on earth (rather than in the heavens) which is reached subjectively as myth through the vertical axis of reality via the pole of the nadir—hence it is placed BELOW the present surface of the earth, though this does not mean that the nadir-land of the origin myths is a hole or cavern as we should understand it. It is *Palátkwapi* 'At the Red Mountains,' a land like our present earth, but to which our earth bears the relation of a distant sky—and similarly the sky of our earth is penetrated by the heroes of tales, who find another earthlike realm above it.

It may now be seen how the Hopi do not need to use terms that refer to space or time as such. Such terms in our language are recast into expressions of extension, operation, and cyclic process provided they refer to the solid objective realm. They are recast into expressions of subjectivity if they refer to the subjective realm—the future, the psychic–mental, the mythical period, and the invisibly distant and conjectural generally. Thus, the Hopi language gets along perfectly without tenses for its verbs.

A LINGUISTIC CONSIDERATION

OF THINKING

IN PRIMITIVE COMMUNITIES *

I

The ethnologist engaged in studying a living primitive culture must often have wondered: "What do these people think? How do they think? Are their intellectual and rational processes akin to ours or radically different?" But thereupon he has probably dismissed the idea as a psychological enigma and has sharply turned his attention back to more readily observable matters. And yet the problem of thought and thinking in the native community is not purely and simply a psychological problem. It is quite largely cultural. It is moreover largely a matter of one especially cohesive aggregate of cultural phenomena that we call a language. It is approachable through linguistics, and, as I hope to show, the approach requires a rather new type of emphasis in lin-

* This paper was found by me in handwritten manuscript form, undated, among the papers left by Whorf to his wife and recently turned over to his son, Robert Whorf. The manuscript appeared to be complete (except for certain footnotes), but it was generally in a somewhat unfinished state, necessitating some editorial work on my part. Notes on the manuscript indicate that Whorf intended to prepare it for publication. He even listed individuals to whom he planned to send reprints including Jung, N(ayán) L(ouise) Redfield, Sapir, Carroll, Wayne Dennis, (Claude) Bragdon, H. G. Wells, and H. L. Mencken. We may date the writing of this article as taking place about late 1936, from two facts: first, it must have occurred after the publication, in early 1936, of his article, "The punctual and segmentative aspects of verbs in Hopi," to which he refers, and, second, it probably preceded the writing (in late 1937) of his article, "Grammatical categories," which gives a somewhat more fully developed notion of cryptotype than occurs in the present paper.

guistics, now beginning to emerge through the work of Sapir, Leonard Bloomfield, and others, though Boas enunciated it decades ago in his introduction to the *Handbook of American Indian languages*.

One of the clearest characterizations of thinking is that of Carl Jung, who distinguishes four basic psychic functions: sensation, feeling (*Gefühl*), thinking, and intuition.[1] It is evident to a linguist that thinking, as defined by Jung, contains a large linguistic element of a strictly patterned nature, while feeling is mainly nonlinguistic, though it may use the vehicle of language, albeit in a way quite different from thinking. Thinking may be said to be language's own ground, whereas feeling deals in feeling values which language indeed possesses but which lie rather on its borderland. These are Jung's two rational functions, and by contrast his two irrational functions, sensation and intuition, may fairly be termed nonlinguistic. They are, it is true, involved in the processes of talking, hearing, and understanding, but only in an infinitesimal part of their entire range. We are thus able to distinguish thinking as the function which is to a large extent linguistic.[2]

The linguistic side of SILENT thinking, thinking without speaking, is of a nature as yet little appreciated. Silent thinking is basically not sup-

[1] To the reader who may not be prepared to accept all of Jung's views, I might say that his conception of these functions is essentially that of earlier psychologists such as Wundt, to which, however, he adds his own penetrative insight and clarification of fundamentals. A distinctive feature in Jung's viewpoint is that his four functions are distinguished not merely qualitatively but as separate energy systems of operation of an energic principle, the Jungian libido, which feature contrasts them with mere processes and complexes. (They are relatively closed systems.) In other words, if I understand Jung rightly, none of the libido or energy available for thinking can pass over into the form of feeling or sensation and vice versa, except by going into the unconscious and receding so far therein that it reaches the primitive undifferentiated state. This libido concept has proved itself of psychiatric value, and it may also have significance for the "linguistics of thinking" if it is true that the psychic energy available for linguistic processes (included in the thinking function) is a differentiated energy, entrained in a closed system and not transferable between such systems. However, such a Jungian viewpoint is by no means necessary for the linguistic approach to thinking which I am here dealing with. [These views of Jung will be found in his *Psychological types* (trans. by Baynes, New York and London, 1923).—JBC]

[2] Some have supposed thinking to be entirely linguistic. Watson, I believe, holds or held this view, and the great merit of Watson in this regard is that he was one of the first to point out and teach the very large and unrecognized linguistic element in silent thinking. His error lies in going the whole hog; also, perhaps, in not realizing or at least not emphasizing that the linguistic aspect of thinking is not a biologically organized process, "speech" or "language," but a cultural organization, i.e., *a* language. Some linguists may also hold the idea that thinking is entirely linguistic.

pressed talking or inaudibly mumbled words or silent laryngeal agitations as some have supposed.[3] Such an explanation merely appears plausible to the linguistically unsophisticated "common sense" view. "Common sense" is unaware that talking itself means using a complex cultural organization, just as it is unaware of cultural organizations in general. Sense or meaning does not result from words or morphemes but from patterned relations between words or morphemes. Isolations of a morpheme, like "John!" or "Come!" are themselves patterns or formulas of a highly specialized type, not bare units.[4] Words and morphemes are motor reactions, but the factors of linkage BETWEEN words and morphemes, which make the categories and patterns in which linguistic meaning dwells, are not motor reactions; they correspond to neural processes and linkages of a NONMOTOR type, silent, invisible, and individually unobservable.[5] It is not words mumbled, but RAPPORT between words, which enables them to work together at all to any semantic result. It is this rapport that constitutes the real essence of thought in-

[3] [No text is available for this footnote. Whorf may have intended to refer again to Watson, who identified thought with subvocal movements of the speech musculature. See his article, "Is thinking merely the action of language mechanisms? (V)," *Brit. J. Psychol.*, 11:87–104 (1920).—JBC]

[4] Apparent isolations of words in a vocabulary list also derive what meaning they have from the patterned "potentials of linkage," which ramify from them and connect them with complex patterns of linguistic formulation.

[5] The pronounced materialist may still be granted leave to regard this matrix of relations as consisting of paths and chains of brain cells or what-not which link and relate themselves by physicochemical processes, but no clue to the nature of the RAPPORT, the structure of the matrix relations, can be obtained in this way, any more than the social organization of a tribe could be worked out from the blood groups of its individuals. It can only be determined by a penetrating study of the LANGUAGE spoken by the individual whose thinking process we are concerned with, and it will be found to be FUNDAMENTALLY DIFFERENT for individuals whose languages are of fundamentally different types. Just as cultural facts are only culturally determined, not biologically determined, so linguistic facts, which are likewise cultural, and include the linguistic element of thought, are only linguistically determined. They are determined not merely by language, but by languages. If the thinkers who are being studied speak our own language (let us say English), then the necessary penetrating study of the English language which is required can be made only by an investigator who has studied and is able to contrast widely differing types of language from English, for only in this way can there be brought into the forefront of consciousness an awareness of the existence of mere bare RELATIONS that do not correspond to any verbalized concepts but nevertheless govern absolutely the linkages of morphemes and shape the channels of thinking. [This footnote is extracted from a preliminary draft, and appears to represent what Whorf intended at this point.—JBC]

sofar as it is linguistic, and that in the last resort renders the mumbling, laryngeal quiverings, etc., semantically *de trop*. The nonmotor processes that are the essential thing are, of their nature, in a state of linkage according to the structure of a particular language, and activations of these processes and linkages in any way, with, without, or aside from laryngeal behavior, in the forefront of consciousness, or in what has been called "the deep well of unconscious cerebration," are all linguistic patterning operations, and all entitled to be called thinking.

Moreover, an analysis of silent thinking into motor quiverings corresponding to suppressed words and morphemes would no more be a real analysis of thinking than the analysis of a language into actual words and morphemes would be a real analysis of the language. The crudest and most amateurish grammar analyzes more effectively than that, and any scientific grammar is necessarily a deep analysis into relations.

For example, gender in English is a system of relations that has an almost minimal outward representation in morphemes. Its only motor reactions are the two pronouns 'he' and 'she.' [6] The motor processes which actualize the gender-linked nouns are undifferentiated in gender, but the linkage between such a motor process and another motor process actualizing the proper pronoun, 'he' or 'she,' is (1) differentiated in gender, (2) a nonmotor process, since the two motor processes are discrete and may even be separated by a prolonged period of rest. The gender nouns, such as boy, girl, father, wife, uncle, woman, lady, including thousands of given names like George, Fred, Mary, Charlie, Isabel, Isadore, Jane, John, Alice, Aloysius, Esther, Lester bear no distinguishing mark of gender like the Latin *-us* or *-a* within each motor process; but nevertheless each of these thousands of words has an invariable linkage-bond connecting it with absolute precision either to the word 'he' or the word 'she,' which however does not come into the overt-behavior picture until and unless special situations of discourse require it. [7] These thousands of linkage processes rallying around the common point of the pronoun and ramifying to all the thousands of nouns of one gender form a sort of psychic complex belonging to (1) the

[6] Including, of course, their inflections 'his, him, her, hers.'

[7] [A marginal note in the MS shows that Whorf intended to point out, in a footnote, that use of gender-linked nouns is not dependent upon knowing any particular individual to which they may refer, although it inevitably classifies such individuals as to sex.—JBC]

nonmotor and nonactualized realm, (2) the thinking function in Jung's definition, (3) the linguistic and cultural order.

There is no evident reason why such a complex should not enter into various functional relations with other material of thought without necessarily requiring the activation of any of the individual words or class marks with which it is connected. We can be thinking of, say, the division of labor between the sexes in a certain culture without having to think of the rather bookish words 'female' and 'male' and to refer continually to them in our meditations upon such a subject. What we more probably do as we run over such a question in our minds is sift the facts in terms of a sort of habitual consciousness of two sex classes as a standing classificatory fact in our thought-world, something which is quite different from sex as a concept or sex as a feeling-value. The basis of this shadowy, abstract, and wordless adumbration of a sex classification is not a word like 'sex' or 'female' or 'women'; it is a linguistic RAPPORT as distinguished from a linguistic UTTERANCE. In English it is probably a rising toward fuller consciousness of the two great complexes of linkage bonds pertaining to the linguistic sex-gender system. It is, one might say, the total pronominal-linkage pressure of the George, Dick, and William class of words, or of the Jane, Sue, and Betty class, that functions in the meditation and NOT a VERBAL concept like 'male' or 'female.' But in a language without sex gender, like Chinese or Hopi, any thinking in terms of a sex classification could not be of this nature; it would presumably operate around a word, or a feeling, or a sexual image, or a symbol, or something else.

A linguistic classification like English gender, which has no overt mark actualized along with the words of the class but which operates through an invisible "central exchange" of linkage bonds in such a way as to determine certain other words which mark the class, I call a COVERT class, in contrast to an OVERT class, such as gender in Latin. Navaho has a covert classification of the whole world of objects based partly on animation and partly on shape. Inanimate bodies fall into two classes which linguists have styled "round objects" and "long objects." [8] These names, of course, misrepresent; they attempt to depict the subtle in terms of the gross, and fail. Navaho itself has no terms which adequately depict the classes. A covert concept like a covert gender is as

[8] [Actually, the Navaho verb system provides for MORE than two classes of inanimate bodies, a fact which makes Whorf's point, if anything, more valid.—JBC]

definable and in its way as definite as a verbal concept like 'female' or feminine, but is of a very different kind; it is not the analog of a word but of a rapport-system, and awareness of it has an intuitive quality; we say that it is sensed rather than comprehended. It is possibly the kind of concept or idea which in Hindu philosophy is called *arūpa*, formless. The Navaho so-called "round" and "long" nouns are not marked in themselves nor by any pronouns. They are marked only in the use of certain very important verb stems, in that a different stem is required for a "round" or a "long" subject or object. Many other verb stems are indifferent to the distinction. A new object, for which the Navaho has no name, will be put into one or the other class by analogy, not analogy as it would seem to us, but as guided by the contents of the two Navaho complexes.

A covert linguistic class may not deal with any grand dichotomy of objects, it may have a very subtle meaning, and it may have no overt mark other than certain distinctive "reactances" with certain overtly marked forms. It is then what I call a CRYPTOTYPE. It is a submerged, subtle, and elusive meaning, corresponding to no actual word, yet shown by linguistic analysis to be functionally important in the grammar. For example, the English particle UP meaning 'completely, to a finish,' as in 'break it up, cover it up, eat it up, twist it up, open it up' can be applied to any verb of one or two syllables initially accented, EXCEPTING verbs belonging to four special cryptotypes. One is the cryptotype of dispersion without boundary; hence one does not say 'spread it up, waste it up, spend it up, scatter it up, drain it up, or filter it up.' [9] Another is the cryptotype of oscillation without agitation of parts; we don't say 'rock up a cradle, wave up a flag, wiggle up a finger, nod up one's head,' etc.[10] The third is the cryptotype of nondurative impact which also includes psychological reaction: kill, fight, etc., hence we don't say 'whack it up, tap it up, stab it up, slam it up, wrestle him up, hate him up.' [11] The fourth is the verbs of directed motion, move, lift, pull, push,

[9] 'Burst' belongs to this cryptotype; the colloquial 'bust' does not.

[10] [In a marginal note, Whorf cites 'shake up,' apparently to point out that this verb implies agitation of parts. The reader should note, incidentally, that this whole discussion concerns only transitive verbs, as is made explicit at the end of the paragraph.—JBC]

[11] [In a marginal note, Whorf alludes to such expressions as 'strike up (a band),' 'hit it up,' but states that they are not true transitives and are not considered. He also refers to verbs such as 'sing, shout, cry' in the same way.—JBC]

put, etc., with which UP has the directional sense, 'upward,' or derived senses, even though this sense may be contradicted by the verb and hence produce an effect of absurdity, as in 'drip it up.' Outside this set of cryptotypes, UP may be freely used with transitives in the completive-intensive sense.

Another English cryptotype is that of the transitive verbs of a covering, enclosing, and surface-attaching meaning, the reactance of which is that UN- may be prefixed to denote the opposite. Hence we say 'uncover, uncoil, undress, unfasten, unfold, unlock, unroll, untangle, untie, unwind,' but not 'unbreak, undry, unhang, unheat, unlift, unmelt, unopen, unpress, unspill.' With the exception of a few words mostly semiarchaic, e.g., 'unsay, unthink, unmake,' the use of UN- as a reversive prefix in true verbs coincides with the centripetal enclosing and attaching meaning.[12] We have no single word in the language which can give us a proper clue to this meaning or into which we can compress this meaning; hence the meaning is subtle, intangible, as is typical of cryptotypic meanings. Nevertheless this formless idea delimits a quite definite class of words and grammatical forms, and may be dredged up from its own plane of thought formations and grasped in a semi-intuitive way. To do this, one needs only meditate on the meaning of the cryptotype, e.g. of the typical verbs which take UN-, or to use methods of free-analogizing akin to the "free-association" methods of Freud and Jung. Thus I can imagine a newly coined verb *flimmick*. If *flimmick* means, let us say, 'tie a tin can to,' then it falls into the cryptotype and I can say, e.g., 'he *unflimmicked* the dog.' But, if it means 'to take apart,' there will be no tendency for anyone to make a form *unflimmick* meaning 'put together'; e.g., 'he *unflimmicked* the set of radio parts.' Such a form will appear strange and unacceptable. Similarly a knowledge of this cryptotype previous to the adoption of the new words 'camouflage' and 'wangle' would have enabled us to predict that it would be possible to say 'uncamouflage it,' but not 'unwangle it.'

[12] [From a marginal note, it is evident that Whorf intended to consider the words 'unstart,' 'unbalance,' and 'undo' in a footnote. Whorf might also have cautioned the reader against being misled by participial or adjectival forms such as 'unbroken, unheated, unopened,' etc. in which the prefix 'un-' does not denote the reverse of an action, but of an adjectivally expressed condition. It is interesting to speculate on the possibility that the reason that words such as 'unsay, unthink, unmake' are now obsolete may be precisely the fact that they had to yield to the pressure of the cryptotype represented by such words as 'uncover, uncoil, undress,' etc.—JBC]

In contrast to the cryptotype I give the name PHENOTYPE to the linguistic category with a clearly apparent class meaning and a formal mark or morpheme which accompanies it; i.e., the phenotype is the "classical" morphological category. The meanings of 'up' and 'un-' are phenotypes, and so are the various tenses, aspects, voices, modes, and other marked forms which all grammars study. Grammatical research up to the present time has been concerned chiefly with study of phenotypes. A certain type of grammar proceeds as if linguistic meaning dwelt wholly in them. The anthropologist should not be satisfied with such a grammar, any more than with an ethnology that described only positive behavior and ignored the patterning of taboos and avoidances. It can be shown that, in some languages at least, linguistic meaning results from the interplay of phenotypes and cryptotypes, not from phenotypes alone.

Thus in Hopi the use of the aspect and tense forms is often governed by cryptotypes. They govern, for instance, the way of expressing the beginning of an action or state, the English 'begins to do,' or 'begins to be' form. First, a different form (phenotype) is used, depending on whether the verb is active or inactive (either passive or static), and this is a cryptotypic distinction, for the formal apparatus of Hopi grammar does not set up any active-versus-inactive contrast. Hopi, moreover, classes being 'in, at, over,' or in some other spatial relationship as ACTIVE, but being 'red, long, little, pretty, turned around, shot,' as INACTIVE. Causal and incausal are really better terms here than active and passive. Next, if the verb is active, the phenotype for beginning depends on which of three active cryptotypes is involved. With most verbs one can use either the inceptive aspect or the future tense. Analysis seems to indicate that Hopi regards the subject of these verbs as working into and through the action by a process of dynamic adjustment. The subject progressively adjusts himself into the action, and throughout the action is maintaining this adjustment either to develop or to stabilize and continue the effect. Hopi includes here [13] sleeping, dying, laughing, eating, as well as most organic functions and most alterative operations, e.g., cutting, bending, covering, placing, and thousands of others. The second cryptotype uses only future tense to express beginning, and includes verbs of straight-line uniform motion, running, fleeing, going, coming, being in or at a place or in any spatial relationship, opening,

[13] [Marginally, Whorf notes that this is "strange at first, but illuminating."]

closing, and certain others. Analysis indicates that here the subject is classed as instantly assuming a full-fledged new status, not as dynamically working into and through a process. The third cryptotype expresses beginning by means of the projective aspect, a phenotype which used elsewhere means 'does with a forward movement.' This cryptotype implies that the subject is seized and assimilated by a field of influence, carried away by it, as it were; and it consists of gravitational and moving-inertia phenomena; 'falling, tumbling, spilling, jumping, whirling,' and also, strange though it seems to us, 'going out' and 'going in.' According to the logic of Hopi linguistics, a person about to enter a house or go outdoors launches off and yields himself to a new influence like one who falls or leaps.

What needs to be clearly seen by anthropologists, who to a large extent may have gotten the idea that linguistics is merely a highly specialized and tediously technical pigeonhole in a far corner of the anthropological workshop, is that linguistics is essentially the quest of MEANING. It may seem to the outsider to be inordinately absorbed in recording hair-splitting distinctions of sound, performing phonetic gymnastics, and writing complex grammars which only grammarians read. But the simple fact is that its real concern is to light up the thick darkness of the language, and thereby of much of the thought, the culture, and the outlook upon life of a given community, with the light of this "golden something," as I have heard it called, this transmuting principle of meaning. As I have tried to show, this amounts to far more than learning to speak and understand the language as the practical language teacher conceives these ends. The investigator of culture should hold an ideal of linguistics as that of a heuristic approach to problems of psychology which hitherto he may have shrunk from considering—a glass through which, when correctly focused, will appear the TRUE SHAPES of many of those forces which hitherto have been to him but the inscrutable blank of invisible and bodiless thought.

II

Awareness of psychological undercurrents is the last thing to arrive in the conquest of linguistic understanding, both in the individual and in history. The attempt to teach one's language to a foreigner results in some awareness of OVERT formal patterns: paradigms and inflected stems.

The earliest grammars known are cuneiform wordlists of this kind, giving equivalents as between Sumerian and the Semitic Akkadian. A
further step did not occur until philosophy, in both Greece and India,
discovered a relation between reasoning and linguistic patterns; this resulted for philosophy in a formal logic, and for grammar in the discovery
of at least the more outstanding categories in the classical Indo-European
tongues. In the Semitic world, grammar remained largely formal, the
classical Hebrew and Arabic grammars consisting mostly of paradigms,
known by code names which made no attempt even to characterize,
much less penetrate, the meanings of these linguistic classes. Even
Latin grammar, with its terms like indicative, subjunctive, passive, etc.,
was psychological by comparison. The discovery of ancient Hindu
grammar by Western scholars in the early nineteenth century impressed
these scholars chiefly by its formal perfection. But it also revealed certain psychological subtleties, such as the recognition of different covert
ideas within word-compounding technique, and the classification of compounds as *tatpurusha, dvandva, bahuvrihi*, and so on.[14]

Even the greatest European grammarians of the nineteenth century
did not go much beyond formal and overt structures except for riding
the classical grammatical and philosophical concepts to the limits of
travel in the languages they studied. To this statement there is one
grand exception—one of those amazing geniuses who baffle their contemporaries and leave no successors. The real originator of such ideas
as rapport-systems, covert classes, cryptotypes, psycholinguistic patterning, and language as part and parcel of a culture was, so far as I can
learn, a French grammarian of the early nineteenth century, Antoine
Fabre d'Olivet (1768–1825),[15] who investigated Semitic languages and
particularly Hebrew, though his work, like that of Mendel in genetics,
made no impress whatsoever on the thought of his time. Unfortunately

---

[14] [The *tatpurusha* compounds are those in which one member modifies the other,
as in such English words as 'self-made, footsoldier,' etc.; the *dvandva* compounds are
those containing coordinate members, the nearest English example being a phrase
like 'bread and butter,' which would have been rendered in Sanskrit by a single compound word; the *bahuvrihi* compounds are adjectival compounds implying a possessive meaning, and may be exemplified by a Sanskrit word which means 'possessing
the brightness of the sun.' See William Dwight Whitney, *Sanskrit grammar* (Harvard University Press, 1931, Chapter XVIII).—JBC]

[15] [I have supplied the dates, which Whorf intended to fill in. They are as given
in the *Grand dictionnaire universel du XIXᵉ siècle*. Note that the surname is Fabre
d'Olivet, not d'Olivet.—JBC]

for its comprehension either then or now, its author was a mystical and religious metaphysician who mingled this side of his nature with the workings of one of the most powerful linguistic intellects of any age. The result was to produce a mystical and gnostic "translation" of Genesis, or rather, an Upanishadic paraphrase that was like some shocking vision of cosmic space alive with terrific hieroglyphs—that got itself promptly placed on the Index. Nor did this repudiation by orthodoxy win any encomiums from what was then the radical left, for his Biblical views were at the same time too iconoclastic and too transcendental to satisfy any possible school of exegesis. But the strictly linguistic part of Fabre d'Olivet's work, embodied in *La langue hébraïque restituée*, which appeared in 1815–16,[16] when separated from his extraordinary Upanishad upon Genesis, can be seen today to be based on purely linguistic criteria and to show great psychological penetration, and ideas far in advance of his time. It must be added that, although mystical almost to the point of a Jacob Boehme or a William Blake, Fabre d'Olivet steered absolutely clear of the cabalistic and numerological hocus-pocus with which the old Jewish tradition of Hebrew was laden. And, while he threw overboard the whole formalistic Hiphil-Hophal conception of grammar, he also declined to foist Latin and Greek patterns upon Hebrew. His Hebrew stands on its own feet as completely as does Boas's Chinook. He reorganized the treatment of verb conjugations on a psycholinguistic basis, considered individual prefixes and suffixes from the standpoint of their meaning and function, went into the semantics of vowel patterns and the semantic coloring of vowels, and showed how many Hebrew stems can be resolved into meaningful fractions, as, e.g., such English words as 'flash, flicker, clash, click, clack, crack, crash, lick, lash' can be so resolved. Refusing to identify the letters of Hebrew writing with the actual phonetic elements and yet perceiving that these elements are not mere sounds, but stereotyped, codified, and patterned semantic sounds, he advanced to a conception of the phoneme, which he called the "sign" or the "vocal sign"—struggling with terminology but showing real in-

[16] [I have supplied the dates, which Whorf left blank in the manuscript. The full title of this scarce work is *La langue hébraïque restituée, et le véritable sens des mots hébreux rétabli et prouvé par leur analyse radicale.* Copies are to be seen in the Library of Congress, the Cornell University Library, and perhaps a few other libraries in the United States. It is probable that Whorf knew the work chiefly from the translation into English by Nayán Louise Redfield, *The Hebraic tongue restored* (New York and London, G. P. Putnam's Sons, 1921).—JBC]

sight into linguistic actualities. He stressed the fact of a complex rapport between signs and between words. A phoneme may assume definite semantic duties as part of its rapport. In English the phoneme ð
(the voiced sound of *th*) occurs initially only in the cryptotype of demonstrative particles (the, this, there, than, etc.). Hence there is a
psychic pressure against accepting the voiced sound of *th* in new or
imaginary words: *thig, thag, thob, thuzzle*, etc. not having demonstrative
meanings. Encountering such a new word (e.g. *thob*) on a page, we will
"instinctively" give it the voiceless sound θ of *th* in "think." But it is
no "instinct." Just our old friend linguistic rapport again. Assign a
demonstrative meaning, let *thag* equal 'over the fence,' for instance, and
we will substitute the voiced phoneme ð of "there." Fabre d'Olivet
knew all about such things.

Moreover, Fabre d'Olivet thought in an anthropological and not
simply a grammatical way; to him, speech was not a "faculty" exalted
on its own perch, but something to be understood in the light of human
behavior and culture, of which it was a part, specialized but involving
no different principle from the rest. The vocal sign (phoneme) was a
highly specialized gesture or symbolic act, language a development of
total somatic behavior becoming symbolic and then diverting its symbolism more and more into the vocal channel—such is his teaching put
into the modern idiom.

No figure so significant for the linguistic approach to thinking again
appears until we come to the Irish linguist James Byrne (1820–97). His
studies were based on the exceedingly valuable idea of a worldwide
survey of grammatical structures in all languages known. His great
work—it at least deserves to be called great in conception, even though
perhaps not in execution—in two volumes, called *General principles of
structure of language*, appeared in 1885.[17] It had the remarkable feature
of presenting condensed grammatical sketches of languages all over the
globe, from Chinese to Hottentot. Almost every linguistic stock outside
of America is represented, and a good number of American ones. On
this survey Byrne based his psychological theory. And it seems to me
at least rather significant that Byrne found, on the basis of language
structure, a similar contrast of two fundamental psychological types to

[17] [I have supplied the date, as also the dates of Byrne's life. Here and later in the
manuscript Whorf gives the name as Thomas Byrne, but this must have been due to
a lapse of memory.—JBC]

that which Jung much later found from psychiatry and called the types of extraversion and introversion. Jung also showed how, all down through history, the irreconcilable opposition of two such types has resulted in fundamental controversies and schisms in successive philosophies and religions. Byrne independently found, or thought he found, a correlation between language structure and two types of mentality, one quick-reacting, quick-thinking, and volatile, the other slow-reacting, slow-thinking, but more profound and phlegmatic. His slow-thinking mentality, suggestive of Jung's introvert, he thought went, on the whole, with languages of a synthetic type having a complex overt morphology and much derivation and word-building, the extreme of the type being polysynthesis. His quick-thinking (extraverted) type went, on the whole, with a simpler morphology, lack of synthesis, an analytic or in the extreme an isolating type of language.

But, while I am sympathetic to the possibility of such a finding, which would indeed be a mighty achievement, and also impressed by Byrne's anticipation of Jung, I find Byrne's general thesis unconvincing, chiefly because I can see how Byrne was working with utterly inadequate materials. It is of the greatest importance to man's knowledge of his own intellectual makeup, especially in future times, that the really colossal task that Byrne so rashly attempted be done as well as possible. This would require not only a survey of many more languages, particularly American ones, than Byrne used, but a grammar of each language worked out scientifically and on the basis of the language's own patterns and classes, and as free as possible from any general presuppositions about grammatical logic. Byrne got his materials from old-fashioned grammars, formal and even "classical" in cut. These grammars might at any juncture quarter a regiment of alien patterns and ideas on the unfortunate tongue. Not one of these grammarians, nor Byrne himself, could have made a *sui generis* configurative report on a language as Fabre d'Olivet had done; that ability had died. But until it again lives as a well-developed scientific technique and is applied to another world survey and comparison, man will remain ignorant of the roots of his intellectual life. He will be debarred from any consideration of human thought on a planetary scale, of what it is in respect to the species.

That ability began to live again with and after the attack made by Boas on the American Indian languages, and especially his statement of principles, and ideals of method, in his justly celebrated introduction to the *Handbook*.[18] And, with Boas, it reappeared in a modern scientific form, and in terms of the acceptable science CULTUS, not as before in terms of an exuberant mystically disposed creative imagination. Boas showed for the second time in history, but for the first in a scientific manner, how a language could be analyzed *sui generis* and without forcing the categories of "classical" tradition upon it. The development of an adequate technique for this new outlook had to come haltingly. When under Boas the American languages first began to reveal the unparalleled complexity and subtlety of their thought categories, the phonemic calculus was still unborn. The American field linguist could not, like Fabre, intuit the phoneme and morphophoneme in a brilliant tour de force of imaginative insight. He had to wait for these concepts to be developed by specialized phoneticians, working at first in the modern-language field, and at first he lacked in psychological penetration.

The new era passes into a second phase, into the truly modern linguistic point of view, with the appearance on the scene of Sapir, and particularly with the publication of his *Language* in 1921.[19] Sapir has done more than any other person to inaugurate the linguistic approach to thinking and make it of scientific consequence, and moreover to demonstrate the importance of linguistics to anthropology and psychology. From this point on it would be a task to mention individual contributors to this dawning realization and growing idea that linguistics is fundamental to the theory of thinking and in the last analysis to ALL HUMAN SCIENCES. The interested reader is referred to the partial and very incomplete bibliography appended.

III

This linguistic consideration of thinking as applied to primitive communities is of significance for anthropology in two ways. First, the ethnological and the psychological-linguistic insights into the same primitive community, especially if made by the same investigator, can be reasonably expected to have a very fertilizing effect upon each other.

[18] [Boas, Franz (ed.). *Handbook of American Indian languages* (Parts 1 and 2). Washington, D. C.: Government Printing Office, 1911–22. (*Bull. 40, Bur. Amer. Ethnol., Smithsonian Institution.*)—JBC]

[19] [I have supplied the date. The full reference is: Sapir, Edward. *Language; an introduction to the study of speech.* New York: Harcourt Brace Co., 1921, vii, 238 pp.—JBC]

We have the testimony and the enlightening teaching of Sapir and others that this is so. The very essence of linguistics is the quest for meaning, and, as the science refines its procedure, it inevitably becomes, as a matter of this quest, more psychological and cultural, while retaining that almost mathematical precision of statement which it gets from the highly systematic nature of the linguistic realm of fact.

Let us suppose that an ethnologist discovers that the Hopi speak about clouds in their rain prayers, etc., as though clouds were alive. He would like to know whether this is some metaphor or special religious or ceremonial figure of speech, or whether it is the ordinary and usual way of thinking about clouds. Here is the sort of problem to which language might be able to give a very meaningful answer, and we immediately turn to it to see if it has a gender system that distinguishes living from nonliving things, and, if so, how it classes a cloud. We find that Hopi has no gender at all. The traditional grammar of the pre-Boas period would stop at this point and think it had given an answer. But the correct answer can only be given by a grammar that analyzes covert as well as overt structure and meaning. For Hopi does distinguish an animate class of nouns AS A CRYPTOTYPE and only as a cryptotype. The crucial reactance is in the way of forming the plural. When members of the Flute Society, e.g., are spoken of as Flutes, this (covertly) inanimate noun is pluralized in the animate way. But the word ʔoˑ'mȧw 'cloud,' is always pluralized in the animate way; it has no other plural; it definitely belongs to the cryptotype of animateness. And so the question whether the animation of clouds is a figure or formality of speech or whether it stems from some more deep and subtly pervasive undercurrent of thought is answered, or at the least given a flood of new meaning.

Language thus should be able to analyze some, if probably not all, of the differences, real or assumed, between the mentality of so-called primitive peoples and modern civilized man. Whether the primitives constitute a unit class of mentality over against modern man, apart from the differences between their cultures and his, as is implied in Lévy-Bruhl's concept of PARTICIPATION MYSTIQUE [20] and in the equation of

[20] [Lévy-Bruhl, Lucien. *Les fonctions mentales dans les sociétés inférieures,* Paris 1912. "Participation mystique" refers to a special kind of psychological relationship with the object, in which the individual cannot clearly perceive a separation between himself and the object.—JBC]

"primitive" to "infantile" used by Freud and Jung; or whether (again apart from general culture) the CIVILIZED MODERN is the unit class of mentality because of the great structural similarity of all the modern civilized Western languages, while over against it are many diverse types of mentality reflecting a rich diversity of speech structure: This is only one of the great psychological world-questions that fall into the domain of linguistics and await the impersonal and positive type of answer that linguistic research can give. We are accustomed to think of such a mentality as is implied by PARTICIPATION MYSTIQUE as less of a thinking mentality, as less rational, than ours. Yet many American Indian and African languages abound in finely wrought, beautifully logical discriminations about causation, action, result, dynamic or energic quality, directness of experience, etc., all matters of the function of thinking, indeed the quintessence of the rational. In this respect they far outdistance the European languages.[21] The most impressively penetrating distinctions of this kind often are those revealed by analyzing to the covert and even cryptotypic levels. Indeed, covert categories are quite apt to be more rational than overt ones. English unmarked gender is more rational, closer to natural fact, than the marked genders of Latin or German. As outward marks become few, the class tends to crystallize around an idea—to become more dependent on whatever synthetizing principle there may be in the meanings of its members. It may even be true that many abstract ideas arise in this way; some rather formal and not very meaningful linguistic group, marked by some overt feature, may happen to coincide very roughly with some concatenation of phenomena in such a way as to suggest a rationalization of this parallelism. In the course of phonetic change, the distinguishing mark, ending, or what not is lost, and the class passes from a formal to a

[21] See for example the Hopi treatment of repetitive and vibrational phenomena in my paper, "The punctual and segmentative aspects of verbs in Hopi," or the instances of [lacuna] in Watkins' Chichewa. [Probably Whorf intended to allude to the Chichewa verb system, which is extremely sensitive to the causative aspects of acts. For example, there are several past tenses, use of which depends not only on the remoteness of the past time being referred to (before or since last night) but also on whether the act continues to have an influence on the present. There are also seven "voices," which express different kinds of relations among subject, verb, and predicate (including object). See pp. 49–57, 72–81 in A grammar of Chichewa, a Bantu language of British Central Africa, by Mark Hanna Watkins, Language Dissertation no. 24, 1937. See also Whorf's later discussion in his article, "Language, mind, and reality" (p. 265 f.).—JBC]

semantic one. Its reactance is now what distinguishes it as a class, and its idea is what unifies it. As time and use go on, it becomes increasingly organized around a rationale, it attracts semantically suitable words and loses former members that now are semantically inappropriate. Logic is now what holds it together, and its logic becomes a semantic associate of that unity of which the CONFIGURATIVE aspect is a bundle of nonmotor linkages mooring the whole fleet of words to their common reactance. Semantically it has become a deep persuasion of a principle behind phenomena, like the ideas of inanimation, of "substance," of abstract sex, of abstract personality, of force, of causation—not the overt concept (lexation) corresponding to the WORD causation but the covert idea, the "sensing," or, as it is often called (but wrongly, according to Jung), the "feeling" that there must be a principle of causation. Later this covert idea may be more or less duplicated in a word and a lexical concept invented by a philosopher: e.g., CAUSATION. From this point of view many preliterate ("primitive") communities, far from being subrational, may show the human mind functioning on a higher and more complex plane of rationality than among civilized men. We do not know that civilization is synonymous with rationality. These primitive tribes may simply have lacked philosophers, the existence of whom may depend on an economic prosperity that few cultures in the course of history have reached. Or perhaps too much rationality may defeat itself, or arouse some strong compensatory principle. These are all questions, essentially anthropological, to which a liaison between ethnology and psychological linguistics would seem to offer the soundest approach.

The second way in which linguistic consideration of thinking is significant for anthropology has more reference to the future, and perhaps most of all to the far distant future of the human species when it will have developed into something other, and let us hope far higher, than present-day man. Turning first to the nearer future, it is desirable that anthropology collaborate in preparation for the time, which cannot be too far postponed, when it will be both possible and urgently necessary to make the cultural and psychological world-survey of languages that is envisioned in the work of James Byrne—this time in a way which will enrich our science with the prodigal wealth of new truth that lies in that field waiting to be discovered.

As time goes on, the type of knowledge that such a survey would unlock becomes more and more a matter of concern and interest outside the world of scholarly pursuits—for it may play a very important part in world history that is now in the making. The problems of achieving mutual understanding, of language barriers, of propaganda and advertising, of education, of the technique of managing human affairs without undue friction, of an intelligence in human relations that can keep pace with the changes brought about by the physical sciences, all run afoul of this matter of language and thought. Everyone is naturally interested in questions of language, although they either do not know it, or know it and think they know all about it. There is for example a movement for the extended use of Ogden's ingenious artificial language called Basic English, which has met with much sympathy among businessmen, educators, people interested in international affairs, and social prophets like H. G. Wells. There is no use sitting aloof and loftily condemning such linguistic movements as unscientific. Unscientific or not, they are linguistic phenomena of today, and why should linguistic science, which alone can handle the vital underlying principles of such movements, stand by in sequestered unconcern and let them blunder along, exercising their crude but vast power to change the thinking of tomorrow? Basic English appeals to people because it seems simple. But those to whom it seems simple either know or think they know English—there's the rub! Every language of course seems simple to its own speakers because they are unconscious of structure. But English is anything but simple—it is a bafflingly complex organization, abounding in covert classes, cryptotypes, taxemes of selection, taxemes of order,[22] significant stress patterns and intonation patterns of considerable intricacy. English is indeed almost in a class by itself as regards prosodic complexity, being one of the most complex languages on earth in this respect; on the whole, it is as complicated as most polysynthetic languages of America, which fact most of us are blissfully unaware of. The complex structure of English is largely covert, which makes it all the harder to analyze. Foreigners learning English have to absorb it unconsciously—a process requiring years—by dint of constant exposure to bombardment by spoken English in large chunks; there exists at this moment no grammar that can teach it. As with Basic English, so with other artificial languages—underlying structures and categories of a few

[22] [The marginal notation appears: "memberships in covert categories of a certain type," and there is a reference to Leonard Bloomfield, *Language* (New York, 1933) where the subject of taxemes is taken up in Chapters 10, 12, and elsewhere.—JBC]

culturally predominant European tongues are taken for granted; their complex web of presuppositions is made the basis of a false simplicity. We say 'a large black and white hunting dog' and assume that in Basic English one will do the same. How is the speaker of a radically different mother tongue supposed to know that he cannot say 'hunting white black large a dog'? The English adjectives belong to cryptotypes having definite position assignments, and their formula is a definite and complex one, but lo, the poor Indian organizes his thinking quite differently. The person who would use Basic English must first know or learn the immensely intricate covert structure of actual "English as she is spoke."

We see here the error made by most people who attempt to deal with such social questions of language—they naïvely suppose that speech is nothing but a piling up of LEXATIONS, and that this is all one needs in order to do any and every kind of rational thinking; the far more important thought materials provided by structure and configurative rapport are beyond their horizons. It may turn out that the simpler a language becomes overtly, the more it becomes dependent upon cryptotypes and other covert formations, the more it conceals unconscious presuppositions, and the more its lexations become variable and indefinable. Wouldn't this be a pretty kettle of fish for the would-be advocates of a "simple" international tongue to have had a hand in stewing up! For sound thinking in such fields we greatly need a competent world-survey of languages.

IV

And now, turning to the more distant future, one may perhaps be permitted to essay a broader view, to look at the subject of linguistics and its bearing upon thinking from the standpoint of the whole human species. In order to do this we must not be afraid to begin with a platitude. Man is distinguished from other animals by language, and by his great development of thinking. So far as we can envision his future, we must envision it in terms of mental growth. We cannot but suppose that the future developments of thinking are of primary importance to the human species. They may even determine the duration of human existence on the planet earth or in the universe. The possibilities open to thinking are the possibilities of recognizing relationships and the discovery of techniques of operating with relationships on the mental or intellectual plane, such as will in turn lead to ever wider and more penetratingly significant systems of relationships. These possibilities are inescapably bound up with systems of linguistic expression. The story of their evolution in man is the story of man's linguistic development—of the long evolution of thousands of very different systems of discerning, selecting, organizing, and operating with relationships. Of the early stages of this evolutionary process, the REALLY PRIMITIVE ROOTS of language, we know nothing. What we are at least in a position to find out is the RESULTS of this evolution as they exist broadcast about the planet in our present day. Only the beginnings of such a knowledge of worldwide linguistic taxonomy are in evidence. In our armchair generalizations about grammar, and the related fields of logic and thought-psychology, we are in the same position as pre-Linnaean botany. We have not yet got anything like a description of existing linguistic species, to use a biological metaphor.

Fortunately for biology, a worldwide systematic taxonomy preceded and laid a foundation for the historical and evolutionary approach. In linguistics as in other cultural studies, we have had unfortunately the reverse situation. The evolutionary concept, having been dumped upon modern man while his notions of language and thought were based on knowledge of only a few types out of the hundreds of very diverse linguistic types existing, has abetted his provincial linguistic prejudices and fostered the grandiose hokum that his type of thinking and the few European tongues on which it is based represent the culmination and flower of the evolution of language! This is as if a pre-Linnaean botanist who had conceived the idea of evolution should suppose that our cultivated wheat and oats represent a higher evolutionary stage than a rare aster restricted to a few sites in the Himalayas. From the standpoint of a matured biology, it is precisely the rare aster which has the better claim to high evolutionary eminence; the wheat owes its ubiquity and prestige merely to human economics and history.

The eminence of our European tongues and thinking habits proceeds from nothing more. The relatively few languages of the cultures which have attained to modern civilization promise to overspread the globe and cause the extinction of the hundreds of diverse exotic linguistic species, but it is idle to pretend that they represent any superiority of type. On the contrary, it takes but little real scientific study of pre-literate languages, especially those of America, to show how much more precise and finely elaborated is the system of relationships in many such tongues than is ours.[23] By comparison with many American languages, the formal systematization of ideas in English, German, French, or Italian seems poor and jejune. Why, for instance, do we not, like the Hopi, use a different way of expressing the relation of channel of sensation (seeing) to result in consciousness, as between 'I see that it is red' and 'I see that it is new'? We fuse the two quite different types of relationship into a vague sort of connection expressed by 'that,' whereas the Hopi indicates that in the first case seeing presents a sensation 'red,' and in the second that seeing presents unspecified evidence from which is drawn the inference of newness. If we change the form to 'I hear that it is red' or 'I hear that it is new,' we European speakers still cling to our lame 'that,' but the Hopi now uses still another relater and makes no distinction between 'red' and 'new,' since, in either case, the significant presentation to consciousness is that of a verbal report, and neither a sensation per se nor inferential evidence. Does the Hopi language show here a higher plane of thinking, a more rational analysis of situations, than our vaunted English? Of course it does. In this field and in various others, English compared to Hopi is like a bludgeon compared to a rapier. We even have to think and boggle over the question for some time, or have it explained to us, before we can see the difference in the relationships expressed by 'that' in the above examples, whereas the Hopi discriminates these relationships with effortless ease, for the forms of his speech have accustomed him to doing so.

BIBLIOGRAPHY

[At the end of the manuscript appears a section entitled "Bibliography (Notes)" which is merely a skeleton of a bibliography; it consists chiefly of names. I have already given footnote references for the following names: Bloomfield, Boas, Byrne, Fabre d'Olivet, Jung, Sapir, Watkins, and Watson. Below I give the citations that Whorf most probably had in mind for the other names; in several cases he was explicit.—JBC]

De Angulo, Jaime. "Tone patterns and verb forms in a dialect of Zapotek."
   Language, 2:238–250 (1926).

[23] [At this point in the manuscript appears a marginal notation: "Conclusion—error supposing function of language to be only the COMMUNICATION of thought." By emphasizing the word communication, Whorf apparently meant to convey the implication that language not only communicates thought but functions in its very inception, a conclusion to which we are forced if we accept the main thesis of this article.—JBC]

Flournoy, Théodore. *Métaphysique et psychologie*. Geneva, 1890. [? This may not be the relevant work.]

Haas, Mary. [Whorf probably referred to unpublished material which he had seen. See her sketch of Tunica, an American Indian language, in H. Hoijer, *Linguistic structures of native America*. New York, 1946.— JBC]

Jones, William, and Michelson, Truman. "Algonquian (Fox)." Pp. 735–873 in Boas, F. (editor). *Handbook of American Indian languages*, Part 1. Washington: Government Printing Office, 1911.

Koffka, K. *Principles of Gestalt psychology*. New York: Harcourt, Brace & Co., 1935.

Lowes, John Livingston. *Road to Xanadu*. Harvard University Press, 1927. [Whorf misremembered the author's name as Dickinson. He comments, "Interesting for illustrations of the dredging up of linguistic material from the unconscious."]

Murdock, George P. *Our primitive contemporaries*. New York: Macmillan, 1934.

Newman, Stanley S. *A grammar of Yokuts, an American Indian language of California*. Unpublished Ph.D. dissertation, Yale Univ. 1932. Also, *Yokuts language of California*. New York, 1944. (Viking Fund Publication in Anthropology, no. 2.)

Morice, Adrian G. *The Carrier language (Dene family); a grammar and dictionary combined*. St. Gabriel-Modling near Vienna, Austria, 1932.

Ogden, Charles K. *Basic English: a general introduction with rules and grammar*. London: K. Paul, Trench, Trubner, 1930. [Whorf's citation is to Ogden and Richards, but I believe he meant to refer to this book about Basic English.]

Swadesh, Morris. [Whorf probably referred to unpublished material which he had seen. See Swadesh's sketch of South Greenland Eskimo in H. Hoijer, *Linguistic structures of native America*. New York, 1946.—JBC]

Trager, George L. "The phonemes of Russian." *Language*, 10:334–344 (1934).

GRAMMATICAL CATEGORIES*

The very natural tendency to use terms derived from traditional grammar, like verb, noun, adjective, passive voice, in describing languages outside of Indo-European is fraught with grave possibilities of misunderstanding. At the same time it is desirable to define these terms in such a way that we can avail ourselves of their great convenience and, where possible, apply them to exotic languages in a scientific and consistent way. To do this, we must re-examine the types of grammatical category that are found in languages, using a worldwide view of linguistic phenomena, frame concepts more or less new, and make needed additions to terminology. These observations apply *pari passu* to English, which hardly less than some American Indian languages is off the pattern of general Indo-European.[1]

In the reaction from conventional grammars of American languages based on classical models, there has been a tendency to restrict attention to the morphemes by which many grammatical forms are marked. This view loses sight of various word-classes that are marked not by mor-

---

* Reprinted from *Language*, 21:1–11 (1945). According to a note supplied by the editor of *Language*, "This paper was written late in 1937 at the request of Franz Boas, then editor of the *Int. J. Amer. Linguistics*. The manuscript was found in the Boas collection by C. F. Voegelin and Z. S. Harris." The Boas collection is cataloged in *Language Monograph* no. 22, 1945.

[1] The author wishes to acknowledge his indebtedness to his colleagues, Dr. George L. Trager and Dr. Morris Swadesh, with whom some of these questions of category have been discussed.

phemic tags but by types of patterning: e.g. by the systematic avoidance of certain morphemes, by lexical selection, by word-order that is also CLASS-ORDER, in general by association with definite linguistic configurations. At the beginning of investigation of a language, the "functional" type of definition, e.g. that a word of a certain class, say a "noun," is "a word which does so-and-so," is to be avoided when this is the ONLY test of distinction applied; for people's conceptions of what a given word "does" in an unfamiliar language may be as diverse as their own native languages, linguistic educations, and philosophical predilections. The categories studied in grammar are those recognizable through facts of a configurational sort, and these facts are the same for all observers. Yet I do not share the complete distrust of all functional definitions which a few modern grammarians seem to show. After categories have been outlined according to configurative facts, it may be desirable to employ functional or operational symbolism as the investigation proceeds. Linked with configurative data, operational descriptions become valid as possible ways of stating the MEANING of the forms, "meaning" in such cases being a characterization which succinctly accounts for all the semantic and configurational facts, known or predictable.

We may first distinguish between OVERT CATEGORIES and COVERT CATEGORIES.

An overt category is a category having a formal mark which is present (with only infrequent exceptions) in every sentence containing a member of the category. The mark need not be part of the same word to which the category may be said to be attached in a paradigmatic sense; i.e. it need not be a suffix, prefix, vowel change, or other "inflection," but may be a detached word or a certain patterning of the whole sentence. Thus in English the plural of nouns is an overt category, marked usually in the paradigm word (the noun in question) by the suffix '-s' or a vowel change, but in the case of words like 'fish, sheep,' and certain gentilic plurals, it is marked by the form of the verb, the manner of use of the articles, etc. In 'fish appeared,' the absence of any article denotes plural; in 'the fish will be plentiful,' a pluralizing adjective denotes it; in 'the Chinese arrived' and 'the Kwakiutl arrived,' the definite article coupled with lack of a singular marker like 'person,' 'Chinaman,' or 'Indian' denotes plural. In all these cases plural is overtly marked, and so, with few exceptions, are all noun plurals in English, so that noun-plural is an overt category in English.[2]   In Southern Paiute the subject-person of a verb is marked by a sublexical element (or "bound morpheme") that cannot stand alone, like English '-s'; but it need not be attached to the verb, it may be attached to the first important word of the sentence.   In English what may be called the potential mode of the verb is an overt category marked by the morpheme 'can' or 'could,' a word separate in the sentence from the verb but appearing in every sentence containing the category.   This category is as much a part of the verb system of morphology as though it were denoted by a bound element in a synthetic Algonkian or Sanskrit verb; its morpheme 'can' may replace coordinate elements in the same modal system, e.g. 'may, will,' but it may not, like a mere lexical item (e.g. 'possibly') be simply added to them.   In Hopi also there is a rigid system of mutually exclusive "modalities" denoted by detached words.

A covert category is marked, whether morphemically or by sentence-pattern, only in certain types of sentence and not in every sentence in which a word or element belonging to the category occurs.   The class-membership of the word is not apparent until there is a question of using it or referring to it in one of these special types of sentence, and then we find that this word belongs to a class requiring some sort of distinctive treatment, which may even be the negative treatment of excluding that type of sentence.   This distinctive treatment we may call the REACTANCE of the category.   In English, intransitive verbs form a covert category marked by lack of the passive participle and the passive and causative voices; we cannot substitute a verb of this class (e.g. 'go, lie, sit, rise, gleam, sleep, arrive, appear, rejoice') into such sentences as 'It was cooked, It was being cooked, I had it cooked to order.'   An intransitive thus configuratively defined is quite a different thing from the "dummy" intransitive used in traditional English grammar; it is a true grammatical class marked by these and other constant grammatical features, such as nonoccurrence of nouns or pronouns after the verb; one

[2] There is of course a minority group of possible or theoretically possible sentences, e.g. 'The fish appeared,' in which plural is not distinguished from singular.   But, in actual speech, such sentences are embedded in a larger context which has already established the plurality or the singularity of the thing discussed.   (Otherwise such a sentence is not likely to occur.)   Such minority types are not considered in the distinction between overt and covert; i.e. they do not prevent a category from being classed as overt.   In covert categories the unmarked forms are relatively numerous, often in the majority, and are undistinguished even by context.

does not say 'I gleamed it, I appeared the table.' Of course compound formations involving these same lexemes may be transitive, e.g. 'sleep (it) off, go (him) one better.' In the American colloquial forms 'go haywire, go South Sea Islander,' etc., the word or phrase after the verb is a covert adjective, cf. 'go completely haywire.'

Another type of covert category is represented by English gender. Each common noun and personal given name belongs to a certain gender class, but a characteristic overt mark appears only when there is occasion to refer to the noun by a personal pronoun in the singular number—or in the case of the neuter class it may be marked by the interrogative and relative pronouns 'what, which.' The grammatical alignment is no less strict than in an overt gender system like that of Latin, where most nouns bear their gender mark. No doubt for many English common nouns a knowledge of actual sex and of scientific biological and physical classification of objects could serve a foreigner in lieu of knowledge of the grammatical classes themselves, but such knowledge would be of only limited use after all, for the greater part of the masculine and feminine classes consists of thousands of personal names, and a foreigner who knows nothing of the cultural background of Western European Christian names must simply learn, i.e. observe, that 'Jane' belongs to the 'she' group and 'John' to the 'he' group. There are plenty of names of overt similarity but contrasted gender, e.g. 'Alice : Ellis, Alison : Addison, Audrey : Aubrey, Winifred : Wilfred, Myra : Ira, Esther : Lester.' [3] Nor would knowledge of any "natural" properties tell our observer that the names of biological classes themselves (e.g. animal, bird, fish, etc.) are 'it'; that smaller animals usually are 'it'; larger animals often 'he'; dogs, eagles, and turkeys usually 'he'; cats and wrens usually 'she'; body parts and the whole botanical world 'it'; countries and states as fictive persons (but not as localities) 'she'; cities, societies, and corporations as fictive persons 'it'; the human body 'it'; a ghost 'it'; nature 'she'; watercraft with sail or power and named small craft 'she'; unnamed rowboats, canoes, rafts 'it,' etc. The mistakes in English gender made by learners of the language, including those whose

[3] There are a very few names of indeterminate or double gender: 'Frances (Francis),' 'Jessie (Jesse),' or 'Jess, Jean (Gene), Jocelyn, Sidney, Wynne,' and perhaps a few others. The number is increased if we include nicknames like 'Bobby, Jerry,' etc.; but, all in all, such instances are relatively so few that they in no way disturb our alignment of facts.

own languages are without gender, would alone show that we have here covert grammatical categories, and not reflections in speech of natural and noncultural differences.

The classes of nouns based actually or ostensibly upon shape, in various American languages, may be either overt or covert. In Navaho they are covert. Some terms belong to the round (or roundish) class, others to the long-object class, others fall into classes not dependent on shape. No overt mark designates the class in every sentence. The class mark as in English gender is a reactance; not a pronoun, however, but a choice between certain verb stems that go definitely with one class and no other, although there are very many verb stems indifferent to this distinction. I doubt that such distinctions, at least in Navaho, are simply linguistic recognitions of nonlinguistic, objective differences that would be the same for all observers, any more than the English genders are; they seem rather to be covert grammatical categories. Thus one must learn as a part of learning Navaho that 'sorrow' belongs in the "round" class. One's first and "common-sense" impression of covert categories like English gender and Navaho shape-class is that they are simply distinctions between different kinds of experience or knowledge; that we say 'Jane went to her house' because we know that Jane is a female. Actually we need not know anything about Jane, Jane may be a mere name; yet having heard this name, perhaps over the telephone, we say 'What about her?'. Common sense may then retreat a step further and say that we know the name Jane to be given only to females. But such experience is linguistic; it is learning English by observation. Moreover it is easy to show that the pronoun agrees with the name only, not with the experience. I can bestow the name 'Jane' on an automobile, a skeleton, or a cannon, and it will still require 'she' in pronominal references. I have two goldfish; I name one 'Jane' and one 'Dick.' I can still say 'Each goldfish likes its food,' but not 'Jane likes its food better than Dick.' I must say 'Jane likes her food.' The word 'dog' belongs to a common gender class with a preference for 'he' and 'it,' but the gender-classed given name of a dog determines its own pronoun; we do not say 'Tom came out of its kennel,' but 'Tom came out of his kennel, Lady came out of her kennel, The female dog came out of its (or her) kennel.' "Doggish" names like 'Fido' are of the 'he' class: 'Towser came out of his kennel.' We say 'See the cat chase her tail,' but never 'See Dick chase her tail.' The words 'child, baby, infant' be-

long to the common class and can take 'it,' but the given names of
children take either 'he' or 'she.' I can say 'My baby enjoys its food,'
but it would be linguistically wrong to say 'My baby's name is Helen—
see how Helen enjoys its food.' Nor can I say 'My little daughter enjoys
its food,' for 'daughter,' unlike 'baby,' is grammatically in the feminine
class.

Likewise with various covert categories of exotic languages: where they
have been thought to be recognitions of objective differences, it may
rather be that they are grammatical categories that merely accord up to
a certain point with objective experience. They may represent experience, it is true, but experience seen in terms of a definite linguistic
scheme, not experience that is the same for all observers. On the other
hand, the distinctions between present and absent, visible and invisible,
made in many American languages, may well represent experiential differences; and again we may have such experiential differences engrafted
upon purely grammatical classifications, yielding mixed classes such as
"experiential-present plus grammatical-feminine."

A covert category may also be termed a CRYPTOTYPE, a name which
calls attention to the rather hidden, cryptic nature of such word-groups,
especially when they are not strongly contrasted in idea, nor marked by
frequently occurring reactances such as pronouns. They easily escape
notice and may be hard to define, and yet may have profound influence
on linguistic behavior. The English intransitive verbs as configuratively
defined above are a cryptotype. A similar cryptotype comprises the
verbs of "copulative resolution" ('be, become, seem, stay, remain,' etc.),
which also lack the passive and causative but may be followed by nouns,
pronouns, and adjectives. Transitives (a cryptotype which includes 'run,
walk, return,' etc.—indeed most English verbs) possess the passive and
causative and may be followed by nouns and pronouns but not by adjectives alone. Names of countries and cities in English form a cryptotype with the reactance that they are not referred to by personal pronouns as object of the prepositions 'in, at, to, from.' We can say 'I live
in Boston' but not 'That's Boston—I live in it.' A word of this cryptotype is referred to by 'there' or 'here' in place of 'in it, at it, to it,' and
by 'from there (here)' in place of 'from it.' In various American languages such place names constitute a grammatical class; in Hopi they
lack the nominative and objective cases, occurring only in locational

cases; in Aztec they bear characteristic endings and exclude the use of certain prepositions.

English adjectives form two main cryptotypes with subclasses. A group referring to "inherent" qualities—including color, material, physical state (solid, liquid, porous, hard, etc.), provenience, breed, nationality, function, use—has the reactance of being placed nearer the noun than the other group, which we may call one of noninherent qualities, though it is rather the residuum outside the first group—including adjectives of size, shape, position, evaluation (ethical, esthetic, or economic). These come before the inherent group, e.g. 'large red house' (not 'red large house'), 'steep rocky hill, nice smooth floor.' The order may be reversed to make a balanced contrast, but only by changing the normal stress pattern, and the form is at once sensed as being reversed and peculiar. The normal pattern has primary stress either on the noun ('steep rocky hi′ll') or on the inherent adjective ('pretty Fre′nch girl'). We cannot simply reverse the order of adjectives and say 'French pre′tty girl'—the form suggests a contrasted 'French plai′n girl' but the pattern of so contrasting adjectives is un-English; the proper contrast is 'plai′n French girl.' We can however reverse the adjectives by altering the stress pattern and say 'Fre′nch pretty girl,' if in contrast with e.g. 'Spa′nish pretty girl,' though such forms are clearly exceptional.

The contrasting term PHENOTYPE may be applied to the overt category and, when no ambiguity results, to the mark which accompanies the overt category in the sentence.

The distinction between overt and covert categories, or PHENOTYPES and CRYPTOTYPES, is one of two distinctions of supreme importance in the theory of grammatical categories. The other is the distinction between what may be called SELECTIVE CATEGORIES and MODULUS CATEGORIES.

A selective category is a grammatical class with membership fixed, and limited as compared with some larger class. A PRIMARY selective category, or LEXEMIC category, is one compared to which the next larger class is the total lexicon of the language. Certain semantic and grammatical properties are assured in the word by selecting it from a certain class of fixed membership not coterminous with the whole vocabulary. In order that a certain grammatical property may be "in the lexeme," it cannot be in all lexemes. The familiar "parts of speech" of most European languages, but not of English, are lexemic categories. The situation in

English is peculiar, and will be touched upon later. Lexemic categories may be either overt or covert. Hopi is an example of a language in which they are covert. Possibly Maya may be another such case, though we lack clear information on that point. In Hopi there is no distinction in the simplex (bare-stem) forms between nouns and verbs, and sentences are possible in which there is no distinction in the sentence. Thus *le·'na* or *pam le·'na* means 'it is a flute,' and *pe·'na* or *pam pe·'na* means 'he writes it.' Hence nouns and verbs MAY BE alike in overt characteristics. But it is easily possible to make sentences· in which *le·'na* appears with case suffixes and in other forms quite impossible for *pe·'na*, and vice versa. One has to learn, and cannot always tell from the sentence, that *le·'na* and *pe·'na* belong to different compartments of the lexicon.

It is probably more common to find lexemic classes that are overt, as in Latin, French, Aztec, Tübatulabal, Taos, and Navaho. In French, *ange* and *mange* belong to different compartments of the vocabulary (noun and verb) and there is always a feature in the sentence that tells which; one does not find such pairs as *il mange* : *il ange*, *c'est un ange* : *c'est un mange*. It may be possible to have *Ange!* versus *Mange!*, but special and abbreviated types of sentence like these with their lack of formal distinctions do not justify calling the categories covert. In Latin, Aztec, Tübatulabal, and Taos, the distinction is marked not only in the sentence, but also usually in the paradigm word itself. Yet this overt mark of the noun, verb, or other "part of speech" cannot usually be transferred to a lexeme outside of the proper group. The mark that goes with a covert lexemic class need not stand for any other category such as case, person, or tense, though it does for example in Latin, Greek, and Sanskrit. The "absolutive suffixes" found attached to lexemic nouns in most Uto-Aztecan languages have basically no other character than that of such class-marks, though in Aztec they are also tied up with number; and needless ingenuity has been wasted in trying to make them out to be "articles" or the like. The absolutive suffixes in Taos go with the selective class of nouns but indicate gender and number also. In Latin the distinction between the nouns (including in this class the adjectives) and the verbs is selective and overt, but that between adjectives and substantives is selective and covert; compare *est gladius* and *est bonus*. As with all covert classes, the distinction is revealed upon forming the proper type of sentence: *est bona* occurs, but not *est gladia*.

Lexemic categories include not only nouns, verbs, adjectives, and other "parts of speech," but also "full" words and "empty" [4] words or stems, as in Chinese and perhaps the Wakashan languages, and still other types of distinction; e.g. in Algonkian the lexemic classes include large groups of stems having different combinatory powers and different positions in the verbal complex.

A modulus category is a nonselective category, i.e. it is generally applicable and removable at will. Depending on its type, it may be applied either to any "major word" (any word excepting small and specialized selective classes, e.g. "particles"), or, more often, to any word coming within a certain prerequisite larger category, which may be either selective or another modulus category. The cases, tenses, aspects, modes, and voices of Indo-European and Azteco-Tanoan [5] languages are modulus categories, applicable at will to words belonging to the proper larger category—cases being moduli of the larger category of nouns; aspects, tenses, etc. moduli of the larger category of verbs. Hence the person versed only in Indo-European types of grammar poses to himself the distinction between selective and modulus classes (or between selectivity and modulation) as the distinction between "parts of speech" on the one hand and "grammatical forms" of the aspect, tense, and voice type on the other. But, in widely different types of speech, these familiar types of meaning and function cease to be associated with selectivity and modulation in the same way; entirely different alignments there hold sway in the grammar, and, until this is recognized, an adequate conception of the grammar cannot be obtained. It is not necessary to have large categories, such as nouns and verbs, in order to have such modulus categories as aspect. In Nitinat [6] (and presumably in the closely related Nootka and Kwakiutl) all major words have aspects, such as durative,

[4] An "empty" word or stem is probably one that is highly specialized for grammatical or syntactic indication, perhaps in a way that does not admit of being assigned a concrete meaning. For example, such a form might have no other meaning than to serve as the reactance of some other category, or as the signature of a modulus category (see the next paragraph).

[5] B. L. Whorf and G. L. Trager, "The relationship of Uto-Aztecan and Tanoan," *Amer. Anthrop.*, 39:609–24 (1937).

[6] See Mary Haas Swadesh and Morris Swadesh, "A visit to the other world: a Nitinat text," *Int. J. Amer. Linguistics*, 7:3–4 (1933).

momentaneous, inceptive, etc.—both the word for 'run' and the word for 'house' always bear some element marking this aspect.

We may use the term "modulus" alone to denote the distinctive class meaning and function of the category; thus the present-participle meaning is a modulus in English. We may also use modulus to mean the grammatical operation of producing one such meaning, and hence, where no ambiguity results, to mean the element or pattern that marks the modulus. Thus we can say that in English the present-participle modulus is the suffixing of '-ing,' or for short that it is '-ing.' Where greater preciseness is desirable, we may call the overt mark the (or a) SIGNATURE of the modulus. This distinction is ultimately important; sometimes it is necessary to distinguish several signatures of the same modulus. In illustrating overt categories we cited the English noun-plural, which is a modulus category. The modulus, or plural type of meaning, is one and the same thing throughout the various examples, but the signatures whereby this plural modulus may be applied to the word 'fish' are different from one example to the next. To these signatures we may add '-s' or '-es,' giving 'fishes.' Since 'sheep, deer, moose, caribou,' etc. belong to a cryptotype that excludes '-s,' and "fishermen's fish" such as 'trout, bass, salmon, mackerel, cod,' etc. (contrasted with "low-grade fish," e.g. 'sharks, skates, eels, sculpins,' etc.) belong to another such cryptotype, we cannot use this last signature for them. As this example shows, it is not necessary to have one-to-one correspondence between moduli and signatures. Where a high degree of such one-to-one correspondence obtains, it has often been the custom to apply the graphic but not very scientific catchword "agglutinative" to the language. Languages of the typical "agglutinative" type, such as Turkish, have been referred to as if they had such one-to-one correspondence, and moreover as if they had no categories but modulus categories. The grammar of Yana (Hokan stock, California) consists largely of moduli, but has also a few selective categories; e.g. a class of stems which must stand first in the verbal complex and a class which must stand second.

A distinction of the same semantic type as that between verbs and nouns in selective categories may be handled by modulus categories instead. That is, the possible moduli include not only voice, aspect, etc., but also VERBATION and STATIVATION.[7] Whenever, as for example in

[7] Stativation is a term used to denote the modulus of forms which are contrasted with verbations in a way similar to that in which nouns, as a selective category, are

Yana, the mere application of certain distinctive suffixes or other signatures makes a "verb" out of any stem, then we do not have a class of verbs in the same sense as in French, Latin, Greek, Hopi, Aztec, Taos, and Navaho: i.e. a selective class. We have verbations instead of such verbs. The so-called verbs and nouns of Semitic are moduli, applicable to lexemes in general by signatures consisting largely of vowel-consonant sequence patterns, though there may be occasional gaps in the universality of lexical applicability. In Hebrew we have *e-e* as one of several signatures for stativation and *ā-a* as one of several for verbation, e.g. *berek* [8] 'knee' : *bārak* 'he kneeled,' *derek* 'road' : *dārak* 'he marched,' *geber* 'man, as virile or strong' : *gābar* 'he was strong,' *hebel* 'cord' : *hābal* 'he bound,' *melek* 'king' : *mālak* 'he reigned,' *qedem* 'antecedence' : *qādam* 'he was before,' *regel* 'foot' : *rāgal* 'he went on foot.' There are no doubt many Hebrew "nouns" for which we do not know the verbation form in texts, but this seems to be so largely because the textual Hebrew that we know does not represent the full resources of the ancient living language; Arabic shows better the general applicability of these moduli to the great majority of lexemes. But verbs and nouns which are modulus categories may be found nearer home than Semitic. The lexicon of English contains two major selective divisions. One division, consisting mostly of long words and words with certain endings, contains selective verbs like 'reduce, survive, undertake, perplex, magnify, reciprocate,' and selective nouns like 'instrument, elephant, longevity, altruism.' A limited number of short words belong also to the group of selective nouns and verbs, e.g. 'heart, boy, street, road, town; sit, see, hear, think.' In this selective vocabulary English is like French or Hopi. The other part of the lexicon, mostly the shorter words but some long ones, contains bare lexemes to which either verbation or stativation may be applied at will, e.g. 'head, hand, stand, walk, ex-

contrasted with verbs in the languages that have such a contrast. It is used here instead of "nomination" or "nominalization," because these terms through past usage have come to suggest derivations rather than moduli, while "stativation" helps us to think of the form not as a noun derived from a verb, but simply as a lexeme which has been affected by a certain meaningful grammatical coloring as a part of certain configurations.

[8] Since these Hebrew examples are used only to illustrate vowel patterns, they are written in approximate morphophonemic orthography, which does not attempt to show the distinction between the stops *b*, *g*, *k*, etc. and the spirants which replace them after vowels under regular statable conditions.

change, sight, skin, weave, dog, surrender, massage,' etc.[9] This part of the vocabulary is like Arabic, though the signatures are of a quite different sort. Those for stativation include the articles, plural signatures, position after possessive pronouns and selective adjectives; those for verbation include position after a nominative pronoun, position before a pronoun, noun, or stativation, the tense forms, the verbal auxiliaries and modal particles, etc.

There may be wide variability in the semantic relations between verbations and stativations in the same language. When contrasted with the corresponding stativations, verbations may seem to add in an inconstant manner such ideas as 'he engaged in' (hunt, jump, dance), 'behave like' (mother, carpenter, dog), 'be in' (lodge, hive), 'put in' (place, seat, pocket, garage), 'make, add, install' (weave, plant, roof, pipe, tin), 'take away' (skin, peel, husk, bone), 'get' (fish, mouse), 'use' (spear, hammer, fiddle, bugle); while on the other hand stativations seem to add inconstantly such ideas as 'result' (weave, plant, form), 'means' (paint, trail), 'action or place' (walk, slide, step, drop), 'instrument' (lift, cover, clasp, clip), etc. This inconstancy, or, better, elasticity, in certain aspects of the meaning, seen in Semitic as well as in English, is characteristic of the simple moduli of verbation and stativation, and it may be contrasted with the condition of having a number of different moduli, each a different specialized type of verbation or stativation, which appears to be the situation in Alaskan Eskimo. It merely means that, in a language with simple primary types of moduli, the meaning of the individual lexeme is more or less under the sway of the entire sentence, and at the mercy of the manifold potentialities of connotation and suggestion which thereby arise.

Can there be languages not only without selective nouns and verbs, but even without stativations and verbations? Certainly. The power of making predications or declarative sentences and of taking on such moduli as voice, aspect, and tense, may be a property of every major word, without the addition of a preparatory modulus. This seems to be the case in Nitinat and the other Wakashan languages. An isolated word is a sentence; a sequence of such sentence words is like a compound sentence. We might ape such a compound sentence in English, e.g.

[9] Adjectivation in English is another modulus which is applied both to bare lexemes and to selective nouns, but there are also selective adjectives, and these are not modulated into substantives.

'There is one who is a man who is yonder who does running which traverses-it which is a street which elongates,' though the exotic sentence consists simply of the predicative lexemes 'one,' 'man,' 'yonder,' 'run,' 'traverse,' 'street,' and 'long,' and the proper translation is 'A man yonder is running down the long street.' Such a structure might or might not be found in an isolating language; again it might or might not be found in a polysynthetic one like Nitinat. The polysynthetic language might or might not fuse some of the lexemes into long synthetic words, but it would doubtless have the power in any case of fusing in a great many aspectual, modal, and connective elements (signatures of moduli). Of such a polysynthetic tongue it is sometimes said that all the words are verbs, or again that all the words are nouns with verb-forming elements added. Actually the terms verb and noun in such a language are meaningless. The situation therein is radically different from for example Hopi, for, though in the latter *le·'na* 'it is a flute' and *pe·'na* 'he writes it' are both complete sentences, they are words which are not equally predicative in all positions of a sentence, and they also belong to selective covert classes of noun and verb that in general take different inflections, and look alike only in particular types of sentence. In Hopi the verb-noun distinction is important on a selective basis; in English it is important on a modulus basis; in Nitinat it seems not to exist.

So far we have dealt with categories which are distinct both configuratively and semantically, and these are the typical formulations of grammar. But we also have word groups which are configuratively distinct and yet have no difference in meaning; these we may call ISOSEMANTIC or purely formal classes. They in turn are of two sorts corresponding to selective and modulus in the semantic categories, but here better styled SELECTIVE and ALTERNATIVE. Selective isosemantic classes are typified by "declensions" and "conjugations," those very common features of languages the world over, richly developed in Latin, Sanskrit, Hopi, and Maya, less developed in Semitic, English ("strong" and "weak" verbs), and Aztec, and almost lacking in Southern Paiute. They also include gender-like classes without semantic difference, as in Bantu and in certain of the genders of Taos (all these might be called "declensions" with pronominal agreement or the like); classes requiring different position in a sentence or complex without difference in type of meaning (stem-position classes in Algonkian); and classes requiring different signatures for the same modulus without difference in type of meaning, e.g. in Hebrew the segholate (*e-e*) "nouns" and parallel stativation groups. Alternative isosemantic classes are what their name implies: e.g. the English group comprising 'don't, won't, shan't, can't,' etc. and the group of 'do not, will not, shall not, cannot.' In this case we could perhaps speak of a modulus of brevity, convenience, or colloquial attitude which is applied in the former group. Alternative classes sometimes show STYLISTIC as opposed to grammatical difference. In other cases there seems to be no GENERALIZABLE difference, as in English 'electrical, cubical, cyclical, historical, geometrical' versus 'electric, cubic, cyclic, historic, geometric.'

There remains another type of distinction: SPECIFIC CATEGORIES and GENERIC ones. A specific category is an individual class existing in an individual language, e.g. English passive voice, Hopi segmentative aspect. A generic category, in the restricted sense of application to a particular language, is a hierarchy formed by grouping classes of similar or (and) complementary types, e.g. case in Latin, voice in Hopi. Here much depends on both the insight and the predilections of the systematizer or grammarian, for it may be easy to build up specific categories into very logical schemes; yet what is rather desired is that such generic categories should represent systems which the language itself contains. We do well to be skeptical of a grammarian's systematization when it is full of ENANTIOMORPHISM, the pairing with every category of an opposite which is merely the lack of it. Specific categories of seemingly opposite meaning such as passive voice and active voice (when this term "active" means merely "nonpassive") should be brought into one generic category ("voice") only when they are more than two, or when, if there are only two, taken together they contrast as a unit with some other system of forms.

Finally, in a still wider sense generic categories may be so formulated as to become equivalent to the concepts of a general science of grammar. Such categories are made by grouping what seem to us to be SIMILAR SPECIFIC CATEGORIES IN DIFFERENT LANGUAGES. Only in such a sense can we speak of a category of "passive voice" which would embrace the forms called by that name in English, Latin, Aztec, and other tongues. Such categories or concepts we may call TAXONOMIC categories, as opposed to DESCRIPTIVE categories. Taxonomic categories may be of the first degree, e.g. passive voice, objective case; or of the second degree, e.g. voice, case. Perhaps those of the second degree are the more important and ultimately the more valuable as linguistic concepts, as generalizations of the largest systemic formations and outlines found in language when language is considered and described in terms of the whole human species.

DISCUSSION OF

HOPI LINGUISTICS *

320 Wolcott Hill Road,
Wethersfield, Conn.

Dear John:

You will be interested to hear that I have been appointed to a part-time lectureship at Yale for the term January to June 1938, Department of Anthropology, to give one 2-hour lecture a week on Problems of American Linguistics. During the fall term my colleague George L. Trager will have the same group in Phonetics, so that I do not plan to devote much of any time to phonetic or phonemic problems per se. I am going to orient my lectures largely toward a psychological direction, and the problems of meaning, thought, and idea in so-called primitive cultures. Methods of investigating language which reveal something of the psychic factors or constants of the American Indians in the given linguistic community will be emphasized. I say psychic instead of mental, since affect as well as thought, insofar as it is linguistic, will be treated. I expect to give a good deal of attention to the subject of the organization of raw experience into a consistent and readily communicable universe of ideas through the medium of linguistic patterns. Altogether I hope to present some conceptions rather exciting to the

* The following, heretofore unpublished, was a draft of a letter addressed to me while I was a student of psychology at the University of Minnesota in the fall of 1937. Even though part of the handwritten draft was copied out on the typewriter, with an original and one carbon, it was apparently never sent, for I never received it. The draft manuscript was found among family papers.

102

cultural anthropologist and to the psychologist, and to have some budding exponents of both disciplines among my students.

In preparing material for the course I should be very glad to have any assistance that you and the University can render, for I know you and they are interested along this linguistic-psychological line. I might outline here certain concepts that I am now working on, based on analysis of the Hopi language, which naturally will be one I shall draw on considerably for examples, though I expect also to devote some time to Aztec and Maya. An introduction to the general problem may be found in the analysis of Hopi categories of verb morphology, especially those which for purposes of convenience may be called aspect and tense, although exactly the same meaning that these terms have in classical European linguistics cannot be taken for Hopi. We have however two distinct morphological categories, the suffixes of which are differently treated and have different positions, the tense suffix coming after the voice suffix. There are three tenses: past (i.e., past up to and including present), future, and generalized (that which is generally, universally, or timelessly true), all of which are mutually exclusive. Of these, the only one to be considered here is the future (suffix *-ni*). A first approximation to its meaning is the English future. There are nine aspects, of which I shall consider chiefly the inceptive (*-va*) and projective (*-to*). The punctual aspect is the aspect of the simplex (stem without suffixes or modification); the past tense is the tense of the simplex. A first approximation to the meaning of the inceptive is 'begins doing' (I shall translate the Hopi past tense by the English present), and to that of the projective is 'does with a forward movement.' Later I shall refer to the progressional resultative or "crescentive" form in *-iwma*. There is another inceptive-like progressional form in *-ʔyma* but I am not including it as it has a noticeably different meaning ('is well on the way to getting it done').

In getting translations of the English 'begins doing it' form with a large number of different verbs, we eventually find that, whereas the Hopi uses the inceptive for the majority of the verbs, for a certain number it uses the projective, and for a considerable number it jumps out of the "aspect" category entirely and uses the FUTURE TENSE (in the punctual or nonspecified aspect). The usage is consistent and does not depend on the formal type ("conjugation") of the verb. Analysis shows that it follows in a curious way the lexical meaning of the verb. The question at once strikes one: Why should a pattern ('begins doing it') which appears to us to be perfectly uniform and of the same nature in all cases present itself to the mind of the bilingual English-speaking Hopi informant as a meaning which switches back and forth between two (or more) fundamental meaning categories of his own language? It is also to be noted that, in almost all the cases where the inceptive is used for 'begins doing,' the Hopi uses not only the suffix -va but also a reduplication. The meaning of reduplication is a durativizing of the punctual to denote a more extended process and hence would seem to be a logical prerequisite to a form denoting the beginning of a process, but nevertheless, where the projective or the future tense translates the 'begins doing,' the reduplication is NOT employed. This tends to confirm one's impression that the Hopi observer conceives the events in a different manner from the one whose native language is English.

Thus in the expressions for 'begins writing, breathing, sleeping, flying, rolling (over and over), laughing, fighting, smoking, singing, swimming, dying, looking, bumping it,[1] turning it, digging it, eating it, breaking it, tearing it, killing it, tying it, gathering it, lifting it, bending it, putting it in, putting it down, picking it up,' and many more, the inceptive (-va on reduplicated base) is used. In those for 'begins running, moving, fleeing, going homeward, going away, going to (a place), going up (or down), talking, opening it, closing it, shooting it (arrow), driving it (car), being in or at (a place),' the future is used. Thus the forms are the same as for 'will run, move, flee,' etc. In the expressions for 'begins going out, going in, coming (= 'arriving' in Hopi), falling down, falling (through space, a different verb), going in a circuit, turning, rotating, splitting open (intransitive), tipping over, spilling,' and others, the projective aspect is used. 'Does with a forward movement' seems appropriate to many of these, but why it is not also appropriate to many of those in the other two groups is not clear, nor why it should be the necessary translation of English 'begins doing' in this third group. The informant himself can give no explanation.

From phenomena of this sort, which are not confined to the inceptive problem but pervade all Hopi grammar, I conclude that there must be to the Hopi speaker a dimly felt relation of similarity between the verb usages in each group having to do with some inobvious facet of their

---

[1] "It" denotes a transitive verb, requiring an object expressed or implied.

meaning, and therefore itself a meaning, but one so nearly at or below the threshold of conscious thinking that it cannot be put into words by the user and eludes translation. To isolate, characterize, and understand the operation of these dimly felt, barely conscious (or even unconscious) meanings is the object of my further analysis. Such an elusive, hidden, but functionally important meaning I call a CRYPTOTYPE.

Thus I would say that the meanings of the Hopi stems translated 'be writing, breathing, sleeping, breaking it,' etc. are similar in that they all contain "cryptotype A," while 'running, moving, going homeward, opening it,' etc. contain "cryptotype B," and 'going in, falling, turning,' etc. "cryptotype C." The mode of lettering is simply a varying and provisional one for each problem. In contrast with the cryptotype, which has no formal mark and whose meaning is not clearly evident, but is rather a submerged meaning shown as an influence, I give the name PHENOTYPE to the categories inceptive, future, projective, etc.; i.e., the phenotype is the "classical" morphological category, having a formal mark and a clearly apparent class-meaning. For schematic purposes, we may refer to inceptive, future, projective, as phenotypes 1, 2, 3, with reference to the present problem. It will be seen that, in a language such as Hopi, the meanings of grammatical forms result from the interplay of phenotype and cryptotype, and not from phenotype alone. This concept is of course extensible to many other languages than Hopi. Linguistics up to now has studied almost entirely the phenotypes. Study of cryptotypes opens up a more psychological phase of linguistics.

So far we have three types of 'begin' forms, A1, B2, C3. If we equate 'begins ——ing' to 'begins to be ——ing' (which is rendered the same in Hopi) and then pass to 'begins to be ——,' where —— is not an -ing form but either (a) an adjective or (b) a past participle, we get an interesting difference. With an adjective, e.g., 'begins to be sweet, red, white, blue, hot, big, short, good, round,' etc. a new phenotype (4), i.e. another inceptive-like morpheme, appears. A form in -iwma is now used. This form is a combination of voice and aspect: the resultative voice ('as a result is sweet') plus the progressional aspect -ma ('does in the course of motion, secondarily "passes" or "goes" into or toward a state or condition'). In the case (b), e.g. 'begins to be torn, bumped, dug, cut, written,' etc., it makes a difference whether the condition is to be considered as resultative or passive, i.e., whether what is beginning is a torn condition, which uses phenotype 4 (-iwma), or what is beginning is a tearing act happening to a passive subject, which uses (2) (future tense, -ni) plus the suffix of the passive voice. If, however, cryptotype C is present, the form is C3 (projective, -to) just as in the previous case without passive meaning, i.e., 'begins to be split open, rotated, spilled,' etc. is the same as 'begins splitting open, rotating, spilling,' although it is possible to use the -iwma form here to give a definitely resultative meaning. In all these 'begin to be ———' forms we see another cryptotype, D, which is evidently the passive-resultative side of the meanings of both A and B, besides also including the ordinary descriptive adjective. D can use two inceptive phenotypes, 4 or 2. Phenotype 4 is really the progressional aspect -ma, -iw- being the sign of the resultative voice corresponding to the sign of the passive used with 2. We have added the types D4, D2.

It may now be noted that D is contrasted with A, B, C as inactive with active. A, B, and C are alike in being active: i.e., actual movement and change is shown going on, or else it is a vital state, a life process, that is shown as in 'sleeping'; the only exception (from our own viewpoint) is 'being in a place,' which is very likely not a real exception but a phase of the same idea. The "role" of the subject is that of actor, even if the actor does nothing but be in a place; this seems to be a common idea to A, B, and C. In D the "role" of the subject is the nonacting substance that serves to display some condition or quality. Perhaps it might be said that, in the first case, the subject is regarded as the causal agent, in the second as not the causal agent, of what I call the 'verbation,' i.e., the manifestation (action, operation, condition, state, status, relation, etc.) announced by the verb. We still cannot state the differences among the A, B, and C cryptotypes, but one factor of cryptotypic meaning has been shown up. The contrast active-inactive or causal-incausal nowhere appears as a phenotype in Hopi. But as a cryptotypic contrast it is decisive in governing the outward form.

If we get renderings for 'begins to do,' distinct differences appear as compared to 'begins doing.' The Hopi now omits the reduplication from the inceptive aspect forms of A1. Evidently the Hopi feels that our -ing form denotes a more extended process than the infinitive. The B cryptotype is however rendered just the same: i.e., -ni for both 'begins moving' and 'begins to move.' The C is also the same: i.e., -to for 'begins going out' and 'begins to go out.' But, moreover, the A cryptotype can now use phenotype 2 (-ni) as well as 1; both forms are possible for the same verb with the same translation. In certain cases a slight difference in meaning creeps out. We have added one more type, A2, which has a slightly different translation from the reduplicated A1, and an even slighter difference in meaning from the unreduplicated A1. This difference is hard to perceive, but is shown in certain examples and is presumably connected with the difference in the phenotypes -*ni* and -*va* (and is not cryptotypic).

Returning to cryptotypes A, B, and C: A and B are related by the fact that A uses both -*va* and -*ni* and B uses -*ni* only. There is then presumably something about the B type of ideas that makes the characteristic inceptiveness of -*va* inappropriate. And there is presumably something about C that makes both -*va* and -*ni* ineligible and demands -*to*. D is characteristically inactive or incausal, and, in contrast, A, B, and C represent three different types of activity or causality. Omitting the space-relational forms and a few others, causality becomes the same as activity. After a prolonged scrutiny and analysis, aided by what grasp I have of Hopi linguistic ideas and viewpoints, I arrive at the following characterization of these cryptotypes A, B, and C. B is an activity, the starting of which implies that there will be a certain amount of actual maintenance thereof, springing from the initial impulse supplied by the subject or actor. B represents acts springing from a subject-initiated impulse, but not necessarily ALL such acts—only those in which the first initiation of a phenomenon by the impulse immediately shows the activity in full-fledged form, a form for which CONTINUING has simply the meaning of adding time, but not of further developing nor of continuously adapting the form. In nearly all cases we may read for "impulse," "volitional impulse" or "will," either actual in an animate actor or "felt into," the rarely occurring inanimate subject. Hence the type includes the subjectively determined kinds of uniform motion like running, fleeing, and "going" of various sorts. Thus, in order to say 'he begins to run,' the activity must already have shown itself in the effective form of running, which will not thereafter be developed and stabilized, but merely continued "as is." "Being," i.e., in Hopi a verbation of spatial relationship like 'in, at, on, along, under, with,' etc., is classed as of the same type as "running." A very few transitive verbs are included, in which the actor transfers his impulse at once to the object in such a way that ITS form of activity is at once completely displayed. Thus, 'he opens it' (no matter how little, it is open and no longer closed); closing it is classed as a converse operation of the same type (the moving of any barrier over the opening is a partial closing which, so far as it goes, has been maintained and will not be changed in form by continuance); so also 'shooting an arrow.'

A however is an activity, the start of which does not mean even a brief maintenance of itself as a result of one first impulse or tendency. If the very first impulse should not be reinforced the laugh would not be a laugh, the writing not a writing but at most a mark, or a pen-grasping, the break not a break but only a strain. The action is felt to consist of a developing train of events or a more than momentary application of the will to action, a following-up sort of participation of the subject necessary to even the briefest establishment of the action in its representative form. Some of the verb meanings of A will at first seem strangely selected from this standpoint, but a little meditation on the matter will often show a peculiar insight revealed in the Hopi cryptotypic meaning. Thus "sleep" is classed here by Hopi as though it felt sleep to be a state which the subject developed into by a continuous readjustment, not one which he launched himself into; while "running" and "talking" are regarded as states launched into, not progressed or adjusted into. All transitive verbs except the few special ones in B are regarded as of this A type—the affecting of an object requires an adjustment to it. Cryptotype A is thus an essentially dynamic or symbolically dynamic concept, even though it may refer to a resting state, and the dynamism emanates from the subject. Cryptotype A is active or symbolically active (actorial) but not dynamic; the subject is simply introjected into a state of uniform motion, or its symbolic equivalent, and left there.

Cryptotype C is an activity (always intransitive), into which the subject needs only to be placed in the initial stage in order to be seized by a natural tendency and carried on beyond the initial state in spite of itself. It is delivered over, as it were, to a realm of tendency, and henceforth is no longer master but must submit to an inevitable development and change of the initial state. Thus the initial state may be losing a support or losing balance, whereupon the subject is delivered over to gravity and 'falls' or 'tips over' or 'spills'; once entered upon this state, it has to "see the finish of it." Or, as in the case of turning, rotating, and other mechanical actions, it may be inertia, momentum, elasticity, or simply some indefinite automatic tendency that seizes the subject, once the first projection of action has, like a trigger, released it. The symbol for this is "being thrown," which is the symbolic image behind the projective aspect -to 'does with a forward movement.' It may at first be thought curious that Hopi puts 'going out' and 'going in' in this category. Actually no external force seizes the subject and moves him, but he does pass over a definite dividing line into another realm, the realm of the exterior, whereas he has been a part of the interior, or vice versa, and once he has made the change he is subject to the laws and nature of the new realm, those of the initial state being absolutely left behind. Thus in a way the verb 'go in' or 'go out' might serve as the symbol of all the other ideas in this cryptotype. Cryptotype C is thus dynamic, or symbolically dynamic, but the dynamism does not emanate from the subject but from the external field. Finally, cryptotype D, as we saw, is not dynamic or even active, but inactive, i.e. either static or passive.

The meaning of a PHENOTYPE, though ostensibly plain, can really not be completely understood in all its subtlety until the cryptotypes that go with it have been dredged up from their submerged state and their effective meanings to some extent brought into consciousness. Thereupon the different effects produced by the same phenotype with different cryptotypes, and vice versa, result in a more pronounced consciousness and clearer understanding of the phenotype itself. We are now in a better position to study the subtle meaning of -va and -ni. In the case of the latter we of course have to begin with a somewhat intuitive study of the tense system as a whole, and then of the "future" tense, denoted by -ni. The "future" tense asserts that expectancy of the event is present, that the subject's will to the event, if it is a voluntary act, is present, and that the very first initial point of the event may have been reached (here context governs), but that all beyond this is not present but future: i.e. the event AS A WHOLE is future. In order that the event as a whole may be future, the tense cannot imply that the subject's tendency will persevere beyond the initial point; otherwise the sense of futurity would be greatly weakened or completely lost; it would mean ONLY 'he is starting his doing of it' or 'he is starting to do it.' On the other hand -va means 'starts with perseverance or gathering impetus to do it'; the initial point is present, the next point swiftly impending, and the follow-through promised. With the A cryptotype, unreduplicated, either -va or -ni may be used with a slight difference in nuance, which is shown by some of the examples to mean 'begins to do it.' The -ni says the activity has gone to the initial point, but the dynamic, perseverating meaning of the cryptotype itself promises that the nondurative condition denoted by the verb will be fairly embarked into. It is the same with -va, except that it makes the embarkation even more positive. But, with the reduplicated or durative A verb, we need -va because the dim crypto-typic perseveration in the A verb is merely sufficient to embark, and, in order to promise a follow-up through a durative action, we need to assert the persevering will or tendency of the subject himself or itself, which is done by means of -va. Thus, to say 'he begins to chop it,' meaning that he swings the axe to make at least one chop (whether he makes any more or decides to quit then and there we don't know), we may use either -ni or -va. But, to say 'he begins chopping it,' meaning that his first chop will be followed by a second and a third and so on, we need the reduplication and -va, not -ni. It is the same if the action is not repetitive but merely continuous: i.e. 'he begins sleeping.'

On the other hand, with cryptotype B, the cryptotypic meaning im-plies that, once the initial point is reached (for which -ni is sufficient), the event is manifested in its typical form and will maintain itself for a time at least in that form; hence the whole question of perseverance by the subject is thrown out of the window, so to say. This means that -va would be redundant and inappropriate, perhaps suggesting more purposive drive than is needed in the bare statement of a B-type activity. There is about the B-cryptotype words a certain bareness and abstract-ness; they announce a type of motion or position and let it go at that. All the 'going' and 'coming' words are particularly abstract, having no really verbal roots but being merely verbalized postpositions or adverbs, 'to, from, away,' etc. It is perhaps a matter of the deep layers of Hopi thought process that this cold bareness should not be spoiled or falsified by the use of an element like -va.

This illustration will show how the meaning of a form in a language like Hopi is capable of being more deeply analyzed by the cryptotype concept, and how the totality of meaning is a joint product of crypto-typic and phenotypic factors. In many languages the cryptotype con-cept would be of little use, but there are languages like Hopi in which much of the influential material of paradigm production lies in this heavily veiled state, just as there are people whose mental life is much less accessible than that of others. Cryptotypes play a much larger part in Hopi than this rather minor problem of inceptive forms, which however yields a neat illustration. I believe I am the first to point out the existence of this submerged layer of meaning, which in spite of its submergence functions regularly in the general linguistic whole.

I am very curious to know what you as a psychologist think of this general idea. How does it bear on the problems you have in hand? The resemblance of the cryptotypes to the concept of the unconscious of Freud, and still more perhaps of Jung, will no doubt strike you, although the parallel should perhaps not be carried too far.

SOME VERBAL CATEGORIES

OF HOPI *

In the earlier stages of work on the Hopi language, I had the pleasant feeling of being in familiar linguistic territory. Here, wondrous to relate, was an exotic language cut very much on the pattern of Indo-European: a language with clearly distinct nouns, verbs, and adjectives, with voices, aspects, tense-moods, and no outré categories, no gender-like classes based on shape of objects, no pronouns referring to tribal status, presence, absence, visibility, or invisibility.

But, in course of time, I found it was not all such plain sailing. The sentences I made up and submitted to my Hopi informant were usually wrong. At first the language seemed merely to be irregular. Later I found it was quite regular, in terms of its own patterns. After long study and continual scrapping of my preconceived ideas, the true patterning emerged at last. I found the experience highly illuminating, not only in regard to Hopi but as bearing on the whole subject of grammatical categories and concepts. It happens that Hopi categories are just enough like Indo-European ones to give at first a deceptive impression of identity marred with distressing irregularities, and just enough different to afford, after they have been correctly determined, a new viewpoint toward the, on the whole, similar distinctions made in many modern and ancient Indo-European tongues. It was to me almost as enlightening to see English from the entirely new angle necessitated in order to translate it into Hopi as it was to discover the meanings of the Hopi

* Reprinted from *Language*, 14:275–286 (1938).

forms themselves. This was notably true for the four types of verbal category herein discussed.

It will be well to outline first the following general distinctions:

1. OVERT CATEGORY: one marked by a morpheme which appears in every sentence containing the category, vs. COVERT CATEGORY: not marked in sentences in general, but requiring a distinctive treatment in certain types of sentence, e.g. English genders.

2. WORD CATEGORY: a category (overt or covert or mixed) which delimits one of a primary hierarchy of word classes, each of limited membership (not coterminous with entire vocabulary), e.g. the familiar "parts of speech" of Indo-European and many other languages, vs. MODULUS CATEGORY: one which modifies either any word of the vocabulary or any word already allocated to a delimited class, e.g. voices, aspects, cases.

3. SPECIFIC CATEGORY: an individual class of any of the above types, e.g. passive voice, durative aspect, vs. GENERIC CATEGORY: a higher hierarchy formed by grouping classes of similar or complementary types, e.g. voice, aspect.

The categories treated in this article are all of the overt and the modulus types, but it should be stated that covert categories and word categories are also of great importance in Hopi grammar. Failure to define such classes would at once give the grammar a very irregular appearance. The generic categories here treated belong to the verb system, and have been designated ASSERTION, MODE, STATUS, and MODALITY.

ASSERTION

Hopi verbs have three assertions: REPORTIVE (zero form), EXPECTIVE (suffix -*ni*), NOMIC (suffix -$\eta^w i$). These translate, more or less, the English tenses.[1] But they do not refer to time or duration. They distinguish three different kinds of information. Assertion, in other words, is a classification that refers the statement to one of three distinct realms of validity. The reportive is simply a reporting statement, telling of the

[1] In "The punctual and segmentative aspects of verbs in Hopi," *Language*, 12 (1936), I referred to the assertions as tenses and called them factual or present-past, future, and generalized or usitative.

historical actuality of a certain situation: e.g. Eng. 'he ran, he is running, I see it.' [2]

The expective declares an expectation or anticipation of a situation. It is translated by the English future, or by 'is going to,' or by 'begins to,' for an attitude may still be one of expectant anticipation, rather than one of reporting a fait accompli, while the action is already beginning. Since the assertions have nothing to do with time as such, an expectant attitude may be projected into an account of past events, giving the translations 'was going to,' 'began to.' A clue to meanings otherwise obscure resides in the rendering 'his doing it is (or was) expected.' Thus, addition of the concursive mode suffix -kaŋ 'while' forms an expective concursive in -nikaŋ, but to translate here by the English future 'while he will do it' would be quite incorrect. The form means 'before he does it': i.e. 'while his doing it is expected.' [3]

The nomic does not declare any particular situation, but offers the statement as a general truth, e.g. English: 'she writes poetry, he smokes

[2] There is no distinction in the reportive between past and present, for both are equally accomplished fact. What we call present tense (not counting our present form which corresponds to the nomic) is from the Hopi standpoint simply a report to others concerning a situation shared with them, this report being either redundant information, or used to call attention to, or tell about some fragment of the situation not fully shared. Thus to the Hopi 'he is running' need not be different from 'he was running,' for, if both the speaker and listener can see the runner, then the 'is' of the former sentence means merely that the listener can see for himself what he is being told; he is being given redundant information, and this is the only difference from the latter sentence. Now the Hopi listener senses no lack in Hopi grammar for its not telling him that the information is redundant, when he can see for himself that it is. If the speaker can see the runner but the listener cannot, then the information is not redundant, but the situation in that case is one of rapidly relaying the information, which rules out the distinctive past meaning of 'was,' and again the Hopi find our tense distinction irrelevant.

[3] The orthography used for Hopi is phonemic and employs the American Anthropological Association symbols generally used for American Indian languages, with the following minor variations: k is somewhat fronted and before a and ε sounds like kʸ; c is the affricate ts; ʔ is glottal stop; v is bilabial and when syllable-final unvoiced, r is retroflex, untrilled, and slightly spirantal, and when syllable-final unvoiced, small capitals denote voiceless consonants which are separate phonemes, a dot under a vowel denotes the short, and lack of a mark the medium grade of the Hopi three-quantity vowel system, ´ ("high accent") denotes raised pitch and fairly strong stress and on monosyllabic words is not marked but to be understood, ` ("low accent") denotes a lower level of pitch and weak stress and is marked where it occurs on monosyllabic words. The mode suffixes and most of the particles have special pausal forms when they stand at the end of sentences; these are not given except for the suffix -qöʔ, which is used in an example.

only cigars, rain comes from the clouds, certain dinosaurs laid eggs in sand.' The three assertion categories are mutually exclusive.

MODE

Mode, in Hopi, is the generic category of the system by which is denoted the nature of the mingled discreteness and connection between a sentence (clause) and the sentence (clause) which follows or precedes it. The INDEPENDENT mode (zero form) implies that the sentence is detached from others, though it is possible to relate such sentences by paratactic connectives like our 'and.' But the Hopi show a great liking for hypotactic constructions. These employ six mutually exclusive DEPENDENT MODES, denoted by suffixes placed after the assertion suffix. Each mode denotes a basic type of relatedness involving both linkage and discreteness, or disparity. With the further addition of qualifying particles, these modes can distinguish a great number of possible relationships, much as in Greek the basic system of three oblique cases can be further developed by a large number of prepositions. However, the mode relationships are not case relations, nor are the modes defective forms like IE infinitives and gerunds, but full verb paradigms.

The names, suffixes, and types of discreteness-connection are as follows: CONDITIONAL ($-\varepsilon^{\jmath}$ eclipsing final vowel of base), condition needed to justify a nonreportive (expective or nomic) assertion in the other clause (Eng. 'when, if') (the mode clause is logically in this same assertion, though it does not bear any assertion suffix); CORRELATIVE ($-qaY$), explanatory justification of the statement of the other clause (Eng. 'because, since, as, for,' gerund construction); CONCURSIVE ($kaŋ, -kakaŋ$), parallel contemporaneous occurrence (Eng. 'while, as, and'); SEQUENTIAL ($-t$), sequence in time (Eng. 'after, . . . and then . . .'); AGENTIVE ($-qa$), qualification of a person or thing in one clause as the subject in the other, the mode clause (Eng. 'who, which,' though not Eng. 'whom'); TRANSRELATIVE ($-q, -qö^{\jmath}$), general relatedness bridging a difference of subject in the two clauses (no Eng. equivalent). Each mode refers to a certain kind of disparity or contrast, as well as of connection, between the two clauses; and a separateness of subjects or performers in the two clauses is itself one basic type of disparity on a level with the other basic types, and necessitates the transrelative mode in one of the clauses.

Hence all the other modes refer to conditions in which the subject of both clauses is the same: i.e. clause-contrast is based on other factors than disparity of subjects. If it is desired to add to the general notion of the transrelative mode an expression of factors like those which are basic in the other modes, this can be done by detached particles. The subject of the transrelative in many constructions and of the agentive in some is in the objective case. That of all other modes is in the nominative. There follow some illustrations of the uses of the modes. In these examples and henceforth throughout this paper, the mode suffix is hyphenated to assist in identifying the dependent verb.

Conditional: *ni'm-ɛˀ mï·'nat tïwą'ni* 'when he goes home he will see the river' (expective); *ni'm-ɛˀ mï·'nat tïwą'ŋʷi* 'when he goes home he sees the river' (nomic).

Correlative: *ni'ma-qaˋY mï·'nat tï̧'wa* 'because he went home he saw the river'; *ni'ma mï·'nat tïwą'ni-qaˋY* 'he went home in order to see the river': i.e. 'he went home because his seeing the river was expected, looked forward to (by him)'; *pą'ŊqaˋW-qaY yaˋw mï·'nat tï̧'wa* 'he said that he saw the river' (by his saying, to quote, 'he saw the river').

Concursive: *ni'ma-kaˋŋ mï·'nat tï̧'wa* 'as (or while) he went home he saw the river'; *wïni'ma-kaˋŋ ta·'wlaˋwï* 'he danced and sang' (at the same time).

Sequential: *ki·y ˀaw pitï̧'-t mï·'nat tï̧'wa* 'after (or when) he arrived at his home he saw the river'; *wïni'ma'-t pï̧ˀ ta·'wlaˋwï* 'he danced and then he sang.'

Agentive: *ta·'qa ni'maˋ-qa mï·'nat tï̧'wa* 'the man who went home saw the river'; *nïˀ tï̧'wa ta·'qat ni'ma-qaˋ-t* 'I saw the man who went home' (the agentive takes noun cases and here is in objective case, as likewise its subject).[4]

Transrelative: *ni'ma-q ta·'qa ˀaw pitï̧'ni* 'when he goes home a man will meet ('arrive to') him'; *ni'ma-q mǫ'ŋᵘi ˀaw pitï̧'ŋʷi* 'when he goes home the chief meets him' (nomic); *ti'yo wïni'ma-q ˀo·'viy ma·'na ta·'wlaˋwï* 'since the boy danced, therefore the girl sang'; *pą'ŊqaˋW-q yaˋw ma·'na ni'ma* 'he said that the girl went home'; *na·t ta·'wlaW-q ma·'na wïni'ma* 'while he sang the girl danced'; *pą'nis wïni'ma'-q pï̧ˀ ma·'na ta·'wlaˋwï* 'right after he (or, as soon as he had) danced the girl

---

[4] This objective-case agentive clause is the one exception to the rule that disparity of subject requires the transrelative.

sang'; *ʔą́'son nï'ma-q mǫ'ŋʷi ʔaw pitï̦'ni* 'after he goes home the chief will meet him.'

Our relative clause with relative pronoun object is transrelative in Hopi, since there is disparity of subject; e.g. *ta·'qat nï̈ʔ tïwą́'-q ni'ma* 'the man whom I saw went home' ('man,' objective dependent on 'my seeing,' 'he went home'). Hopi treats 'man' as the object of the seeing clause, while the subject of the going-home clause is 'he' expressed in the verb. English makes very little distinction between this construction and the one expressed in Hopi by the agentive, often using the same connective, 'that' or 'which,' for both, so that bewildering changes of construction may result, in translating a number of outwardly similar relative clauses into Hopi. These changes however are perfectly transparent to a Hopi; even a bilingual Hopi, when given the two propositions dressed in the same garb of English form, 'the man that I saw went home' and 'the man that saw me went home,' will instantly react with two completely dissimilar patterns: *ta·'qat nï̈ʔ tïwą́'-q ni'ma*, and *ta·'qa nïy tïwä̈"qa ni'ma*. Hopi also produces transrelative forms that translate our relative pronoun object of a preposition; and here the remoteness from our pattern is extreme: e.g. *yamą́'kpitʔ ąŋ wa·'yma-q lɛ"pɛ* 'the bridge on which he was walking collapsed' ('bridge [objective] on-it being his walking, it collapsed'). Most bewildering of all to the usual Indo-European view is the manner in which Hopi combines modes with modalities according to a systematic logic of its own, of which more presently.

Lest the omission of "imperative" from the modes seem peculiar, I may say that it belongs to a category of INJUNCTIVES (imperative, semi-imperative, optative, vetative), defective paradigms that are neither modes nor modalities.

STATUS

The status categories have been named AFFIRMATIVE (zero form, declarative sentence), NEGATIVE, INTERROGATIVE, INDEFINITIVE. The negative is formed in the reportive and nomic by the particle *qa*` 'not' before the verb, in the expective by *sǫ'ʔon* before the verb. The interrogative is the status of asking a question for a yes-or-no answer. It is formed by the particle *pï*` as the first word in the sentence, e.g. *pï*` *ma·'na ti'yot tï̦'wa* 'did the girl see the boy?' There is no different intonation from any other type of sentence. The reply-forms are *ʔowi·ˆy* 'yes,' *qaʔʔe* or *qaʔɛ·ˆy* 'no,' *pi·'hi·ˆy*, an unanalyzable word meaning 'I don't know.' The indefinitive is the status of the sentence containing an "interrogative" (better, indefinitive) pronoun, adverb, or verb (e.g. the verb 'do what'). It need not be necessarily a true question, because such interrogative words are also indefinites (i.e. the words 'what?' and 'something' are the same); or, better said, the meaning of the word is an indefinite suggestion that implies also a more or less inquisitive attitude 'something—I wonder what?' The Hopi sentence *hi·'mï pɛ'wiʔ* 'something is coming' could be rendered psychologically as an 'I-wonder-what is coming.' Whether this is to be interpreted as a request for information or merely as an interesting remark will depend on the context, which may include the general behavior of the speaker.

MODALITY

Modality in Hopi is in rough terms the sort of thing that is referred to by the subjunctive and some other moods of IE languages. But of course we ought not to rest content with this "sort of" sort of definition. I would say that the modalities of Hopi are moduli of moduli, that is, they are methods of further modifying and amplifying the three-assertion system that distinguishes three basic realms of validity, so that in effect many more than three realms and subrealms of validity are distinguished—again, much as prepositional relationships in Greek amplify a basic system of case relationships. Modalities are to ASSERTIONS what the particles *na·t, ʔą'son*, etc. in our mode examples are to MODES. They are denoted by particles designated MODALIZERS. The word-category of modalizers is more abundant in morphemes than the category of modality strictly considered. While there are many particles of the modalizer type, it seems necessary to distinguish eight (perhaps more) as mutually coordinated to the point of forming a system of eight modalities, to which on schematic grounds we may add as ninth the INDICATIVE modality or zero form. The line between the modalities and the lexical use of other modalizers is not sharp; yet on the whole the modalities are a set of mutually exclusive forms (with certain exceptions), while the other modalizers are used more freely along with each other or with the modality modalizers, occur in less frequent and less formally patterned uses, and are perhaps most conveniently treated as lexical items (see examples at end of this paper). The modalities have been named: INDICATIVE, QUOTATIVE, INHIBITIVE, POTENTIAL, INDETERMINATE, ADVISORY, CONCESSIVE, NECESSITATIVE, IMPOTENTIAL.

QUOTATIVE: modalizer *ya'w*. The assertion becomes the assertion of a linguistic report. In telling a folk-tale *ya'w* is used like the English 'so' or 'and so' at the beginning of almost every long sentence; it there means 'so' in the sense of 'according to the story.' In the simple independent sentence it adds the idea 'they say,' 'on dit que.' It is placed immediately after a direct quotation, the last word in which then receives high stress on the last syllable, this combination being equivalent to spoken quotation marks. It is used in indirect discourse, the verb of saying, hearing, etc., being in correlative or transrelative mode (see examples under these modes). Contrast *nï² navǫ't-q ya'w mï'nï* 'I heard that he fell down' (by verbal report) with *nï² navǫ't-q mï'nï* 'I heard him fall down' (heard the sound of his fall). However the quotative cannot imply the confirmation or concede the truth of the report, which is the function of the concessive modality (*kïr*); hence *nï² navǫ't-q kïr mï'nï* 'I heard (of the fact) that he fell down' (which is conceded to have actually happened).

INHIBITIVE: modalizer *kïrhï'n*. This means that the subject is blocked or prevented from producing the effect specified by the verb, with complete lack of implication about the cause of this condition, as to whether it lie in the ability of the subject or externally, etc. It is translated simply by 'cannot.'

POTENTIAL: This formulation strikes the English speaker at first as topsy-turvy, if not positively weird. It is translated by 'can,' but is simply the negative of the inhibitive, donated by *kïrhï'n qa'*. Yet analysis shows the form to be remarkably logical. By this means the Hopi produce a perfectly neutral, potential 'can' that does not merely refer to personal ability, but denotes that the way is entirely open for the subject to turn potentiality into action if he chooses. (For the 'can' of personal or technical ability, 'knowing how,' there is a definite verb, used with the expective correlative of the action verb.) But how could such a neutral potential 'can' be better expressed than by a negative form which declares simply the absence of all inhibitive or frustrative checks between the subject and action?

INDETERMINATE: modalizer *sęn*. This indicates uncertainty, corresponding to 'perhaps, possibly, maybe,' or in the expective to 'may': e.g. *ni'm-ε? sęn mǫ'ŋ*ʷ*it ?aw piti̧'ni* 'when he goes home he may meet the chief' (and again he may not). The uncertainty is like that of a balancing between about equal positive and negative probabilities; hence, e.g. *nï? ?aw tï'viŋta`-q sęn ni'mą̧'ni* 'I asked him if (whether) he were about to go home' (transrelative construction). Here at first *sęn* seems to play the role of Eng. 'if,' but it is not so. It answers only to the indeterminacy expressed by the 'if,' whereas the linking and relating function of the 'if' is performed by the transrelative mode relation; *sęn* itself is quite unable to effect any linkage.

ADVISORY: modalizer *kε*. It denotes an uncertainty like *sęn*, but stresses slightly the possibility of the positive rather than the negative outcome. If this positive possibility is being asserted in the presence of a somewhat opposing attitude, or a dread of such an outcome, it gives the feeling of our 'might,' 'may nevertheless,' or in the reportive 'might have done so.' Thus, *ta·'qa tïw-ę'? kε wa·'ya'ni* 'when the man sees it he may run away' (his possible running away is the thing to be kept in mind). Hence the sentence containing *kε* has an advisory character, since it does not merely adumbrate an uncertainty, but calls attention to one possible outcome thereof. Logically enough, our 'may not' is *kε qa`*, not *sęn qa`*, e.g. *ni'm-ε? kε qa` tïwą̧'ni* 'when he goes home he may not see it.'

CONCESSIVE: modalizer *kir̲*. It denotes that the assertion is given validity as a concept rather than validity as an objective experience: [5] e.g. 'it is

[5] We may not here read "sensory" for "objective," for experiences which psychology would place at the level of percepts rather than sensations, or even at the level of simple concepts, do not require the concessive, though they are treated differently from sensations. They are the percepts (or simple concepts) of seeing an action or phenomenon of a type having a lexical name (verb), and are put in the indicative transrelative, while it is now the verb of seeing that is in the independent mode, e.g., *nï? ti̧'wa wa·'ya'-qö?* 'I saw him run away,' *nï? ti̧'wa ci̧'rot mi̧'?a-qö`?* 'I saw him shoot the bird.' It is a remarkable fact that the Hopi seem to recognize, in their language, a distinction of four types of received information which correspond roughly to gradings made by psychology: (1) sensory, e.g. 'I see that it is red,' 'I hear him fall,' sensing verb in transrelative, information verb in indicative; (2) perceptual-conceptual, e.g. 'I see him fall,' sensing verb in independent, information verb in transrelative; (3) overt linguistic, e.g. 'I heard that he fell' (unconceded), sensing verb in transrelative, information verb in quotative; (4) pure conceptual, e.g. 'I see that it is new.' 'I heard that he fell' (a conceded truth), sensing verb in transrelative, information verb in concessive.

conceded, granted, inferred from the evidence at hand, assumed, considered as known,' etc. In the independent sentence it may be rendered 'it seems that, evidently, apparently,' or merely 'so': e.g. kịr moʻŋʷi niʼma 'so the chief went home' (I gather). It is in complex sentences that its subtle importance stands out. Consider the transrelative pattern; niʔ tïwạ́ʼ-q paʼla 'I see that it is red' (by my seeing it is red), niʔ tïwạ́ʼ-q rïpiʼpita 'I see that it sparkles.' The Hopi refuse to use this pattern as it stands for, e.g. 'I see that it is new,' which demands the concessive in the clause expressing newness, i.e. niʔ tïwạ́ʼ-q kịr pï·ʼhï (by my seeing it is inferentially new). In other words newness is not a visual sensation like redness or light; it is not seen directly, but is inferred or assumed, kịr, from seen data. To us this seems like psychological analysis, but to the Hopi it is a clear and practical distinction. The ordinary English conditional 'if' construction requires in Hopi that the conditional or transrelative mode which represents the linking function of our 'if' be also concessive to represent the hypothecating function of the 'if'; otherwise the mode would be translated 'when' and not 'if.' Thus, kịr niʼm-εʔ mï·ʼnat tïwạʼni 'if he goes home he will see the river' (assuming that he goes home, etc.). The contrary-to-fact 'if' is another matter (ʔạs, see below).

NECESSITATIVE: modalizer soʼʔon qa. It means 'necessarily, naturally, inevitably,' and seems queer from the IE standpoint in being simply a double negative, which in Hopi always makes a positive. It is a combination of qa 'not' and soʼʔon 'expective not' and thus means that there can be no expectancy of a negative. It often translates English 'must' and 'have to' but is not tinged with any notions of compulsion, duty, or obligation, being entirely neutral and abstract. It is often used in the conclusion of conditional statements to indicate a necessary consequence: e.g. kịr niʼm-εʔ soʼʔon qa mï·ʼnat tïwạʼni 'if he goes home he will see the river' (as a necessary consequence).

IMPOTENTIAL: modalizer ʔạs. This modality is very difficult to express in terms of our ways of thinking. It indicates what I might call teleological ineffectiveness. We go part way along the road with the Hopi by recognizing forms of assertion, like 'may' and 'can,' that are on a different plane from the bare 'does' and 'does not,' and as compared with these more rudimentary assertions have a status that combines the qualities of affirmative and negative, of reality and unreality. They are on a middle ground between these opposites, even though formally cast in an affirmative pattern. But all our middle-ground expressions refer to the realm of latency; the reason for the statement's dual positive-negative character is that its truth is that of a latency, of which the manifestation belongs to the future. The Hopi also have middle-ground expressions of this sort, as we have seen. But they have, further, a middle-ground expression in which the dual positive-negative character is not a matter of latency, but is ascribed to events that have already happened. Moreover an expression referring to something that never happened at all can be assigned to this same realm of quasireality, along with references to actual happenings. The criterion that fastens this particular stigma, as it were, of quasireality upon the subject matter of discourse is ineffectiveness in terms of the purpose, goal, drive, need, function, etc. (a variety of concepts in our own ideology are here applicable) that originally formed the grounds for the action. If a Hopi is reporting a train of events in which a man ran away from his pursuers but was eventually captured by them, he will use the impotential, and say *ta·'qa ʔas wa·'ya* 'the man ran away' (implying that 'ran away' cannot here be held to mean 'escaped'). If the man ran away and escaped, the statement would be simply *ta·'qa wa·'ya*. *Nïʔ ma'qto* is 'I went hunting'; *nïʔ ʔas ma'qto* is the same, except that it implies that I came back empty-handed or practically so. We could convey such information by saying 'well, I went hunting!' in a disgusted tone, but the Hopi sentence is not really comparable to this. It is a quite unemotional statement; *ʔas* is not an expression of affect but is intellectual, and would be used whether the speaker be unmoved, displeased, or pleased; e.g. *cö·'viw ʔas wa·'ya* 'the deer fled' (but I caught him just the same). My name for this modality, "impotential," refers to the connotation of impotence that it gives to the statement of actions and attempts. In the expective, it changes the translation from 'will' to 'tries to': e.g. *ma·'na ʔas wïni'ma̧'ni* 'the girl tries to dance' (but does not for the present succeed). However, expective impotential does not imply that later attempts will not succeed. When the expective refers to the past of narration, its impotential refers to a frustrated attempt at some event that did not actually happen: e.g. *ʔas wa·'ya'ni* 'he tried to escape,' of a prisoner who failed to escape. When the impotential is expective in a dependent mode (i.e. when it is conditional or transrelative and the other clause is expective), the reality is further attenuated to a never-realized theoretical past possibility. Thus our contrary-to-fact condition is impotential in Hopi: e.g. *ʔɑs ni'm-ɛʔ sọ'ʔon qɑ` mï·'nat tïwɑ'ni* 'if he had gone home he would have seen the river' ('when in not-to-be-realized capacity of going home he was in necessitous expectancy of seeing the river'). Here the concessive may be added to the impotential, especially if the mode is transrelative: e.g. *kïr ʔɑs ni'ma-q sọ'ʔon qɑ` mọ'ŋʷi ʔaw pitï'ni* 'if he had gone home the chief would have met him.' Our 'although, but, yet,' etc. indicate a tension of some sort between two conflicting tendencies. The Hopi unerringly discriminate whether one of these tendencies has actually aborted the other (the impotential meaning) or whether the opposition is of the sort to be indicated by *kɛ, sɛn*, or some other means. Thus, in concursive, *nï ʔɑs qatï'-kaŋ ma·'ŋï'ʔi* 'although I was sitting I felt tired'; in transrelative, *ʔɑs wa·'ya'-q nï ŋï'ʔa* 'although he fled I caught him.' On the other hand, *ʔɑs* would be wrong in 'although he was running he was singing,' since neither action has aborted the purpose of the other; here a Hopi would say simply *wa'rikï`w-kaŋ ta·'wla`wï* 'while he was running he was singing,' or perhaps add to this an element denoting mild surprise. In the sequential form *ʔɑs pitï'-t qɑ` wïni'ma* 'although he had arrived he did not dance,' *ʔɑs* implies that the function of coming was to dance; he might as well not have come.[6]

The disparity of pattern from Indo-European appears in that, while all these modalities resemble the IE subjunctive, not one aligns with it. The Hopi interpret our subjunctive in various ways according to a recognition of relationships of which we are not linguistically conscious. Thus, in 'if I were king,' 'were' from the Hopi viewpoint is impotential; in 'to see if he were brave,' 'were' is indeterminate; in 'though he be stubborn,' 'be' is advisory; in 'if he be right,' 'be' is concessive. Or is the pattern so very different from Indo-European after all? It remains a fact that the Uto-Aztecan languages in general, and Hopi especially, are for American languages unusually reminiscent of IE in their type of grammar. Could it be possible that in ancient forms of IE, perhaps in Hittite, patterns of syntactic construction may exist that would lend themselves to an analysis following somewhat the Hopi outline?

[6] The realm of the might-as-well-not-have-been is, in a nutshell, that middle ground between positive and negative which the impotential represents. What we call the might-have-been is to the Hopi simply a part of this realm. It is the expectancy (potency, tendency, possibility, wish) that might as well not have been.

OTHER MODALIZERS

There are a number of modalizers having uses less definitely formal than those of the modality system. Their wide range of expression is shown by the following samples:

ʔi'ra: memory, recollection—'according to recollection it is so.'

ʔi'snïntiˋq: probability, reasonable expectation, justifiable assumption or hope—'supposedly'—and in the expective is like our 'if all goes well.'

na'wïs: obligation to voluntary action without compulsion; differs from our 'ought to, should' by greater promise that the action will be performed; may sometimes be rendered 'has to,' but, according to my informant, corresponds to our expression 'can't very well refuse to.'

pɛ·v: 'almost, nearly,' *pɛ·v kɛ* 'possibly almost,' 'almost may.'

piˋ: acceptance of conditions as they are or must be, undeniable fact, inevitability; sometimes corresponds to English word stress, e.g. *pạm pitiˊni* 'he will arrive,' *piˋ pạm pitiˊni* '*he* will arrive,' 'he, at least, will arrive.' It also corresponds to 'after all,' and still more to our shrug of the shoulders, while *pay piˋ* 'already,' *piˋ* indicates philosophic resignation to unchangeable reality—*pay piˋ wa·'ya* 'he ran away, and that's that.' Also common are the combinations with negative (*piˋ qaˋ*) and necessitative (*sọ'ʔon piˋ qaˋ*).

ta'tam: necessity to which one resigns oneself with a self-sacrificing feeling; 'must,' or 'may as well' imbued with this feeling; implies that the subject is sacrificing his own interests or preferences.

tịr: intention without clear resolve, vaguer than 'wants to' or 'intends to'; more like 'is (was) thinking of ——ing,' 'would,' 'would like to.'

The extent to which "modal feeling" is diversified and the finesse of its application differ markedly in different languages, but probably few languages have gone so far into these fields as Hopi.

LANGUAGE: PLAN AND
CONCEPTION OF ARRANGEMENT

Editor's note: In 1938, Whorf circulated this table and accompanying outline in manuscript form among selected colleagues. It was written as a supplement to the *Outline of cultural materials* prepared by George P. Murdock and his colleagues at the Department of Anthropology at Yale University as a guide to ethnological field workers, and is referred to in the brief "Language" section of that outline.

In several places in his writings Whorf mentions the desirability of a "world-survey" of languages; this outline was doubtless intended by him as a suggested standard framework for collecting the information on particular languages which would be needed for such a survey.

The reader's attention should be directed first to the table on page 126, which displays the whole scheme of language as conceived by Whorf. The subsequent outline, which presents an expansion of the semasiology section of the table, is thus only an appendage to the table, even though it contains most of the meat. The material is printed with only minor alterations and corrections of the original manuscript, which was furnished by Professor Norman McQuown of the University of Chicago.

[EXPANSION OF *Semasiology* SECTION OF THE TABLE]

A. *The sentence*

1. Sentence-end marking: **by**
   intonation (one pattern, several **patterns**)
   pause **forms**

LANGUAGE

PLAN AND CONCEPTION OF ARRANGEMENT

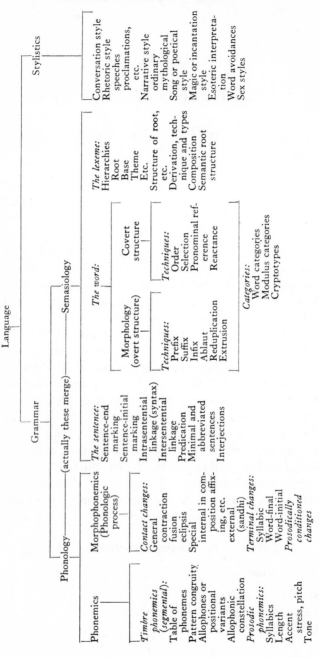

special marking elements
word order
affective marking.   Intonations or other elements marking sentence end
and also denoting, e.g., emphasis, interest, surprise, doubt, interroga-
tion, force of conviction, affective diminution, or augmentation, etc.

2. Sentence-initial marking: by
word order, e.g., verb always first, etc.
sentence introducers
intonation
others
absent

3. Intrasentential linkage (syntax) (integrating principle within the sentence)
word order.   Expansion of word order, subject-predicate order, adjacent
order (modifier before, modifier after, mixed), interrupted order
(tmesis), e.g., English split infinitive.
functional categories (e.g., nouns, verbs, predicators, etc.) variously
marked.   See categories under B, The word.
marking of relationships, e.g., by cases, pre- or postpositions, action direc-
tors (i.e., different markings of action-goal or cause-effect, transitives,
applicatives) et al.
subsumption (reference within verb or other keyword to the syntax)
pronominal incorporation or reference, noun incorporation
directive and instrumental elements, and body-part elements, etc.
verb a nuclear sentence (e.g. Navaho)
holophrastic sentence (form of polysynthesis in which verb takes in
most of the sentence)
sentence harmony, i.e., agreement of formal classes, e.g., agreement in
gender, number, etc.   (Bantu is an extreme instance)

4. Intersentential linkage (external syntax) (addition of sentence to sentence)
Paratactic (coordinating)
juxtaposition of sentences
coordinating elements
prosodic (intonations, etc.)
sublexical (suffixes, etc.)
particles (enclitics or words, e.g., 'and')
Hypotactic (subordinating) (use of dependent clauses) by
order
prosodic means (intonation, etc., e.g., the English comma intonation)
sublexical marking, including special verb forms, gerundials
subordinating particles, conjunctions

5. Predication
Techniques
word order or sentence pattern (the isolating type)
sublexical predicators (i.e., suffixes, etc., which make a "verb" out of

anything to which they are added. Here the suffix, not the whole "verb" is the predicator)

predicating word-classes (verbs and various types of quasiverbs; the predicative force is fused with a lexical meaning, e.g., 'eat, kill, stand') (See categories under *B*, The word)

verbal sentence only

verbal and nominal sentences—nominal sentences designated by order pattern, sublexically, etc.

operators (words specialized for predication, otherwise lexical meaning blank ['be, become, cause, do'] or vague ['make, turn, get,' etc.]).

auxiliary verbs.

mixtures of techniques

Categories of predication

copulative (be)

general

inherent (Spanish *ser*), or subjective

objective (Spanish *estar*)

general verbal, including all the following:

causal

active–causal

intransitive—mediopassive

transitive

inactive–causal

intransitive

transitive

incausal

static

resultative

passive

others (the above may be stated differently according to the pattern of language, e.g., instrumental verb, etc.)

6. Minimal and abbreviated sentences

abbreviated sentences

retrospective forms, e.g., 'I did.' 'Will you?'

elliptic forms, e.g., 'But tomorrow—!'

social formulas ('thank you, hello, please,' etc.)

minimal sentences

vocative type ('John! Mother!')

imperative type ('Come!')

others

'yes' and 'no'

interjections

ordinary ('oh, ouch, alas,' etc.)

"swear words"
other types with special cultural force

B. *The word (the word as part of the sentence)*

1. Morphology (overt structure)
   Techniques (of overt marking) (if possible, state degree, e.g., slight, moderate, abundant, profuse)
   prefixing
   suffixing
   infixing
   vocalic ablaut
    change of 1 vowel of stem, of 2 or more
    ablaut elision, length-change, quavering
   consonantal ablaut
   accent and (or) tone changes
   reduplication (total, partial, initial-syllabic, final-syllabic, vocalic, reduplication with interpolation)
   extrusion (commonly called reduplication)
    vocalic, initial (*tak—atak*), final (*lem—leme*)
    consonantal, initial (*lem—leml*), final (*lem—mlem*)
    mixed (e.g., *lem—lemel*)
   vowel-harmony accompanying other techniques
   Categories, morphological. See 3. Categories
2. Covert structure and relationship
   Techniques
   selection * (e.g., difference between 'John, come, dog, kill')
   suppletion (e.g., 'go, went')
   order (in phrase or sentence)
   pronominal reference (e.g., used in English to mark gender-class)
   reference by key-word not a pronoun
   reactance (word with the covert relation governs choice of certain other words, e.g., round- vs. long-object terms in Navaho, governs choice of verb stem)
   Categories, covert. See 3. Categories
3. Categories
   May be either overt or covert. If possible, say which and how marked, or mixed, e.g., verbs, suffixing; nouns, pure selection; nouns, absence of other marking.†

---

* Selection, i.e., pure selection. Selection also accompanies all other marking of word-categories. Pure selection requires existence of covert word-categories (q.v.).

† Where possible, state avoidance of commonly found categories, e.g., no plural, no gender.

I. Word categories
    a. Functional–lexical
        noun
        verb
        adjective
        adverb
        none (it must be remembered that any or all of these types may not exist; e.g., it may be impossible to have a "verb" without a suffix of verbation which can be applied to ANY stem. There is then no class of verbs, but only the "modulus category" (q.v.) of verbation.)
    b. Functional
        pronouns (personal, state kinds of—demonstrative, directive—state ideas connoted—interrogative, negative, indefinite, relative, etc.)
        particles (words used in marking or linking the SENTENCE, q.v., end-markers, initial-markers (inceptors), pro- and postpositions, conjunctions, modal particles, predicators, operators, etc.)
        articles. See II,*c.* definite–indefinite
    c. Reference categories (which imply a classification of experience, different kinds of things, state, or action)
        genders (many different kinds, masculine, feminine, animate, inanimate, personal, rational, irrational, integral, etc.)
        multireference categories (many gender-like classes, often with indistinguishable meaning, e.g., Bantu)
        social status and rank classes
        shape classes (e.g., Navaho, Haida)
        presence–absence
        visibility
        locus and extension classes
    d. Purely formal classes, e.g., conjugations and declensions
    e. Personal name classes, gender, age, respect, etc.
II. Modulus categories. (These do not delimit word-classes in themselves; they MODIFY, either ANY class, or classes already delimited by other means)
    a. Generally applicable
        predication
        verbation (predication other than 'be')
        "nomination" or noun-designation
            absolutive suffixes, nominative articles, zero-marking, etc.
        adjectivization
    b. Mixed application—sometimes generally applied, sometimes specially applied
        number (kinds 1, 2, 3, several, many, plural)

    collectivity and distribution

    duration

    tension (extension–duration)

    time or tense

    comparison, e.g., of adjectives

    see also reference categories; the same ideas may be applied as moduli

c. Special application

    Applied usually to verbs (or along with verbation)

        categories of predication, q.v. A. *The sentence*

            voice: active, passive, etc.

            resolution: transitive, intransitive, passive (voice and resolution merge)

        aspect (duration, extension, etc., e.g., punctual, durative, perfective, imperfective, inceptive, continuative, progressive, frequentative, iterative, usitative, etc.)

        intensives

        tense systems

        mode (mood), e.g., indicative, subjunctive, inferential, dubitative, optative, potential, permissive, concessive, adversative, et al.

        status, e.g., interrogative, negative, quotative, emphatic

        exclamative and other affective forms

        address-forms, e.g., imperative, vetative (negative imperative), hortative, etc.

        gerundials or subordinators (cross-refer to A4)

    Applied usually to nouns (or along with nomination)

        state (i.e., possessed, unpossessed, pronominally possessed forms)

        case (various cases)

        adjectivization (also given under general)

        definite-indefinite (articles, etc.)

        partitives (some or any)

        generality, e.g., 'man, woman, canis,' as opposed to 'a man, a woman, a dog'

        continual, e.g., 'wood, metal,' as opposed to 'stick, piece of metal'

        individuative, e.g., 'stick'

        others—See Reference categories, into which these merge

d. Affective modulus categories (express speaker's feelings rather than an idea)

    affective diminution (diminutives)

    affective augmentation

    respect forms

emphasis, exclamative, and other forms—what classes of words is the affective modulus applied to?

III. Cryptotypes. Covert word categories with subtle meaning marked only by reactances. Skip this in the survey except for obvious cases, as determination of cryptotypes usually requires deep study of a language.

C. *The lexeme (the word or stem as an item of the vocabulary, and as a part analyzed or abstracted from sentence words)*

1. Lexical hierarchies
   a. The language possesses distinctions between roots and derivative formations (stems, bases, themes). In this case the minimal irreducible base is called ROOT.
   b. The language may have only one sort, or one main sort, of lexical element. In this case such an element is usually called STEM— e.g., stems in Algonkin, Yana. Characterize language in this way if possible.
   c. Lexeme may be identical with word (word in sentence).
   Lexeme always different from word. Lexeme occurs in sentence—
      1. with morphological elements
      2. in polysynthetic composition
2. Root and stem types
   polymorphous (no particular form for root or stem—however, this is rare; apt to be appearance based on insufficient analysis, e.g., as regards roots, English is not polymorphous)
   monomorphous. One characteristic root type, or 1 or 2 related types, e.g., CV, CVC, etc.
   restricted. Type with considerable freedom of form with certain restrictions, e.g., limitation on the kind and position of consonant clusters within root or within stem, e.g., English. Indicate the restrictions on clusters, etc. if possible.
3. Derivation (formation of secondary lexemes, i.e., word bases, from roots)
   Techniques. Overt. These are similar to morphological techniques; e.g., prefixing, suffixing, etc.
   Covert techniques—transfer to a different covert class and change of meaning with covert marking, e.g., '(to) stand, (a) stand (position), (a) stand (pedestal)'
   Degree of derivation—none, slight, moderate, great, cumulative (piling of derivative upon derivative, e.g., the mock-learned 'honorificabilitudinity'; this is found in Aztec, less so in Sanskrit and Greek, possibly in Magyar and Turkish)
   Derivational types ‡

‡ These may merge into or become identical with morphological categories, and in some languages this section is to be transferred from the LEXEME to the WORD: morphology.

Noun types from verb-like bases
    action and state nouns, abstract nouns
    agentives—nouns of the doer
    instrumentives—nouns of instrument
    place nouns
    nomen patientis $\begin{cases} \text{noun of one affected} \\ \text{noun of state produced} \end{cases}$
    adjectival nouns
    others—there are many possibilities
Verb types from nounlike bases
    verbs of activation, of possession, etc.

4. Composition

Compounding (essentially binary complexes; the 2 main parts may also be separate)
    modifier types. Does modifier come before or after?
        types: noun–noun, verb–noun, noun–verb, etc.
    coordinate types, e.g., 'space-time' in 'space-time relationships'
Polysynthetic composition
    composition of many stems with rules of order, e.g., Algonkin
        a further possibility is: no distinction between stems (lexemes) and markers of modulus categories. In this case cross-refer to modulus categories.
Mixed types, e.g., "interrupted synthesis"
    in Athabascan—may be skipped as often difficult to analyze
Nonisolatable lexemes—few, many, or all lexemes thus

5. Semantic root-structure

root analyzable into more or less vague parts and meanings, e.g., '*tr*ead, *tr*ack, *tr*ip.' Root-nucleus (e.g., *tr*) and root-determinative
phonemic symbolism (correspondence between sound and sense)
    recurrence of the same phoneme or phoneme-group with a type of meaning
    overt manipulation of phonemes for semantic and affective results (e.g., childish forms in some NW coast languages)
    roots susceptible of considerable intra-radical analysis.

THE RELATION OF HABITUAL

THOUGHT AND BEHAVIOR

TO LANGUAGE *

Human beings do not live in the objective world alone, nor alone in the world of social activity as ordinarily understood, but are very much at the mercy of the particular language which has become the medium of expression for their society. It is quite an illusion to imagine that one adjusts to reality essentially without the use of language and that language is merely an incidental means of solving specific problems of communication or reflection. The fact of the matter is that the "real world" is to a large extent unconsciously built up on the language habits of the group. . . . We see and hear and otherwise experience very largely as we do because the language habits of our community predispose certain choices of interpretation.

—Edward Sapir

There will probably be general assent to the proposition that an accepted pattern of using words is often prior to certain lines of thinking and forms of behavior, but he who assents often sees in such a statement nothing more than a platitudinous recognition of the hypnotic power of philosophical and learned terminology on the one hand or of catchwords, slogans, and rallying cries on the other. To see only thus far is to miss the point of one of the important interconnections which Sapir saw between language, culture, and psychology, and succinctly expressed in the introductory quotation. It is not so much in these

* Reprinted from pp. 75–93, *Language, culture, and personality, essays in memory of Edward Sapir*, edited by Leslie Spier (Menasha, Wis.: Sapir Memorial Publication Fund, 1941). The article was written in the summer of 1939.

special uses of language as in its constant ways of arranging data and its most ordinary everyday analysis of phenomena that we need to recognize the influence it has on other activities, cultural and personal.

THE NAME OF THE SITUATION AS AFFECTING BEHAVIOR

I came in touch with an aspect of this problem before I had studied under Dr. Sapir, and in a field usually considered remote from linguistics. It was in the course of my professional work for a fire insurance company, in which I undertook the task of analyzing many hundreds of reports of circumstances surrounding the start of fires, and in some cases, of explosions. My analysis was directed toward purely physical conditions, such as defective wiring, presence or lack of air spaces between metal flues and woodwork, etc., and the results were presented in these terms. Indeed it was undertaken with no thought that any other significances would or could be revealed. But in due course it became evident that not only a physical situation *qua* physics, but the meaning of that situation to people, was sometimes a factor, through the behavior of the people, in the start of the fire. And this factor of meaning was clearest when it was a LINGUISTIC MEANING, residing in the name or the linguistic description commonly applied to the situation. Thus, around a storage of what are called "gasoline drums," behavior will tend to a certain type, that is, great care will be exercised; while around a storage of what are called "empty gasoline drums," it will tend to be different—careless, with little repression of smoking or of tossing cigarette stubs about. Yet the "empty" drums are perhaps the more dangerous, since they contain explosive vapor. Physically the situation is hazardous, but the linguistic analysis according to regular analogy must employ the word 'empty,' which inevitably suggests lack of hazard. The word 'empty' is used in two linguistic patterns: (1) as a virtual synonym for 'null and void, negative, inert,' (2) applied in analysis of physical situations without regard to, e.g., vapor, liquid vestiges, or stray rubbish, in the container. The situation is named in one pattern (2) and the name is then "acted out" or "lived up to" in another (1), this being a general formula for the linguistic conditioning of behavior into hazardous forms.

In a wood distillation plant the metal stills were insulated with a composition prepared from limestone and called at the plant "spun limestone." No attempt was made to protect this covering from excessive heat or the contact of flame. After a period of use, the fire below one of the stills spread to the "limestone," which to everyone's great surprise burned vigorously. Exposure to acetic acid fumes from the stills had converted part of the limestone (calcium carbonate) to calcium acetate. This when heated in a fire decomposes, forming inflammable acetone. Behavior that tolerated fire close to the covering was induced by use of the name "limestone," which because it ends in "-stone" implies non-combustibility.

A huge iron kettle of boiling varnish was observed to be overheated, nearing the temperature at which it would ignite. The operator moved it off the fire and ran it on its wheels to a distance, but did not cover it. In a minute or so the varnish ignited. Here the linguistic influence is more complex; it is due to the metaphorical objectifying (of which more later) of "cause" as contact or the spatial juxtaposition of "things"—to analyzing the situation as 'on' versus 'off' the fire. In reality, the stage when the external fire was the main factor had passed; the overheating was now an internal process of convection in the varnish from the intensely heated kettle, and still continued when 'off' the fire.

An electric glow heater on the wall was little used, and for one workman had the meaning of a convenient coathanger. At night a watchman entered and snapped a switch, which action he verbalized as 'turning on the light.' No light appeared, and this result he verbalized as 'light is burned out.' He could not see the glow of the heater because of the old coat hung on it. Soon the heater ignited the coat, which set fire to the building.

A tannery discharged waste water containing animal matter into an outdoor settling basin partly roofed with wood and partly open. This situation is one that ordinarily would be verbalized as 'pool of water.' A workman had occasion to light a blowtorch near by, and threw his match into the water. But the decomposing waste matter was evolving gas under the wood cover, so that the setup was the reverse of 'watery.' An instant flare of flame ignited the woodwork, and the fire quickly spread into the adjoining building.

A drying room for hides was arranged with a blower at one end to make a current of air along the room and thence outdoors through a vent at the other end. Fire started at a hot bearing on the blower, which blew the flames directly into the hides and fanned them along the room, destroying the entire stock. This hazardous setup followed naturally from the term 'blower' with its linguistic equivalence to 'that which blows,' implying that its function necessarily is to 'blow.' Also its function is verbalized as 'blowing air for drying,' overlooking that it can blow other things, e.g., flames and sparks. In reality, a blower simply makes a current of air and can exhaust as well as blow. It should have been installed at the vent end to DRAW the air over the hides, then through the hazard (its own casing and bearings), and thence outdoors.

Beside a coal-fired melting pot for lead reclaiming was dumped a pile of "scrap lead"—a misleading verbalization, for it consisted of the lead sheets of old radio condensers, which still had paraffin paper between them. Soon the paraffin blazed up and fired the roof, half of which was burned off.

Such examples, which could be greatly multiplied, will suffice to show how the cue to a certain line of behavior is often given by the analogies of the linguistic formula in which the situation is spoken of, and by which to some degree it is analyzed, classified, and allotted its place in that world which is "to a large extent unconsciously built up on the language habits of the group." And we always assume that the linguistic analysis made by our group reflects reality better than it does.

GRAMMATICAL PATTERNS AS INTERPRETATIONS OF EXPERIENCE

The linguistic material in the above examples is limited to single words, phrases, and patterns of limited range. One cannot study the behavioral compulsiveness of such material without suspecting a much more far-reaching compulsion from large-scale patterning of grammatical categories, such as plurality, gender and similar classifications (animate, inanimate, etc.), tenses, voices, and other verb forms, classifications of the type of "parts of speech," and the matter of whether a given experience is denoted by a unit morpheme, an inflected word, or a syntactical combination. A category such as number (singular vs. plural) is an attempted interpretation of a whole large order of experience, virtually of the world or of nature; it attempts to say how experience is to be segmented, what experience is to be called "one" and what "several." But the difficulty of appraising such a far-reaching influence is great because of its background character, because of the difficulty of standing aside from our own language, which is a habit and a cultural *non est disputandum*, and scrutinizing it objectively. And if we take a very dissimilar language, this language becomes a part of nature, and we even do to it what we have already done to nature. We tend to think in our own language in order to examine the exotic language. Or we find the task of unraveling the purely morphological intricacies so gigantic that it seems to absorb all else. Yet the problem, though difficult, is feasible; and the best approach is through an exotic language, for in its study we are at long last pushed willy-nilly out of our ruts. Then we find that the exotic language is a mirror held up to our own.

In my study of the Hopi language, what I now see as an opportunity to work on this problem was first thrust upon me before I was clearly aware of the problem. The seemingly endless task of describing the morphology did finally end. Yet it was evident, especially in the light of Sapir's lectures on Navaho, that the description of the LANGUAGE was far from complete. I knew for example the morphological formation of plurals, but not how to use plurals. It was evident that the category of plural in Hopi was not the same thing as in English, French, or German. Certain things that were plural in these languages were singular in Hopi. The phase of investigation which now began consumed nearly two more years.

The work began to assume the character of a comparison between Hopi and western European languages. It also became evident that even the grammar of Hopi bore a relation to Hopi culture, and the grammar of European tongues to our own "Western" or "European" culture. And it appeared that the interrelation brought in those large subsummations of experience by language, such as our own terms 'time,' 'space,' 'substance,' and 'matter.' Since, with respect to the traits compared, there is little difference between English, French, German, or other European languages with the POSSIBLE (but doubtful) exception of Balto-Slavic and non-Indo-European, I have lumped these languages into one group called SAE, or "Standard Average European."

That portion of the whole investigation here to be reported may be summed up in two questions: (1) Are our own concepts of 'time,' 'space,' and 'matter' given in substantially the same form by experience to all men, or are they in part conditioned by the structure of particular languages? (2) Are there traceable affinities between (*a*) cultural and behavioral norms and (*b*) large-scale linguistic patterns? (I should be the

last to pretend that there is anything so definite as "a correlation" between culture and language, and especially between ethnological rubrics
such as 'agricultural, hunting,' etc., and linguistic ones like 'inflected,'
'synthetic,' or 'isolating.' [1] When I began the study, the problem was
by no means so clearly formulated, and I had little notion that the
answers would turn out as they did.

PLURALITY AND NUMERATION IN SAE AND HOPI

In our language, that is SAE, plurality and cardinal numbers are
applied in two ways: to real plurals and imaginary plurals. Or more
exactly if less tersely: perceptible spatial aggregates and metaphorical
aggregates. We say 'ten men' and also 'ten days.' Ten men either are
or could be objectively perceived as ten, ten in one group perception [2]—
ten men on a street corner, for instance. But 'ten days' cannot be
objectively experienced. We experience only one day, today; the other
nine (or even all ten) are something conjured up from memory or
imagination. If 'ten days' be regarded as a group it must be as an
"imaginary," mentally constructed group. Whence comes this mental
pattern? Just as in the case of the fire-causing errors, from the fact that
our language confuses the two different situations, has but one pattern
for both. When we speak of 'ten steps forward, ten strokes on a bell,'
or any similarly described cyclic sequence, "times" of any sort, we are
doing the same thing as with 'days.' CYCLICITY brings the response of
imaginary plurals. But a likeness of cyclicity to aggregates is not un-
mistakably given by experience prior to language, or it would be found
in all languages, and it is not.

Our AWARENESS of time and cyclicity does contain something immediate and subjective—the basic sense of "becoming later and later." But,
in the habitual thought of us SAE people, this is covered under something quite different, which though mental should not be called subjective. I call it OBJECTIFIED, or imaginary, because it is patterned on

[1] We have plenty of evidence that this is not the case. Consider only the Hopi
and the Ute, with languages that on the overt morphological and lexical level are as
similar as, say, English and German. The idea of "correlation" between language
and culture, in the generally accepted sense of correlation, is certainly a mistaken one.

[2] As we say, 'ten at the SAME TIME,' showing that in our language and thought we
restate the fact of group perception in terms of a concept 'time,' the large linguistic
component of which will appear in the course of this paper.

the OUTER world. It is this that reflects our linguistic usage. Our tongue makes no distinction between numbers counted on discrete entities and numbers that are simply "counting itself." Habitual thought then assumes that in the latter the numbers are just as much counted on "something" as in the former. This is objectification. Concepts of time lose contact with the subjective experience of "becoming later" and are objectified as counted QUANTITIES, especially as lengths, made up of units as a length can be visibly marked off into inches. A 'length of time' is envisioned as a row of similar units, like a row of bottles.

In Hopi there is a different linguistic situation. Plurals and cardinals are used only for entities that form or can form an objective group. There are no imaginary plurals, but instead ordinals used with singulars. Such an expression as 'ten days' is not used. The equivalent statement is an operational one that reaches one day by a suitable count. 'They stayed ten days' becomes 'they stayed until the eleventh day' or 'they left after the tenth day.' 'Ten days is greater than nine days' becomes 'the tenth day is later than the ninth.' Our "length of time" is not regarded as a length but as a relation between two events in lateness. Instead of our linguistically promoted objectification of that datum of consciousness we call 'time,' the Hopi language has not laid down any pattern that would cloak the subjective "becoming later" that is the essence of time.

NOUNS OF PHYSICAL QUANTITY IN SAE AND HOPI

We have two kinds of nouns denoting physical things: individual nouns, and mass nouns, e.g., 'water, milk, wood, granite, sand, flour, meat.' Individual nouns denote bodies with definite outlines: 'a tree, a stick, a man, a hill.' Mass nouns denote homogeneous continua without implied boundaries. The distinction is marked by linguistic form; e.g., mass nouns lack plurals,[3] in English drop articles, and in French take the partitive article *du, de la, des.* The distinction is more wide-

[3] It is no exception to this rule of lacking a plural that a mass noun may sometimes coincide in lexeme with an individual noun that of course has a plural; e.g., 'stone' (no pl.) with 'a stone' (pl. 'stones'). The plural form denoting varieties, e.g., 'wines' is of course a different sort of thing from the true plural; it is a curious outgrowth from the SAE mass nouns, leading to still another sort of imaginary aggregates, which will have to be omitted from this paper.

spread in language than in the observable appearance of things. Rather few natural occurrences present themselves as unbounded extents; 'air' of course, and often 'water, rain, snow, sand, rock, dirt, grass.' We do not encounter 'butter, meat, cloth, iron, glass,' or most "materials" in such kind of manifestation, but in bodies small or large with definite outlines. The distinction is somewhat forced upon our description of events by an unavoidable pattern in language. It is so inconvenient in a great many cases that we need some way of individualizing the mass noun by further linguistic devices. This is partly done by names of body-types: 'stick of wood, piece of cloth, pane of glass, cake of soap'; also, and even more, by introducing names of containers though their contents be the real issue: 'glass of water, cup of coffee, dish of food, bag of flour, bottle of beer.' These very common container formulas, in which 'of' has an obvious, visually perceptible meaning ("contents"), influence our feeling about the less obvious type-body formulas: 'stick of wood, lump of dough,' etc. The formulas are very similar: individual noun plus a similar relator (English 'of'). In the obvious case this relator denotes contents. In the inobvious one it "suggests" contents. Hence the 'lumps, chunks, blocks, pieces,' etc., seem to contain something, a "stuff," "substance," or "matter" that answers to the 'water,' 'coffee,' or 'flour' in the container formulas. So with SAE people the philosophic "substance" and "matter" are also the naïve idea; they are instantly acceptable, "common sense." It is so through linguistic habit. Our language patterns often require us to name a physical thing by a binomial that splits the reference into a formless item plus a form.

Hopi is again different. It has a formally distinguished class of nouns. But this class contains no formal subclass of mass nouns. All nouns have an individual sense and both singular and plural forms. Nouns translating most nearly our mass nouns still refer to vague bodies or vaguely bounded extents. They imply indefiniteness, but not lack, of outline and size. In specific statements, 'water' means one certain mass or quantity of water, not what we call "the substance water." Generality of statement is conveyed through the verb or predicator, not the noun. Since nouns are individual already, they are not individualized by either type-bodies or names of containers, if there is no special need to emphasize shape or container. The noun itself implies a suitable type-body or container. One says, not 'a glass of water' but *ka·yi* 'a water,' not 'a pool of water' but *pa·hǝ*,[4] not 'a dish of cornflour' but *ŋǝmni* 'a (quantity of) cornflour,' not 'a piece of meat' but *sikʷi* 'a meat.' The language has neither need for nor analogies on which to build the concept of existence as a duality of formless item and form. It deals with formlessness through other symbols than nouns.

PHASES OF CYCLES IN SAE AND HOPI

Such terms as 'summer, winter, September, morning, noon, sunset' are with us nouns, and have little formal linguistic difference from other nouns. They can be subjects or objects, and we say 'at sunset' or 'in winter' just as we say 'at a corner' or 'in an orchard.' [5] They are pluralized and numerated like nouns of physical objects, as we have seen. Our thought about the referents of such words hence becomes objectified. Without objectification, it would be a subjective experience of real time, i.e. of the consciousness of "becoming later and later"—simply a cyclic phase similar to an earlier phase in that ever-later-becoming duration. Only by imagination can such a cyclic phase be set beside another and another in the manner of a spatial (i.e. visually perceived) configuration. But such is the power of linguistic analogy that we do so objectify cyclic phasing. We do it even by saying 'a phase' and 'phases' instead of, e.g., 'phasing.' And the pattern of individual and mass nouns, with the resulting binomial formula of formless item plus form, is so general that it is implicit for all nouns, and hence our very generalized formless items like 'substance, matter,' by which we can fill out the binomial for an enormously wide range of nouns. But even these are not quite generalized enough to take in our phase nouns. So for the phase nouns we have made a formless item, 'time.' We have made it by using 'a time,' i.e. an occasion or a phase, in the pattern of a mass noun, just as from 'a summer' we make 'summer' in the pattern of a mass noun. Thus with our binomial formula we can say and think 'a moment of time, a second

---

[4] Hopi has two words for water quantities; *kǝ·yi* and *pa·hǝ*. The difference is something like that between 'stone' and 'rock' in English, *pa·hǝ* implying greater size and "wildness"; flowing water, whether or not outdoors or in nature, is *pa·hǝ*; so is 'moisture.' But, unlike 'stone' and 'rock,' the difference is essential, not pertaining to a connotative margin, and the two can hardly ever be interchanged.

[5] To be sure, there are a few minor differences from other nouns, in English for instance in the use of the articles.

of time, a year of time.' Let me again point out that the pattern is simply that of 'a bottle of milk' or 'a piece of cheese.' Thus we are assisted to imagine that 'a summer' actually contains or consists of such-and-such a quantity of 'time.'

In Hopi however all phase terms, like 'summer, morning,' etc., are not nouns but a kind of adverb, to use the nearest SAE analogy. They are a formal part of speech by themselves, distinct from nouns, verbs, and even other Hopi "adverbs." Such a word is not a case form or a locative pattern, like 'des Abends' or 'in the morning.' It contains no morpheme like one of 'in the house' or 'at the tree.' [6] It means 'when it is morning' or 'while morning-phase is occurring.' These "temporals" are not used as subjects or objects, or at all like nouns. One does not say 'it's a hot summer' or 'summer is hot'; summer is not hot, summer is only WHEN conditions are hot, WHEN heat occurs. One does not say 'THIS summer,' but 'summer now' or 'summer recently.' There is no objectification, as a region, an extent, a quantity, of the subjective duration-feeling. Nothing is suggested about time except the perpetual "getting later" of it. And so there is no basis here for a formless item answering to our 'time.'

TEMPORAL FORMS OF VERBS IN SAE AND HOPI

The three-tense system of SAE verbs colors all our thinking about time. This system is amalgamated with that larger scheme of objectification of the subjective experience of duration already noted in other patterns—in the binomial formula applicable to nouns in general, in temporal nouns, in plurality and numeration. This objectification enables us in imagination to "stand time units in a row." Imagination of time as like a row harmonizes with a system of THREE tenses; whereas a system of TWO, an earlier and a later, would seem to correspond better to the feeling of duration as it is experienced. For if we inspect consciousness we find no past, present, future, but a unity embracing complexity. EVERYTHING is in consciousness, and everything in conscious-

[6] 'Year' and certain combinations of 'year' with name of season, rarely season names alone, can occur with a locative morpheme 'at,' but this is exceptional. It appears like historical detritus of an earlier different patterning, or the effect of English analogy, or both.

ness IS, and is together. There is in it a sensuous and a nonsensuous. We may call the sensuous—what we are seeing, hearing, touching—the 'present' while in the nonsensuous the vast image-world of memory is being labeled 'the past' and another realm of belief, intuition, and uncertainty 'the future'; yet sensation, memory, foresight, all are in consciousness together—one is not "yet to be" nor another "once but no more." Where real time comes in is that all this in consciousness is "getting later," changing certain relations in an irreversible manner. In this "latering" or "durating" there seems to me to be a paramount contrast between the newest, latest instant at the focus of attention and the rest—the earlier. Languages by the score get along well with two tenselike forms answering to this paramount relation of "later" to "earlier." We can of course CONSTRUCT AND CONTEMPLATE IN THOUGHT a system of past, present, future, in the objectified configuration of points on a line. This is what our general objectification tendency leads us to do and our tense system confirms.

In English the present tense seems the one least in harmony with the paramount temporal relation. It is as if pressed into various and not wholly congruous duties. One duty is to stand as objectified middle term between objectified past and objectified future, in narration, discussion, argument, logic, philosophy. Another is to denote inclusion in the sensuous field: 'I SEE him.' Another is for nomic, i.e. customarily or generally valid, statements: 'We SEE with our eyes.' These varied uses introduce confusions of thought, of which for the most part we are unaware.

Hopi, as we might expect, is different here too. Verbs have no "tenses" like ours, but have validity-forms ("assertions"), aspects, and clause-linkage forms (modes), that yield even greater precision of speech. The validity-forms denote that the speaker (not the subject) reports the situation (answering to our past and present) or that he expects it (answering to our future) [7] or that he makes a nomic statement (answering

---

[7] The expective and reportive assertions contrast according to the "paramount relation." The expective expresses anticipation existing EARLIER than objective fact, and coinciding with objective fact LATER than the status quo of the speaker, this status quo, including all the subsummation of the past therein, being expressed by the reportive. Our notion "future" seems to represent at once the earlier (anticipation) and the later (afterwards, what will be), as Hopi shows. This paradox may hint of how elusive the mystery of real time is, and how artificially it is expressed by a linear relation of past–present–future.

to our nomic present). The aspects denote different degrees of duration and different kinds of tendency "during duration." As yet we have noted nothing to indicate whether an event is sooner or later than another when both are REPORTED. But need for this does not arise until we have two verbs: i.e. two clauses. In that case the "modes" denote relations between the clauses, including relations of later to earlier and of simultaneity. Then there are many detached words that express similar relations, supplementing the modes and aspects. The duties of our three-tense system and its tripartite linear objectified "time" are distributed among various verb categories, all different from our tenses; and there is no more basis for an objectified time in Hopi verbs than in other Hopi patterns; although this does not in the least hinder the verb forms and other patterns from being closely adjusted to the pertinent realities of actual situations.

DURATION, INTENSITY, AND TENDENCY IN SAE AND HOPI

To fit discourse to manifold actual situations, all languages need to express durations, intensities, and tendencies. It is characteristic of SAE and perhaps of many other language types to express them metaphorically. The metaphors are those of spatial extension, i.e. of size, number (plurality), position, shape, and motion. We express duration by 'long, short, great, much, quick, slow,' etc.; intensity by 'large, great, much, heavy, light, high, low, sharp, faint,' etc.; tendency by 'more, increase, grow, turn, get, approach, go, come, rise, fall, stop, smooth, even, rapid, slow'; and so on through an almost inexhaustible list of metaphors that we hardly recognize as such, since they are virtually the only linguistic media available. The nonmetaphorical terms in this field, like 'early, late, soon, lasting, intense, very, tending,' are a mere handful, quite inadequate to the needs.

It is clear how this condition "fits in." It is part of our whole scheme of OBJECTIFYING—imaginatively spatializing qualities and potentials that are quite nonspatial (so far as any spatially perceptive senses can tell us). Noun-meaning (with us) proceeds from physical bodies to referents of far other sort. Since physical bodies and their outlines in PERCEIVED SPACE are denoted by size and shape terms and reckoned by cardinal numbers and plurals, these patterns of denotation and reckoning extend to the symbols of nonspatial meanings, and so suggest an IMAGINARY SPACE. Physical shapes 'move, stop, rise, sink, approach,' etc., in perceived space; why not these other referents in their imaginary space? This has gone so far that we can hardly refer to the simplest nonspatial situation without constant resort to physical metaphors. I "grasp" the "thread" of another's arguments, but if its "level" is "over my head" my attention may "wander" and "lose touch" with the "drift" of it, so that when he "comes" to his "point" we differ "widely," our "views" being indeed so "far apart" that the "things" he says "appear" "much" too arbitrary, or even "a lot" of nonsense!

The absence of such metaphor from Hopi speech is striking. Use of space terms when there is no space involved is NOT THERE—as if on it had been laid the taboo teetotal! The reason is clear when we know that Hopi has abundant conjugational and lexical means of expressing duration, intensity, and tendency directly as such, and that major grammatical patterns do not, as with us, provide analogies for an imaginary space. The many verb "aspects" express duration and tendency of manifestations, while some of the "voices" express intensity, tendency, and duration of causes or forces producing manifestations. Then a special part of speech, the "tensors," a huge class of words, denotes only intensity, tendency, duration, and sequence. The function of the tensors is to express intensities, "strengths," and how they continue or vary, their rate of change; so that the broad concept of intensity, when considered as necessarily always varying and/or continuing, includes also tendency and duration. Tensors convey distinctions of degree, rate, constancy, repetition, increase and decrease of intensity, immediate sequence, interruption or sequence after an interval, etc., also QUALITIES of strengths, such as we should express metaphorically as smooth, even, hard, rough. A striking feature is their lack of resemblance to the terms of real space and movement that to us "mean the same." There is not even more than a trace of apparent derivation from space terms.[8] So, while Hopi

[8] One such trace is that the tensor 'long in duration,' while quite different from the adjective 'long' of space, seems to contain the same root as the adjective 'large' of space. Another is that 'somewhere' of space used with certain tensors means 'at some indefinite time.' Possibly however this is not the case and it is only the tensor that gives the time element, so that 'somewhere' still refers to space and that under these conditions indefinite space means simply general applicability, regardless of either time or space. Another trace is that in the temporal (cycle word) 'afternoon' the element meaning 'after' is derived from the verb 'to separate.' There are other such traces, but they are few and exceptional, and obviously not like our own spatial metaphorizing.

in its nouns seems highly concrete, here in the tensors it becomes abstract almost beyond our power to follow.

HABITUAL THOUGHT IN SAE AND HOPI

The comparison now to be made between the habitual thought worlds of SAE and Hopi speakers is of course incomplete. It is possible only to touch upon certain dominant contrasts that appear to stem from the linguistic differences already noted. By "habitual thought" and "thought world" I mean more than simply language, i.e. than the linguistic patterns themselves. I include all the analogical and suggestive value of the patterns (e.g., our "imaginary space" and its distant implications), and all the give-and-take between language and the culture as a whole, wherein is a vast amount that is not linguistic but yet shows the shaping influence of language. In brief, this "thought world" is the microcosm that each man carries about within himself, by which he measures and understands what he can of the macrocosm.

The SAE microcosm has analyzed reality largely in terms of what it calls "things" (bodies and quasibodies) plus modes of extensional but formless existence that it calls "substances" or "matter." It tends to see existence through a binomial formula that expresses any existent as a spatial form plus a spatial formless continuum related to the form, as contents is related to the outlines of its container. Nonspatial existents are imaginatively spatialized and charged with similar implications of form and continuum.

The Hopi microcosm seems to have analyzed reality largely in terms of EVENTS (or better "eventing"), referred to in two ways, objective and subjective. Objectively, and only if perceptible physical experience, events are expressed mainly as outlines, colors, movements, and other perceptive reports. Subjectively, for both the physical and nonphysical, events are considered the expression of invisible intensity factors, on which depend their stability and persistence, or their fugitiveness and proclivities. It implies that existents do not "become later and later" all in the same way; but some do so by growing like plants, some by diffusing and vanishing, some by a procession of metamorphoses, some by enduring in one shape till affected by violent forces. In the nature of each existent able to manifest as a definite whole is the power of its own mode of duration: its growth, decline, stability, cyclicity, or creativeness. Everything is thus already "prepared" for the way it now manifests by earlier phases, and what it will be later, partly has been, and partly is in act of being so "prepared." An emphasis and importance rests on this preparing or being prepared aspect of the world that may to the Hopi correspond to that "quality of reality" that 'matter' or 'stuff' has for us.

HABITUAL BEHAVIOR FEATURES OF HOPI CULTURE

Our behavior, and that of Hopi, can be seen to be coordinated in many ways to the linguistically conditioned microcosm. As in my fire casebook, people act about situations in ways which are like the ways they talk about them. A characteristic of Hopi behavior is the emphasis on preparation. This includes announcing and getting ready for events well beforehand, elaborate precautions to insure persistence of desired conditions, and stress on good will as the preparer of right results. Consider the analogies of the day-counting pattern alone. Time is mainly reckoned "by day" (*taɹk, -tala*) or "by night" (*tok*), which words are not nouns but tensors, the first formed on a root "light, day," the second on a root "sleep." The count is by ORDINALS. This is not the pattern of counting a number of different men or things, even though they appear successively, for, even then, they COULD gather into an assemblage. It is the pattern of counting successive reappearances of the SAME man or thing, incapable of forming an assemblage. The analogy is not to behave about day-cyclicity as to several men ("several days"), which is what WE tend to do, but to behave as to the successive visits of the SAME MAN. One does not alter several men by working upon just one, but one can prepare and so alter the later visits of the same man by working to affect the visit he is making now. This is the way the Hopi deal with the future—by working within a present situation which is expected to carry impresses, both obvious and occult, forward into the future event of interest. One might say that Hopi society understands our proverb 'Well begun is half done,' but not our 'Tomorrow is another day.' This may explain much in Hopi character.

This Hopi preparing behavior may be roughly divided into announcing, outer preparing, inner preparing, covert participation, and persistence. Announcing, or preparative publicity, is an important function in the hands of a special official, the Crier Chief. Outer preparing is preparation involving much visible activity, not all necessarily directly useful within our understanding. It includes ordinary practicing, rehearsing, getting ready, introductory formalities, preparing of special food, etc. (all of these to a degree that may seem overelaborate to us), intensive sustained muscular activity like running, racing, dancing, which is thought to increase the intensity of development of events (such as growth of crops), mimetic and other magic, preparations based on esoteric theory involving perhaps occult instruments like prayer sticks, prayer feathers, and prayer meal, and finally the great cyclic ceremonies and dances, which have the significance of preparing rain and crops. From one of the verbs meaning "prepare" is derived the noun for "harvest" or "crop": *na'twani* 'the prepared' or the 'in preparation.' [9]

Inner preparing is use of prayer and meditation, and at lesser intensity good wishes and good will, to further desired results. Hopi attitudes stress the power of desire and thought. With their "microcosm" it is utterly natural that they should. Desire and thought are the earliest, and therefore the most important, most critical and crucial, stage of preparing. Moreover, to the Hopi, one's desires and thoughts influence not only his own actions, but all nature as well. This too is wholly natural. Consciousness itself is aware of work, of the feel of effort and energy, in desire and thinking. Experience more basic than language tells us that, if energy is expended, effects are produced. WE tend to believe that our bodies can stop up this energy, prevent it from affecting other things until we will our BODIES to overt action. But this may be so only because we have our own linguistic basis for a theory that formless items like "matter" are things in themselves, malleable only by similar things, by more matter, and hence insulated from the powers of life and thought. It is no more unnatural to think that thought contacts everything and pervades the universe than to think, as we all do, that light kindled outdoors does this. And it is not unnatural to suppose that thought, like any other force, leaves everywhere traces of effect. Now, when WE think of a certain actual rosebush, we do not suppose that our thought goes to that actual bush, and engages with it, like a searchlight turned upon it. What then do we suppose our conscious-

[9] The Hopi verbs of preparing naturally do not correspond neatly to our "prepare"; so that *na'twani* could also be rendered 'the practiced-upon, the tried-for,' and otherwise.

ness is dealing with when we are thinking of that rosebush? Probably we think it is dealing with a "mental image" which is not the rosebush but a mental surrogate of it. But why should it be NATURAL to think that our thought deals with a surrogate and not with the real rosebush? Quite possibly because we are dimly aware that we carry about with us a whole imaginary space, full of mental surrogates. To us, mental surrogates are old familiar fare. Along with the images of imaginary space, which we perhaps secretly know to be only imaginary, we tuck the thought-of actually existing rosebush, which may be quite another story, perhaps just because we have that very convenient "place" for it. The Hopi thought-world has no imaginary space. The corollary to this is that it may not locate thought dealing with real space anywhere but in real space, nor insulate real space from the effects of thought. A Hopi would naturally suppose that his thought (or he himself) traffics with the actual rosebush—or more likely, corn plant—that he is thinking about. The thought then should leave some trace of itself with the plant in the field. If it is a good thought, one about health and growth, it is good for the plant; if a bad thought, the reverse.

The Hopi emphasize the intensity-factor of thought. Thought to be most effective should be vivid in consciousness, definite, steady, sustained, charged with strongly felt good intentions. They render the idea in English as 'concentrating, holding it in your heart, putting your mind on it, earnestly hoping.' Thought power is the force behind ceremonies, prayer sticks, ritual smoking, etc. The prayer pipe is regarded as an aid to "concentrating" (so said my informant). Its name, na'twanpi, means 'instrument of preparing.'

Covert participation is mental collaboration from people who do not take part in the actual affair, be it a job of work, hunt, race, or ceremony, but direct their thought and good will toward the affair's success. Announcements often seek to enlist the support of such mental helpers as well as of overt participants, and contain exhortations to the people to aid with their active good will.[10] A similarity to our concepts of a sympathetic audience or the cheering section at a football game should

[10] See, e.g., Ernest Beaglehole, *Notes on Hopi economic life* (Yale University Publications in Anthropology, no. 15, 1937), especially the reference to the announcement of a rabbit hunt, and on p. 30, description of the activities in connection with the cleaning of Toreva Spring—announcing, various preparing activities, and finally, preparing the continuity of the good results already obtained and the continued flow of the spring.

not obscure the fact that it is primarily the power of directed thought, and not merely sympathy or encouragement, that is expected of covert participants. In fact these latter get in their deadliest work before, not during, the game! A corollary to the power of thought is the power of wrong thought for evil; hence one purpose of covert participation is to obtain the mass force of many good wishers to offset the harmful thought of ill wishers. Such attitudes greatly favor cooperation and community spirit. Not that the Hopi community is not full of rivalries and colliding interests. Against the tendency to social disintegration in such a small, isolated group, the theory of "preparing" by the power of thought, logically leading to the great power of the combined, intensified, and harmonized thought of the whole community, must help vastly toward the rather remarkable degree of cooperation that, in spite of much private bickering, the Hopi village displays in all the important cultural activities.

Hopi "preparing" activities again show a result of their linguistic thought background in an emphasis on persistence and constant insistent repetition. A sense of the cumulative value of innumerable small momenta is dulled by an objectified, spatialized view of time like ours, enhanced by a way of thinking close to the subjective awareness of duration, of the ceaseless "latering" of events. To us, for whom time is a motion on a space, unvarying repetition seems to scatter its force along a row of units of that space, and be wasted. To the Hopi, for whom time is not a motion but a "getting later" of everything that has ever been done, unvarying repetition is not wasted but accumulated. It is storing up an invisible change that holds over into later events.[11] As we have seen, it is as if the return of the day were felt as the return of the same person, a little older but with all the impresses of yesterday, not as "another day," i.e. like an entirely different person. This principle

[11] This notion of storing up power, which seems implied by much Hopi behavior, has an analog in physics: acceleration. It might be said that the linguistic background of Hopi thought equips it to recognize naturally that force manifests not as motion or velocity, but as cumulation or acceleration. Our linguistic background tends to hinder in us this same recognition, for having legitimately conceived force to be that which produces change, we then think of change by our linguistic metaphorical analog, motion, instead of by a pure motionless changingness concept, i.e. accumulation or acceleration. Hence it comes to our naïve feeling as a shock to find from physical experiments that it is not possible to define force by motion, that motion and speed, as also "being at rest," are wholly relative, and that force can be measured only by acceleration.

joined with that of thought-power and with traits of general Pueblo
culture is expressed in the theory of the Hopi ceremonial dance for
furthering rain and crops, as well as in its short, piston-like tread, repeated thousands of times, hour after hour.

SOME IMPRESSES OF LINGUISTIC HABIT IN WESTERN CIVILIZATION

It is harder to do justice in few words to the linguistically conditioned
features of our own culture than in the case of the Hopi, because of both
vast scope and difficulty of objectivity—because of our deeply ingrained
familiarity with the attitudes to be analyzed. I wish merely to sketch
certain characteristics adjusted to our linguistic binomialism of form
plus formless item or "substance," to our metaphoricalness, our imaginary space, and our objectified time. These, as we have seen, are
linguistic.

From the form-plus-substance dichotomy the philosophical views most
traditionally characteristic of the "Western world" have derived huge
support. Here belong materialism, psychophysical parallelism, physics—
at least in its traditional Newtonian form—and dualistic views of the
universe in general. Indeed here belongs almost everything that is
"hard, practical common sense." Monistic, holistic, and relativistic
views of reality appeal to philosophers and some scientists, but they are
badly handicapped in appealing to the "common sense" of the Western
average man—not because nature herself refutes them (if she did, philosophers could have discovered this much), but because they must be
talked about in what amounts to a new language. "Common sense,"
as its name shows, and "practicality" as its name does not show, are
largely matters of talking so that one is readily understood. It is sometimes stated that Newtonian space, time, and matter are sensed by
everyone intuitively, whereupon relativity is cited as showing how mathematical analysis can prove intuition wrong. This, besides being unfair
to intuition, is an attempt to answer offhand question (1) put at the
outset of this paper, to answer which this research was undertaken.
Presentation of the findings now nears its end, and I think the answer
is clear. The offhand answer, laying the blame upon intuition for our
slowness in discovering mysteries of the Cosmos, such as relativity, is

the wrong one. The right answer is: Newtonian space, time, and matter are no intuitions. They are recepts from culture and language. That is where Newton got them.

Our objectified view of time is, however, favorable to historicity and to everything connected with the keeping of records, while the Hopi view is unfavorable thereto. The latter is too subtle, complex, and ever-developing, supplying no ready-made answer to the question of when "one" event ends and "another" begins. When it is implicit that everything that ever happened still is, but is in a necessarily different form from what memory or record reports, there is less incentive to study the past. As for the present, the incentive would be not to record it but to treat it as "preparing." But OUR objectified time puts before imagination something like a ribbon or scroll marked off into equal blank spaces, suggesting that each be filled with an entry. Writing has no doubt helped toward our linguistic treatment of time, even as the linguistic treatment has guided the uses of writing. Through this give-and-take between language and the whole culture we get, for instance:

1. Records, diaries, bookkeeping, accounting, mathematics stimulated by accounting.

2. Interest in exact sequence, dating, calendars, chronology, clocks, time wages, time graphs, time as used in physics.

3. Annals, histories, the historical attitude, interest in the past, archaeology, attitudes of introjection toward past periods, e.g., classicism, romanticism.

Just as we conceive our objectified time as extending in the future in the same way that it extends in the past, so we set down our estimates of the future in the same shape as our records of the past, producing programs, schedules, budgets. The formal equality of the spacelike units by which we measure and conceive time leads us to consider the "formless item" or "substance" of time to be homogeneous and in ratio to the number of units. Hence our prorata allocation of value to time, lending itself to the building up of a commercial structure based on time-prorata values: time wages (time work constantly supersedes piece work), rent, credit, interest, depreciation charges, and insurance premiums. No doubt this vast system, once built, would continue to run under any sort of linguistic treatment of time; but that it should have been built at all, reaching the magnitude and particular form it has in the Western world, is a fact decidedly in consonance with the patterns of the SAE languages. Whether such a civilization as ours would be possible with widely different linguistic handling of time is a large question—in our civilization, our linguistic patterns and the fitting of our behavior to the temporal order are what they are, and they are in accord. We are of course stimulated to use calendars, clocks, and watches, and to try to measure time ever more precisely; this aids science, and science in turn, following these well-worn cultural grooves, gives back to culture an ever-growing store of applications, habits, and values, with which culture again directs science. But what lies outside this spiral? Science is beginning to find that there is something in the Cosmos that is not in accord with the concepts we have formed in mounting the spiral. It is trying to frame a NEW LANGUAGE by which to adjust itself to a wider universe.

It is clear how the emphasis on "saving time" which goes with all the above and is very obvious objectification of time, leads to a high valuation of "speed," which shows itself a great deal in our behavior.

Still another behavioral effect is that the character of monotony and regularity possessed by our image of time as an evenly scaled limitless tape measure persuades us to behave as if that monotony were more true of events than it really is. That is, it helps to routinize us. We tend to select and favor whatever bears out this view, to "play up to" the routine aspects of existence. One phase of this is behavior evincing a false sense of security or an assumption that all will always go smoothly, and a lack in foreseeing and protecting ourselves against hazards. Our technique of harnessing energy does well in routine performance, and it is along routine lines that we chiefly strive to improve it—we are, for example, relatively uninterested in stopping the energy from causing accidents, fires, and explosions, which it is doing constantly and on a wide scale. Such indifference to the unexpectedness of life would be disastrous to a society as small, isolated, and precariously poised as the Hopi society is, or rather once was.

Thus our linguistically determined thought world not only collaborates with our cultural idols and ideals, but engages even our unconscious personal reactions in its patterns and gives them certain typical characters. One such character, as we have seen, is CARELESSNESS, as in reckless driving or throwing cigarette stubs into waste paper. Another of different sort is GESTURING when we talk. Very many of the gestures made by English-speaking people at least, and probably by all SAE speakers, serve to illustrate, by a movement in space, not a real spatial reference but one of the nonspatial references that our language handles by metaphors of imaginary space. That is, we are more apt to make a grasping gesture when we speak of grasping an elusive idea than when we speak of grasping a doorknob. The gesture seeks to make a metaphorical and hence somewhat unclear reference more clear. But, if a language refers to nonspatials without implying a spatial analogy, the reference is not made any clearer by gesture. The Hopi gesture very little, perhaps not at all in the sense we understand as gesture.

It would seem as if kinesthesia, or the sensing of muscular movement, though arising before language, should be made more highly conscious by linguistic use of imaginary space and metaphorical images of motion. Kinesthesia is marked in two facets of European culture: art and sport. European sculpture, an art in which Europe excels, is strongly kinesthetic, conveying great sense of the body's motions; European painting likewise. The dance in our culture expresses delight in motion rather than symbolism or ceremonial, and our music is greatly influenced by our dance forms. Our sports are strongly imbued with this element of the "poetry of motion." Hopi races and games seem to emphasize rather the virtues of endurance and sustained intensity. Hopi dancing is highly symbolic and is performed with great intensity and earnestness, but has not much movement or swing.

Synesthesia, or suggestion by certain sense receptions of characters belonging to another sense, as of light and color by sounds and vice versa, should be made more conscious by a linguistic metaphorical system that refers to nonspatial experiences by terms for spatial ones, though undoubtedly it arises from a deeper source. Probably in the first instance metaphor arises from synesthesia and not the reverse; yet metaphor need not become firmly rooted in linguistic pattern, as Hopi shows. Nonspatial experience has one well-organized sense, HEARING—for smell and taste are but little organized. Nonspatial consciousness is a realm chiefly of thought, feeling, and SOUND. Spatial consciousness is a realm of light, color, sight, and touch, and presents shapes and dimensions. Our metaphorical system, by naming nonspatial experiences after spatial ones, imputes to sounds, smells, tastes, emotions, and thoughts qualities like the colors, luminosities, shapes, angles, textures, and motions of spatial experience. And to some extent the reverse transference occurs;

for, after much talking about tones as high, low, sharp, dull, heavy, brilliant, slow, the talker finds it easy to think of some factors in spatial experience as like factors of tone. Thus we speak of "tones" of color, a gray "monotone," a "loud" necktie, a "taste" in dress: all spatial metaphor in reverse. Now European art is distinctive in the way it seeks deliberately to play with synesthesia. Music tries to suggest scenes, color, movement, geometric design; painting and sculpture are often consciously guided by the analogies of music's rhythm; colors are conjoined with feeling for the analogy to concords and discords. The European theater and opera seek a synthesis of many arts. It may be that in this way our metaphorical language that is in some sense a confusion of thought is producing, through art, a result of far-reaching value—a deeper esthetic sense leading toward a more direct apprehension of underlying unity behind the phenomena so variously reported by our sense channels.

HISTORICAL IMPLICATIONS

How does such a network of language, culture, and behavior come about historically? Which was first: the language patterns or the cultural norms? In main they have grown up together, constantly influencing each other. But in this partnership the nature of the language is the factor that limits free plasticity and rigidifies channels of development in the more autocratic way. This is so because a language is a system, not just an assemblage of norms. Large systematic outlines can change to something really new only very slowly, while many other cultural innovations are made with comparative quickness. Language thus represents the mass mind; it is affected by inventions and innovations, but affected little and slowly, whereas TO inventors and innovators it legislates with the decree immediate.

The growth of the SAE language-culture complex dates from ancient times. Much of its metaphorical reference to the nonspatial by the spatial was already fixed in the ancient tongues, and more especially in Latin. It is indeed a marked trait of Latin. If we compare, say Hebrew, we find that, while Hebrew has some allusion to not-space as space, Latin has more. Latin terms for nonspatials, like *educo, religio, principia, comprehendo*, are usually metaphorized physical references: lead out, tying back, etc. This is not true of all languages—it is quite untrue of Hopi. The fact that in Latin the direction of development happened to be from spatial to nonspatial (partly because of secondary stimulation to abstract thinking when the intellectually crude Romans encountered Greek culture) and that later tongues were strongly stimulated to mimic Latin, seems a likely reason for a belief, which still lingers on among linguists, that this is the natural direction of semantic change in all languages, and for the persistent notion in Western learned circles (in strong contrast to Eastern ones) that objective experience is prior to subjective. Philosophies make out a weighty case for the reverse, and certainly the direction of development is sometimes the reverse. Thus the Hopi word for "heart" can be shown to be a late formation within Hopi from a root meaning think or remember. Or consider what has happened to the word "radio" in such a sentence as "he bought a new radio," as compared to its prior meaning "science of wireless telephony."

In the Middle Ages the patterns already formed in Latin began to interweave with the increased mechanical invention, industry, trade, and scholastic and scientific thought. The need for measurement in industry and trade, the stores and bulks of "stuffs" in various containers, the typebodies in which various goods were handled, standardizing of measure and weight units, invention of clocks and measurement of "time," keeping of records, accounts, chronicles, histories, growth of mathematics and the partnership of mathematics and science, all cooperated to bring our thought and language world into its present form.

In Hopi history, could we read it, we should find a different type of language and a different set of cultural and environmental influences working together. A peaceful agricultural society isolated by geographic features and nomad enemies in a land of scanty rainfall, arid agriculture that could be made successful only by the utmost perseverance (hence the value of persistence and repetition), necessity for collaboration (hence emphasis on the psychology of teamwork and on mental factors in general), corn and rain as primary criteria of value, need of extensive PREPARATIONS and precautions to assure crops in the poor soil and precarious climate, keen realization of dependence upon nature favoring prayer and a religious attitude toward the forces of nature, especially prayer and religion directed toward the ever-needed blessing, rain—these things interacted with Hopi linguistic patterns to mold them, to be molded again by them, and so little by little to shape the Hopi world-outlook.

To sum up the matter, our first question asked in the beginning (p. 138) is answered thus: Concepts of "time" and "matter" are not given in substantially the same form by experience to all men but depend upon the nature of the language or languages through the use of which they have been developed. They do not depend so much upon ANY ONE SYSTEM (e.g., tense, or nouns) within the grammar as upon the ways of analyzing and reporting experience which have become fixed in the language as integrated "fashions of speaking" and which cut across the typical grammatical classifications, so that such a "fashion" may include lexical, morphological, syntactic, and otherwise systemically diverse means coordinated in a certain frame of consistency. Our own "time" differs markedly from Hopi "duration." It is conceived as like a space of strictly limited dimensions, or sometimes as like a motion upon such a space, and employed as an intellectual tool accordingly. Hopi "duration" seems to be inconceivable in terms of space or motion, being the mode in which life differs from form, and consciousness *in toto* from the spatial elements of consciousness. Certain ideas born of our own time-concept, such as that of absolute simultaneity, would be either very difficult to express or impossible and devoid of meaning under the Hopi conception, and would be replaced by operational concepts. Our "matter" is the physical subtype of "substance" or "stuff," which is conceived as the formless extensional item that must be joined with form before there can be real existence. In Hopi there seems to be nothing corresponding to it; there are no formless extensional items; existence may or may not have form, but what it also has, with or without form, is intensity and duration, these being nonextensional and at bottom the same.

But what about our concept of "space," which was also included in our first question? There is no such striking difference between Hopi and SAE about space as about time, and probably the apprehension of space is given in substantially the same form by experience irrespective of language. The experiments of the Gestalt psychologists with visual perception appear to establish this as a fact. But the CONCEPT OF SPACE will vary somewhat with language, because, as an intellectual tool,[12] it

---

[12] Here belong "Newtonian" and "Euclidean" space, etc.

is so closely linked with the concomitant employment of other intellectual tools, of the order of "time" and "matter," which are linguistically conditioned. We see things with our eyes in the same space forms as the Hopi, but our idea of space has also the property of acting as a surrogate of nonspatial relationships like time, intensity, tendency, and as a void to be filled with imagined formless items, one of which may even be called 'space.' Space as sensed by the Hopi would not be connected mentally with such surrogates, but would be comparatively "pure," unmixed with extraneous notions.

As for our second question (p. 138): There are connections but not correlations or diagnostic correspondences between cultural norms and linguistic patterns. Although it would be impossible to infer the existence of Crier Chiefs from the lack of tenses in Hopi, or vice versa, there is a relation between a language and the rest of the culture of the society which uses it. There are cases where the "fashions of speaking" are closely integrated with the whole general culture, whether or not this be universally true, and there are connections within this integration, between the kind of linguistic analyses employed and various behavioral reactions and also the shapes taken by various cultural developments. Thus the importance of Crier Chiefs does have a connection, not with tenselessness itself, but with a system of thought in which categories different from our tenses are natural. These connections are to be found not so much by focusing attention on the typical rubrics of linguistic, ethnographic, or sociological description as by examining the culture and the language (always and only when the two have been together historically for a considerable time) as a whole in which concatenations that run across these departmental lines may be expected to exist, and, if they do exist, eventually to be discoverable by study.

GESTALT TECHNIQUE

OF STEM COMPOSITION

IN SHAWNEE *

C. F. Voegelin has accomplished the difficult and signal work of analyzing an immense number of baffling stem compounds of Shawnee into their component lexemes (stems) and other morphemes (formatives), classifying them according to formal categories of Shawnee grammar, and discovering an important native semantic relation, that of the occurrent, a lexeme that has some pervasive semantic influence that induces the native to cling to translation of the occurrent even when he neglects specific translation of the other lexemes in the compound.

Voegelin has asked me to illustrate the application of a different aspect of linguistic method, which can be applied only after a formal grammatical analysis has been made, but which then can sometimes show the principles by which lexemes of differing meaning are placed in certain sequences to produce semantic effects, whether in compounds or in syntactic constructions.

Linguists have studied the Indo-European languages so long that they have been able to generalize their most typical sequences and resultant semantic effects into such general formulas as subject and predicate, actor, action, and goal, attribute and head, and exocentric versus endocentric; also to tag and handle relations that have a superficial similarity in languages that may otherwise differ greatly from Indo-European. But

* Reprinted from the appendix, pp. 393–406, to C. F. Voegelin, *Shawnee stems and the Jacob P. Dunn Miami dictionary*. Indianapolis: Indiana Historical Society, 1940. (*Prehistory Research Series*, vol. I, no. 9, April 1940).

this last ability must turn out in many cases to be only a happy, or at times perhaps an unhappy accident. When the principles of composition are themselves widely different, these schematizations break down and cannot account for either the rules of sequence or the resulting semantic effects. Let me give a simple instance from a language not widely removed from the syntactic type of Indo-European—Aztec, belonging to the Uto-Aztecan stock. Here an apparent attribute-head relationship is very definite, and the attribute term or modifier always precedes the head or modified term (why this is a necessary conclusion would require some length to explain). Yet many expressions follow the type of 'narrow road,' *o?-picak-tli*, in which 'narrow' has to be expressed by a sort of verbal passive participle, 'narrowed' (*-picak-*), and such a participle is placed last, hence after 'road' (*-o?-*). The complete correlation of attribute and head with word order in this language forces us to conclude that 'narrow' is the head and 'road' is the attribute, as it is in English 'roadside.' Yet if one wished to say 'new road, good road, brick road,' in these 'road' would be 'head' and would come last. Of what use then, to one wishing to compose in Aztec, is the category of attribute and head, when it cannot say whether such a simple notion as 'road' is attribute or head in semantic effects that seem so closely parallel as 'narrow road' and 'good road'? One concludes that such categories are but linguistic kinship systems, and like social kinship systems do not follow any universal norm.

It is the same with the schematizations of subject–predicate, actor–action, and action–goal. Even in English, the description of such a sentence as 'the tree stood here' as 'actor–action' is rather forced, even if it is formally parallel to 'the boy ran.' A hypothetical American language X might use three or more lexemes instead of two for the latter; perhaps (1) movement-of-foot (2) over-a-surface (3) manifestation-of-boy-occurs-quickly. Perhaps (3) might bear formatives that make it formally a verb, or an 'action,' but again such formatives might be 'operators' applying to the whole sentence, no more to one lexeme than another. Such a sentence cannot really be broken into a subject and a predicate, not even when it consists of just two formal words. Nevertheless it has an analysis, and the parts correspond to certain essentials that have been segregated out of the situation reported: i.e., the situation does contain something that might be called a surface and something that can be called moving feet, besides something that can be called a boy. Our problem is to determine how different languages segregate different essentials out of the same situation. This is often a crucial question in the description of a language, and it must not be supposed that it has been answered by an account of the formal rules for combination into sentences of the lexemes and other morphemes that represent the language's segregation of essentials out of situations. Our hypothetical language X might express the sentence (1)-(2)-(3) by a polysynthetic compounding of stems and formatives into one formal word, as often in Shawnee, or by a number of words arranged into a sentence as analytic as one of English; yet in either case the really important difference from English is the same, viz., that it has isolated the peculiar group of essentials (1), (2), (3), and ignored our own isolation of 'boy (as actor)' and 'ran.' So, where we speak of 'cleaning (a gun) with a ramrod,' Shawnee does not isolate any rod or action of cleaning, but directs a hollow moving dry spot by movement of tool (*Shawnee stems*, part III, 157). This is what makes Shawnee so strange and baffling from the standpoint of English, and not at all the mere fact that it is polysynthetic. A language can be polysynthetic and still say 'clean with a ramrod' polysynthetically, thereby remaining quite transparent from the standpoint of English.

To compare ways in which different languages differently "segment" the same situation or experience, it is desirable to be able to analyze or "segment" the experience first in a way independent of any one language or linguistic stock, a way which will be the same for all observers. This cannot be done by describing the situation in terms of subject–predicate, actor–action, attribute–head, etc., for any scientific use of such terms contemplates that they shall have a variable meaning as defined for each particular language, including the possibility that for some languages their meaning shall be nil. Neither can it be done wholly by familiar terms ranging from the common-sense type to the quasiscientific, as by trying to break up the situation into 'things, objects, actions, substances, entities, events.' Cautious use of such terms may be helpful, perhaps unavoidable, but it must be remembered that in their ranges of meaning they are but the creatures of modern Indo-European languages and their subsidiary jargons, and reflect the typical modes of segmenting experience in these tongues. They do not become scientific for linguistics because they may happen to be used in physics or chemistry. When they refer to psychological experience, like the terms 'thoughts, ideas, concepts,' they require no less caution in use, but they are under no specially strong taboo for being "mentalistic" or "mystical." Mystical in the proper sense they certainly are not, but are merely "lexations," no better and no worse than 'gravitation' or 'cheese.'

There is one thing on which all observers of the appearance of a running boy will agree, at least after questioning or experimental testing—that it can be divided into parts—and they will all make the division in the same way. They will all divide it into (1) a figure or outline having more or less of motion (the boy) and (2) some kind of background or field against which, or in which, the figure is seen (that is, if we define observation in its common visual sense and so leave out the blind "observers").

A discovery made by modern configurative or Gestalt psychology gives us a canon of reference for all observers, irrespective of their languages or scientific jargons, by which to break down and describe all visually observable situations, and many other situations, also. This is the discovery that visual perception is basically the same for all normal persons past infancy and conforms to definite laws, a large number of which are fairly well known. It is impossible here to do more than touch on these laws, but they bring out clearly that the basal fact of visual perception is the relation of figure and ground, that perceptions are largely in the nature of outlines, contrasted more or less with the grounds, fields, and fillings of outlines, and that perception of motion or action is figural in type, or connected with the perception of at least a vague outline quality.

To say that the facts are essentially the same for all observers is not to deny that they have their fringe of aberrations and individual differences, but these are relatively minor. Brain lesions and eye defects produce distortions; special skills or mental effort can rearrange emphases and sometimes change the figure-ground roles of certain items, as when one "wills" the drawing of a cube seen edgewise to look like a hexagon with three radii. Color blindness and unequal sensitivity to colors are such marginal variations; impression of size, too, has marginal variation, as when the moon looks to one person the size of a nickel, to another as big as a house, yet always subtends on the retina less than a pencil at arm's length. When it comes to shape, the variations are still more marginal and slight. All these variations operate within the

frame of known laws, and so do not hinder a normative account of perceived data. The FACTS may differ slightly; the LAWS are the same for
all. If the perceptual influences are such as to cause one normal person
to see a definite outline, they will cause all other normal persons to see
the same outline. For example, all people see the constellation Ursa
Major as the outline which we call dipper-shaped, though they may not
call it a dipper or have such a utensil in their culture, and though there
are, of course, no lines connecting the stars into this or any other outline.

But how do these laws of vision give any canon of reference for non-
visual experience? By process of elimination. Everything that "takes
up space" can be shown to be known directly or indirectly through
vision. Everything unvisual is unspatial in character (and vice versa)
and is felt as immediate to the experiencer. Touch alone is somewhat
fused with visual material, and, when it tells us form, contour, and texture, it is indirectly visual. Visual experience is projected and constitutes space, or what we shall call the external field of the observer; unvisual experience is introjected and makes up what we shall call, following some Gestalt psychologists, the ego field, or egoic field, because the
observer or ego feels himself, as it were, alone with these sensations and
awarenesses. Hence in referring a certain experience to the egoic field,
because it is not in the visual field, or to the ambivalent borderland, as
when a sensation is known by both modes as within the observer's body,
we are classing it as all observers class it, regardless of their language,
once they understand the nature of the distinction. Moreover, the
egoic field has its own Gestalt laws, of sense quality, rhythm, etc., which
are universal. We can unhesitatingly class the referent of a lexeme of
hearing, tasting, or smelling along with those of thinking, emotions,
etc., in the egoic realm and apart from any lexeme referring to an
experience having outline or motion. The difference between light and
darkness, and the referent of seeing, not of what is seen, also, is either
borderland or of the egoic field, because the sensation quality is introjected though the figure-ground quality is projected; the referent of
saying something is also egoic, because the observer introjects both his
own and other people's speech, equating an essential from it to his egoic
field of hearing or sound; and the referent of possessing or having is also
egoic.

This principle of classifying referents is nonlinguistic and nonsemantic
in the ordinary sense of semantic. An isolate of experience in either the
external or the egoic field, e.g., a shape or a noise, is not a meaning.

Nevertheless a language may sometimes have a principle of classifying groups of morphemes and their semantic effects which is coordinated with this universal principle. Thus, in English, verbs referring to the subject's ego-field experience use the simple present tense for momentary present fact, and not the present progressive. Other verbs employ the present progressive tense for either momentary or continued present fact, and the simple present (except in special locutions like 'here he comes') for the nomic or customary tense aspect. Foreigners learning English do not know this, and hence may say 'I am hearing you, he is seeing it.' English speakers say 'I hear you, he sees it, he feels sick, I say that—, I think that—'; but, on the contrary, 'I am working' (not 'I work'), 'the boy is running' (not 'the boy runs,' which is nomic, e.g., 'the boy runs whenever—').[1]

I have found this Gestalt method of describing referents and situations of so much service toward understanding puzzling points of languages, as different in viewpoints as English, Hopi, Aztec, and Maya, that I decided to try it on Shawnee, though I know nothing of Shawnee or any other Algonkian language except from what Voegelin has published in the present series and his manuscript for the remainder of the series, which will complete his lexicon of Shawnee and Miami. The results are as follows, and it is for Algonkianists to say whether they have any significance or utility.

A fairly simple rough general rule applies to formation of a Shawnee stem compound. It may be likened in applicability to the rough general rule for noun-phrase composition in English: modifier precedes modified. Neither rule is absolute; e.g., in English 'brick buildings' represents the typical case where the general rule applies, 'buildings brick except for frame porches' one of the overriding special rules. The English rule is a good rough guide to a modern European, learning to compose English, because his own language is sufficiently similar so that he understands what is meant by modifier and modified: his language makes a similar classification of experience, and at most, as in French, merely reverses the order.[2] The phraseology of modifier and

---

[1] Cf. 'he is feeling (outlining) it'—external field visual touch, and 'he feels it'—egoic field sensation.

[2] Yet sometimes the non-English speaker makes a Gestalt error, as when a Mexican translated for me *desierto de los leones* as 'lion desert.' Normal English does not say 'lion wilderness' or 'fish ocean' because of an overriding rule that a small compact figure does not modify a total external-field ground, or in vernacular 'a little object can't modify all out-of-doors.'

modified does not work for Shawnee stem compounds that result in a verb, as they usually do. The rough general rule (aside from the over-riding rules) for Shawnee is: figure precedes external field, the more figural precedes the less figural, but the egoic field generally precedes all these. The chief overriding rules are: (1) a group of stems of vague figure (vague movement, texture, size, etc.) precedes everything; (2) non-initial stems must be preceded somehow, even in contravention of the general principle, although they generally comply in being less figural than what precedes; (3) when the result is a noun (but not a bahuvrihi or sentence used like a noun) the rule is reversed, and ground or field characters precede the figural; (4) two themes each compounded according to all the foregoing may be placed together, sometimes result-ing in irregular sequences within the total formation; (5) such a theme is sometimes used like a stem.

The descriptions of the reference of stems will be:

svf   special stem of vague figure (often of vague motion, direction, texture or plasticity of surface or mass, size, etc.).

ef   egoic field reference.

f   figure—this group expresses outline and space distribution more than the others; it does not necessarily imply movement but movement may be present, and an f stem may be used after some more figural f stem to denote relative external field, ground, or filling quality of the latter.

frg   figure as relative ground, as in preceding description, often a body part.

mf   movement figure, the 'idea' or image of a certain outline of movement.

fcm   figure containing movement, a vaguely outlined field which is relatively stationary but has movement or "coming to rest" within it.

xf   external field or ground, with a minimum of figural or outline quality.

i   instrumental, a special small group of elements.

This is the normal order of position, i.e., svf, ef, f, frg, mf, fcm, i— although there is nothing very rigid about the relative order of frg, mf, fcm, with respect to each other. Formatives will be denoted:

s   (formative of) subject.

o   object and/or transitive.

t   transitive element.

m   miscellaneous formatives.

In a broad sense the group f, frg, mf, fcm, xf, is one, and sometimes the same stem can fill any one of these positions if it is preceded or followed by stems in such a way that the progression of decreasing figural quality and increasing ground or field quality is carried out.

Examples of svf stems are: *paʔ-* 'going, moving thither'; *paak-* 'hard, firm, staccato movement'; *tep-* 'acquiring'; *kt-* 'big, superlative'; *kaʔk-* 'rough, dry'; *laakeet-* 'lightly, easily, quickly'; *laašiwe-* 'down, off from, above'; *loʔθee-* 'go out, off, through'; *liil-* 'diversity.'

Examples of ef stems are: *paʔpa-* 'tapping sound' (ef because a sound); *petškw-* 'aversion, repugnance'; *petθak(y)-* 'trouble, nuisance, intricate, difficult, confused, excited'; *pt-* 'accidental, unintentional, erroneous'; *teepwe-* 'truth'; *tepaat-* 'satisfactory'; *čiʔθ-* 'fear'; *kiš-* 'warm, hot'; *-kiiškwe-* 'consciousness'; *katawi-* 'ability'; *katow-* 'ask, beg'; *lalalwee-* 'rattling noise'; *miimʔkaw-* 'discovered, remembered'; *wiyakowee-* 'anger'; *waaši-* 'intentional'; *halan-* 'notifying'; *-eele-* 'thought.'

Examples of the (f——xf) group of the first degree, operating chiefly as f, are: *pap-* 'roomy configuration'; *pat-* 'moist spot or mass'; *Ppeʔt-* 'weakly propping configuration'; *petekw-* 'rounded, around, roll'; *petakw-* 'covering, top, above'; *piit-* 'interior outline, inside, hole'; *piʔtaw-* 'in-between figure'; *pakw-* 'plantlike, leafshaped'; *peekw-* 'dry spot'; *peʔkw-* 'cluster, bunched together'; *poʔk(y)-* 'broken, smashed condition'; *pašk(y)-* 'emergence from opening'; *poškw-* 'irregular fraction, halved, broken'; *tepilahi* 'straight (outline)'; *tepet(w)-* 'together, in a group'; *čee-* 'matched pair or combination, equal, even'; *kip-* 'covered, closed up'; *kotekwi* 'turning, winding'; *kakaanwi* 'long (long outline)'; *kooky-* 'immersed in water'; *šaapw-* 'in and out, through'; *škote* 'fire (fiery figure)'; *laa-* 'midst of area'; *leep-* 'tapering at base'; *liipiik-* 'settled liquid'; *—lʔpw-* 'contracted, pounded down'; *lakaʔkwa* 'ribbed contour, like washboard or palate'; *lekw-* 'covered with ground or ashes'; *liiky-* 'dismantled, apart'; *leʔθawaa-* 'forked'; *laal-* 'hanging down, away from'; *lelʔky-* 'torn outline, tear cloth, etc.'; *waawiyaa-* 'circle.'

Some f stems often operating as frg are: *(-)leč-* 'finger, hand, in the fingers, on the hand'; *-eče-* 'belly, body' (in fact, all body and body-part terms are usually frg); *-aʔkwi-* '(mass of) vegetation, flora, wood'; *-aalaka* 'hole, hollowness'; *-kamekwi* 'house, in the house'; *-šee-* 'cloth, clothing'; *-wale* 'back pack'; *-api* 'sitting configuration, sitting.'

Some mf stems are: *peteki* 'back in time or space' (movement or path); *-pho* 'picking up while running'; *ptoo-* 'running'; *čiip-* 'conveying in, conveying secretly'; *čiʔčiip-* 'shaking'; *-ʔtan-* 'flowing, floating'; *-ke-* 'general bodily movement'; *-eška-* 'initiating bodily movement'; *-eka* 'dancing'; *-kawi* 'dripping'; *-ʔθa-* 'flying'; *loop-* 'swinging'; *lek-* 'dissolving, melting'; *miil-* 'giving'; *hee-* 'going'; *-ʔθen* 'breaking off from moving thing.'

Some fcm stems are: *piʔte-* 'foaming'; *pootawe* 'burning wood'; *-eʔtekwi* 'stream'; *kapee-* 'crossing stream'; *kalawi-* 'talking (person talking)'; *kon-* 'swallowing'; *kwaap-* 'lifting from water'; *kwaškw-* 'recoiling'; *kwke-* 'movement of hook in water'; *-a-* 'teeth movement'; *-ʔši-*, *-ʔšin-* 'coming to rest'; *-laa-* 'boiling.'

Examples of stems chiefly operating as xf are: *-piiwe* 'hair, feathers'; *-aapo* 'liquid'; *-pki* 'scattering over level surface, level surface'; *tepki* 'swampy, marshy terrain'; *tepeʔki* 'night'; *-taškwi* 'flora'; *-la* 'color'; *-kami* 'expanse of water'; *-ʔki* 'expanse, abundance'; *-ʔkwatwi* 'sky'; *-šwaa-* 'space, room'; *-ʔškw-atwi* 'herbage'; *-aam-* 'soil, ground'; *-ʔho-* 'water, wetness'; *-ʔšk(y)-* 'softness, sliminess.'

Examples are hardly needed of the small group of very common i stems (instrumentals) indicating operation by hand, foot, tool, heat, etc.

A few examples of composition may be explained in detail. In *Shawnee Stems*, part III, 289, under *kip-*, *kipw-*, stem of f type, an outline of closure or of something covered up is placed or 'pictured' on a ground or in a setting of: (*a*) buckskin, (*b*) a path, (*c*) the eye region, (*d*) the eye region with movement of hand (*-kip-iikwee-n-*, -f-frg-i-), also in the anus region, the mouth, the ear, etc. Or consider the way of saying 'among the swamps.' Our own manner of lexation is to isolate from the experience an essential that we call 'swamp,' in the form of a typical English noun. As such a noun, it slides in the grammatical grooves prepared for all nouns, is treated as a typical "thing," referred to as having individual separation, singularity, plurality, suitability for article and preposition treatment. There is little difference in linguistic treatment between a swamp and a butterfly, in spite of the enormous difference in the perceptual experience. In Shawnee we have to forget the English type of lexation and fall back on the perceptual situation. The referent of our preposition 'among' becomes actually the part of the picture with the most quality of outline—a limited, defined spot in the midst of an indefinite field—which is a field of swampiness. The picture is, as it were, rough sketched by placing first the figural element *laa-* 'midst of area' followed by its ground or setting *tepki* 'swampy terrain,' > *laa-teepki* (f-xf) '(spot) among the swamps, in the swamp' (part II, 137).

In part II, 157, we have for 'I clean or dry gun by running ramrod in it,' *ni-peekw-aalak-h-a*, s-f-frg-i-o. The figural center of the composition is a dry or clean spot (*peekw*) which is placed in a setting of hollowness or 'hole' by the stem *-aalak-*, frg, a figure serving as relative ground or field for the first figure; the figural center is then activated or given motion by the instrumental *-h-* 'by movement of tool,' and denoted as transitive with inanimate object by the formative *-a*. In part II, 143, the f-stem *čee-* sets up a basic outline for the composition, the configuration of a matched pair, or matching units. Essentials of filling quality for the matched pair are given by xf stems signifying 'certain kind or type, general appearance, color,' or by frg stem 'person-s,' or by xf-xf, e.g., 'color plus body hair,' and 'color plus water.' Thus the words mean 'of the same type, looking alike, of the same color,' etc. In *ni-Ppeθ-k-a*, s-f-mf-o, part I, 69, 'I lean against it to hold it up,' the basic outline of propping, visually often something like a rough T or a lower-case lambda, is given by *Ppeθ* (< *Ppeʔt*), and the vague figural quality of a moving animate body is imparted by the mf stem *-k-* 'bodily movement.' In *ni-Ppeč-ši-m-a*, s-f-fcm-t-o, 'I put him there (on some support) to keep him from falling,' the second figure *-ši-*, a vague outline of motion coming to rest within an area, comes to rest in or on (as filling of) the basic prop outline, and is made transitive with animate object.

Many further examples of stem compounding are briefly analyzed in the list at the end of this appendix. It remains to speak of noun compounding and theme compounding, which are here regarded as overriding the basic rule of stem compounding. When the result of compounding is a noun, the rule is reversed: field or ground precedes figure, the less figural precedes the more figural. Since this is also commonly the case in the usual type of attribute-head relation in English, the Shawnee noun (unlike the verb) can usually be understood in terms of such a relation; e.g., part III, 290, *kopeleko-miyeewi*, xf-f, 'iron road (railroad).' The thing mentally associated with the head term or figure precedes it, again as in English; in this type of analysis it is regarded as a datum of the speaker's egoic field due to memory, and hence is denoted efm. Thus, part II, 139, *takhwaan-ekaawe*, efm-f, 'bread dance'; p. 141, *taamin-aapo* 'corn liquid (whisky)'; p. 143, *čiipa-yeemo*, efm-f, 'spirit bee'; p. 145, *čaki-yʔkweeθa*, frg-f, 'small woman,' where the vague figure, awareness of degree of size, precedes the more definite outline.

Two compound themes may be compounded with each other, but what rule if any governs the order I am unable to say. The examples seem few compared to the huge number of ordinary stem compounds. Thus in part I, 67, is a form that can perhaps be analyzed as *waašinitaši-paʔlenaweewi-či*, theme-theme-s. The first theme would be *waaši-nitaši*, ef-f 'intentionally at a spot there,' the second *paʔlenaweewi*, svf-ef 'going thither, living.' On the other hand, perhaps we have here a theme preceded by two stems.

It may be that there are two kinds of lexemes in Shawnee, stems and themes, and two kinds of compounding techniques, one for stems and one for themes. According to such a theory, stem compounds would use the principle of figure before ground and would result in a verbal theme, which if ending the word makes it a verb or normal sentence, or else a nomic sentence used as a noun (a bahuvrihi form). Theme compounds would use the principle of ground before figure, the result being whatever the last theme is, verb or noun. It would then appear that certain lexemes although not analyzable are always themes, e.g., fundamentally nominal lexemes and the svf and ef lexemes. These svf and ef elements, being themes, precede the f——xf verbal theme, as less figural. This is, of course, very tentative.

Nothing treated in this appendix explains which stem the native regards as most pervasive: i.e., as the occurrent. This may be a question quite apart from that of the method of compounding. I might hazard a guess that it may depend on the degree of analogic pressure behind the various stems in a combination. Some stems in the nature of the case would be more productive of combinations than others. The stem with the greatest number of close parallels to the combination in question might be felt by the native as nuclear.

There follows a list of analyzed combinations from parts I, II, III, each preceded by page number and followed by formula and translation, often reworked from Voegelin's to illustrate the technique, with occasional comments on the semantic effect.

Part I: 67 *pa-kwke*, svf-fcm 'he went to condition of water with hook moving in it, he went fishing.' 67 *ni-paʔ-pem-ʔθe-ʔto*, s-svf-f-mf-o 'I pass it (the resolution) along (around).' 67 *yeʔ-paʔ-nekot-θee-θi-ya*, m-svf-f-mf-m-s 'when I go there alone.' 68 *papi-šwaa-wi*, f-xf-s 'figure of roomy occupancy in field of general space occurs, it has plenty of room.' 69 *ni-pat-šk-a-m-a*, s-f-xf-fcm-t-o 'I kissed him' (f moist spot, xf general softness, fcm lip mvt., stem -a- can be called fcm but is perhaps also i). 69 *ni-pat-šk-aʔh-w-a*, s-f-xf-i-t-o 'I made him wet with mud' (i, mvt. of tool or means). 70 *ni-peteko-n-a*, s-f-i-o 'I roll it.' 70 *peteko-če-ška*, f-frg-mf 'he doubled up his body' (rolled outline in relative ground of body or belly, general bodily mvt.). 70 *taʔpetekiši-miimʔkaweele-ta-m-akwe*, theme-theme-t-o-s < *taʔ-peteki-ši*, svf-mf-m 'back to that place,' *miimʔkaw-eele*, ef-ef 'remember.' 71 *ni-petškw-eele-m-a*, s-ef-ef-t-o 'I hate him.' 71 *petθaki-lee-θa*, ef-f-m '(person who) is a nuisance.' 71 *ni-petako-l-aw-a*, s-f-mf-t-o 'I shot above him' (outline of superposition, projectile mvt.). 71 *ni-pt-a-m-a*, s-ef-fcm-t-o 'I accidentally bit him.' 72 *piič-θe-ʔθen-wi*, f-mf-fcm-s 'it breaks off and flies in.' 72 *piiči-leče-ʔšin-wa*, f-frg-fcm-s 'he laid his hand inside.' 72 *ni-piiči-miil-a*, s-f-mf-o 'I gave it to him through a hole.' 72 *piit-alwa*, f-frg (interiority figure, bullet filling) = 'bullet sack.' 72 *piʔteewi-laate*, fcm-fcm as relative ground 'it foams when boiling.' 73 *ni-piʔtawiše-ʔθe-to*, s-theme-fcm-o 'I joined pieces of cloth,' *piʔtawi-še*, f-xf 'juncture (f) in cloth (xf).' 73 *piimi-pooteθ-wa*, ef-f-s 'he makes error in smoking.' 74 *paak-aameʔki*, svf-xf 'it is a hard spot (svf) of ground (xf). 74–75 *ni-paak-eele-m-a*, s-svf-ef-t-o 'I think of his strength.' 76 *ni-paki-kaw-ʔto*, s-svf-mf-o 'I make it drip.' 77 *ni-pkw-eʔko-ta*, s-f-fcm-o 'I cut a piece off it.' 83 *leelawi-piikwa*, f-xf 'central point (f) of undergrowth (xf) occurs.' 83 *kinwi-piikwa*, f-xf 'long narrow area (f) of brush (xf) occurs, brush extends along.' 83 *ni-poʔki-če-el-aw-a*, s-f-frg-mf-t-o 'I caused breech (f) in body (frg) with projectile mvt. (mf) to him, I shot him in the body.' 83 *poʔk-iikwe*, f-frg 'he has breech (f) in one-side-of-face (frg), he has one eye out.' 87 *ni-poškwi-piye-en-a*, s-f-frg-i-o 'I caused irregular fraction (f) of long extension (frg) by hand mvt. (i) of it (tree), I broke a limb of the tree.' 87 *ni-poškwi-nʔke-ʔši-m-a*, s-f-frg-fcm-t-o 'I broke (f) his arm (frg) by motion coming to rest (fcm), by throwing him against something.' 91 *ni-paalači-we-l-a*, s-f-mf-t-o 'I carry (mf) him downward (f).' 91 *ni-pele-še-en-a*, s-f-frg-i-o 'I ripped the seam of it.' 92 *meelawaači-paam-ʔθe*, ef-f-mf 'he was tired (ef) of running (mf) around (f).' 99 *piyet-aalak-θen-wi*, svf-f-xf-s 'it lies (is in xf) with hole (f) this way (svf).'

Part II: 135 *ni-tephikan-ʔθe-to*, s-f-fcm-o 'I put it in jar-s.' 135 *ni-tepi-kiiškwe*, s-svf-ef 'I returned to consciousness.' 136 *paʔ-tepowee-ki*, svf-ef-s 'they went to council (counseling).' 137 *ni-tepeto-kalawi-pe*, s-f-fcm-m 'they were talking (fcm) in a group, together (f).' 137 *tepeto-ptoo-ki*, f-mf-s 'they were running in a group.' 138 *tetep-aʔkwi*, f-frg 'rolling outline of flora' = 'grapevine.' 138 *ni-waawiyaa-tap-šk-a*, s-f-mf-i-o 'I rolled (mf) it in a circle (f) by kicking (i).' 141 *ni-meʔči-tehe*, s-svf-ef 'I have thought.' 149 *ni-θaki-čaalee-pi-l-a*, s-f-frg-fcm-t-o 'I cause holding-outline (f) on nose (frg) with tying (fcm), I put halter on him.'

Part III: 289 *kape-ho-kwi*, fcm-xf-s 'he crosses floating.' 293 *kotekw-aakami*, f-xf 'water (xf) is in a winding (f) channel.' 295 *ni-kakaanwi-leče*, s-f-frg 'I have long hands.' 297 *ni-kooki-tepe-en-a*, s-f-frg-i-o 'I dipped his head (frg, filling of the immersion-figure) in the water.' 298 *ni-Kki-lečee-pi-l-a*, s-f-frg-fcm-t-o 'I put (binding action, fcm) a ring (circular outline, f) on his finger (frg). 300 *kaško-ʔše*, f-frg 'he has sharp ears.' 300 *ni-kišw-eele-m-a*, s-ef-ef-t-o 'I regard him as worthy, permit him.' 301 *kiišoo-kwaam-wa*, ef-ef-s or svf-ef-s he 'sleeps warmly.' 303 *ni-kilek-a-m-a*, s-f-fcm-t-o 'I caused mixed configuration (f) with mvt. in mouth (fcm), I mix it in my mouth.' 304 *kolep-šin-wa*, f-fcm-s 'he turned over lying down.' 306–307 *ni-kaawat-eele-m-a*, s-theme-ef-t-o 'I think of him as round' (*kaaw-at-* theme, hence can precede ef?). 308 *ni-kwaško-l-aw-a*, s-fcm-mf-t-o 'I knocked him down by shooting him.' 308 *ni-kwaškwi-tepe-en-a*, s-fcm-frg-i-o (irregular order but fcm could be considered f) 'I pushed his head away.' 310 *šaapot-aalakat-wi*, f-frg-s 'it has a hole through to the other side.' 319 *θaak-ho-ʔθen-wi*, f-xf-xf-s 'it is partly immersed sticking out of the water.' 320 *ni-θak-aalow-een-a*, s-f-frg-i-o 'I caught him by his tail.'

DECIPHERMENT OF THE

LINGUISTIC PORTION OF THE

MAYA HIEROGLYPHS *

The Maya were the only fully literate people of the aboriginal American world. The buildings and monuments of stone that they left are covered with their writings—writings of which little has yet been read except the dates with which they begin. Moreover, they wrote many books and manuscripts, and three such books of fairly late period have been preserved. These are the famous three Maya codices, and I propose, before the end of this paper, to read a very brief extract from one of them, and to show, in a very plain and simple way, what the Maya writing system was like, and how its signs were put together.

Included in this writing system is a group of signs and combinations of signs referring to a special kind of subject matter. These are signs denoting numerals, periods of time, and terms of the calendar, between which mathematical relations exist and the use of which constitutes a system of mathematics. The mathematical references of these signs have been determined from these mathematical relations that are observed to exist between them, and thus we can read the dates and the positions of the solar-lunar calendar that are recorded at the beginning of most inscriptions. Besides this mathematical record, there is the purely linguistic portion of the writings, between the parts of which we can observe grammatical or linguistic relations, but no mathematical

* Reprinted from pp. 479–502 of the *Smithsonian Report for 1941* (Washington: Government Printing Office, 1942). This paper was read before the Section on Anthropological Sciences of the Eighth American Scientific Congress, Washington, D. C., May 10–18, 1940.

relations. These purely linguistic portions are those with which I shall deal. I shall deal, moreover, with the writing in the codices, not that of the inscriptions, though the inscriptional writing is generally similar to that of the codices. It may surprise many to know that, in the codices, the nonmathematical, linguistic signs outnumber the mathematical ones by more than a hundred to one (not counting repetitions of the same sign). So much for the belief that the Maya writings are mainly mathematical.

When Champollion began the decipherment of Egyptian writing, he was in the relatively fortunate position of not having to oppose an extensive body of established doctrine holding that the markings were not writing but a nonlinguistic symbolism. To be sure there were the fantastic speculations of Athanasius Kircher, concerned wholly with the religious and mystical symbolism which he read into the hieroglyphs, but these were upheld by none of the scholarly disciplines and quickly went down before Champollion's irrefutable logic. At that time the philologist and literary scholar reigned supreme in the study of ancient cultures. Champollion therefore had only to prove the linguistic logic of his results to philologists; he needed not to advocate his methods to archaeologists, for there were none, except philologists. There was not then the specialized separation of disciplines which prevails now. At that time philology led the way, read inscriptions, and stimulated archaeology.

It is popularly supposed that the success of Champollion's effort was wholly due to the discovery of the Rosetta Stone with its bilingual inscription and that there is nothing corresponding to the Rosetta Stone in Maya hieroglyphs. Both suppositions are wrong. Champollion would have ultimately succeeded without a Rosetta Stone, for the inscriptions happened to be in a language that he knew. He knew Egyptian, that is Coptic, the late form of the language and still essentially the same tongue, which the ancient Egyptians spoke and wrote. Just so the Central American writings happen to be in a language that it is possible to know. They might have been in a dead language, and then the case would indeed have been difficult, but fortunately they are in Maya, which is still spoken and can be studied from many sources. But how do we know they are in Maya? This will be quite clear to a linguistic scholar, who appreciates that, if texts in an unknown character are in a language that he knows, it is likely that he can detect that fact from the nature and frequency of repeated collocations of signs. In addition, the meaning of various clusters of signs in the Maya system is known from tradition (e.g., the glyphs of the months) and others from pictures that accompany them in the codices. The hieroglyphs record a language in which the writings for a certain month and for 'sitting position' begin with the same sign, which is the image of a feather. This condition is satisfied only by the Maya language, in which the roots of these particular words and the root of the word 'feather' all begin with the same syllable. Again, it is a language in which the writings for 'snake, fish,' and a certain time period all begin with the same or with mutually interchangeable signs, a condition also satisfied by Maya. It is a language in which the writings for 'honeybee, earth,' and the name of a day begin the same, in which 'hold in the hand' and 'nothing' begin the same, in which 'spear' and 'noose' begin with the same sign, which is also found in the clusters that mean 'jaguar,' 'nine,' and 'lunar month,' and so on. The evidence mounts and becomes at last overwhelming. Not even Cholti or Tzeltal, the languages closest to Maya, can satisfy the requirements; only Maya can do so.

There exists also a lesser equivalent of the Rosetta Stone, i.e., the preserved names of the ancient months and other calendar terms with the sign clusters for writing them, the ways of writing the numerals, the 27 characters recorded by Bishop Landa, the sign clusters for the cardinal directions, the colors, quite a number of animals, and various gods—a collection of odd bits that, when gathered together, make a not inconsiderable total. Finally there are many texts in the codices in which the meaning is almost as plain as though a translation ran beside it, because of the detailed pictures that run parallel with the text and illustrate it. Thus we really do have a Maya Rosetta Stone, as well as a knowledge of the language of the texts, so that, given linguistic scholarship like that of Champollion, it is perfectly feasible to decipher and translate some of the texts NOW, and eventually all of them.

But, on the other hand, the linguistic decipherer today has to contend with the chasm that now exists between American archaeology and philology. The philological viewpoint, with its scholarly interest in texts simply as texts, has become rather strange and incomprehensible to modern American archaeology, with its high development, along the scientific side, of the logical correlating of strictly material evidence, the while its popular side and its financing is largely connected with the esthetic interest, and with the interest that attaches to concrete human subject matter, particularly that of an exotic kind. Now the linguistic and philological interest is to be distinguished both from the materially and physically scientific interest and from the estheticohuman one; for, while it is not entirely divorced from either, and it cannot live in a vacuum, yet it finds its main concern upon a different level, a level of its own. The linguistic scholar is interested in a text as the monument of a language arrested and preserved at a certain point of time. He is not primarily interested in the subject matter of the text, as either history, folklore, religion, astronomy, or whatnot, but in its linguistic form, which to him is the supreme interest of interests. From this proceeds his type of objectivity, an earnest that his reading will not be affected by theories concerned with the content of the writing. He puts aside content to concentrate on linguistic form. He aims to reconstruct the language as it actually was, with its consonants and vowels in their actual places in words, its paradigms of declension and conjugation and its patterns of syntax, thereby adding a new body of facts to the whole domain of linguistic taxonomy. A by-product of his research is the reading of history and culture, but it may be questioned if his discovery of strictly linguistic fact in a time perspective is not the more important. The decipherment of Hittite has proved to be far more important for the light it has thrown on the development of the Indo-European languages than for all the accounts of Hittite reigns and conquests. The battles and politics of the Hittites are as dead as a nail in Hector's coffin, but their verb forms and pronouns and common words are matters of live interest in American universities at this moment, since the accurate facts of the Hittite language revealed by careful decipherment are completely revolutionizing our concepts of Indo-European linguistics. This authoritative knowledge of Hittite could not have come about if the deciphering scholars had not been linguists who had slowly and carefully ascertained, by scholarly methods, with profound respect for the text as a text, the exact words and grammar, conceiving this as their paramount duty. It could not have come about if they had conceived their duty as that of reading off a sweeping survey of Hittite history and culture, or even of clothing the dry bones of archaeology with the flesh of human narrative, important as these things are.

The desiderata for Maya decipherment are no different. Reading Maya texts must be a slow, careful investigation of linguistic forms, regardless of the interest or lack of interest of their subject matter. We must not conceive it our task to read off sweepingly the Maya literature for the sake of the information on history, culture, religion, or whatever else may be contained in it. The annals of this subject are cumbered by such attempts to read off or "interpret" the whole corpus of the Maya codices at one fell swoop, from Brasseur de Bourbourg to one very recent such an attempt. Such amusements proceed from a longing for glamour and quick results, misconceiving what is the most valuable thing to be obtained from the results. On the other hand, much of the work of Cyrus Thomas and various bits of linguistic data pointed out by Morley and others have been at least in the right direction—they seem to have understood what the problem really is.

The Maya writing system was a complex but very natural way—natural to minds just beginning to exploit the idea of fixing language in visual symbols—of using small picture-like signs to represent the sounds of fractions of utterances (usually of a syllable or less in extent), combining these signs so that the combined fractions of utterance outlined the total utterance of a word or a sentence. Past study of this system has been considerably retarded by needless and sterile logomachy over whether the system, or whether any particular sign, should be called phonetic or ideographic. From a configurative linguistic standpoint, there is no difference. "Ideographic" is an example of the so-called mentalistic terminology, which tells us nothing from a linguistic point of view. No kind of writing, no matter how crude or primitive, symbolizes ideas divorced from linguistic forms of expression. A symbol when standing alone may symbolize a "pure idea," but, in order to represent an idea as one in a definite sequence of ideas, it must become the symbol for a linguistic form or some fraction of a linguistic form. All writing systems, including the Chinese, symbolize simply linguistic utterances. As soon as enough symbols for utterances have been assembled to correspond uniquely to a plainly meaningful sequence (phrase or sentence, e.g.) in the language being written, that assembly of signs will inevitably convey the meaning of that linguistic sequence to the reader native to that language, no matter what each sign may symbolize in isolation. Meaning enters into writing, writing of any kind, only in this way, and in no other. The meaning of any linear or temporal succession of symbols is not the sum of any symbolisms or denotations that the symbols may have in isolation, but is the meaning of the total linguistic form which that succession suggests. Hence the fact that some individual signs look like pictures of the things or ideas denoted by the words of the utterance plays no real part in the reading; those signs are just as much symbolic, learned, and at bottom arbitrary signs for fractions of utterance as any other characters or letters. On the other hand, resemblance to an object or picture may be really im-

Number	Sound	Symbol	Probable Object-Source	Maya Name of Object-Source
1.	ha, -a, -ah		scraper 'cepillo, o qualquier instrumento para raspar'	haab
2.	b		perforations 'pequeñas agujereados'	bis
3.	e		points, dots 'punta'	e
4.	h		opening, door 'abrir como puertas'	he
5.	haw hw		(face of) chief 'rey'	aháw
6.	hu hw -u		letter, book 'carta o libro'	huun
7.	i		nipples (of animal) 'teta de mujer y de qualquier animal'	im
8.	ka		pan 'lebrillo'	kat
9.	kak ka		no. 8 enlarged and doubled (?)	
10.	ka		lid tied on 'cerrar con cerradura, obrochar, atrancar'	kal
11.	kum		feather 'pluma de ave'	kukúm

Number	Sound	Symbol	Probable Object-Source	Maya Name of Object-Source
12.	l, le		loop, noose 'lazo para cozar'	le
13.	l, le		double loop (No. 12 doubled)	le
14.	l, lu, lo		drinking-cup (& loop) 'vaso para beber'	luč
15.	m ma		grasp of the hand 'asir, tomar con las manos, o empuñar'	mač
16.	mn men		?	?
17.	n, -an ne		tail 'cola'	ne
18.	s, sa		woven work in loom 'tela en el telar'	sakal
19.	si sin		stretched strings 'estender paños o cueros, colgar estendiendo, ormar lazos'	sin 'stretch or string'
20.	š, ša		road-crossings 'encrucijada de camino'	šay
21.	to, tu		flames (?) 'quemar'	took 'burn'
22.	s̨(ts)		face of dog (?) 'porro liso sin pelo'	som (from) 'hairless dog'
23.	u		crescent moon ? 'luna'	u 'moon'

Figure 3.   Examples of Maya symbols having phonetic values.

portant in decipherment, as a clue to how the sign came to be invented, to the logic of its original use, and hence to the fraction of utterance, i.e., sound, which answers to it in reading—a clue to be tested by how well that proposed fraction, or sound, fits into each proposed reading.

Figure 3 shows 23 symbols selected out of the several hundreds found in the whole Maya literature. These particular ones have been chosen because they enter into the written words and the codex sentence used as examples of decipherment in this paper. The fractions of utterance to which these signs regularly correspond have been identified by comparative evidence—running back ultimately to that body of evidence which I have called the Maya Rosetta Stone. Signs 1, 2, 3, 7, 8, 12,

17, 22, are also given by Landa with the same values (1, 7, 12, 17 being slightly altered in form) in his book *Relación de las cosas de Yucatán*, a first-hand account of the Maya shortly after the Conquest. The left-hand column shows in alphabetic order the fraction of utterance, i.e., sound which regularly [1] corresponds to the appearance of the sign in a written form. The next column to the right shows the usual appearance of the written sign, with common variants added in some cases. The list includes less than a third of all the signs the phonetic values of which I consider fairly well established. The column headed "Probable Object Source" names the thing or condition of which the written sign was probably at one time a picture. However, these theories of pictorial origins, while they seem probable and have a substantiating value, are not the evidence for the phonetic values, and their being proved wrong would not invalidate the latter nor alter the readings, but would merely mean that the ORIGIN of the sign was other than I have supposed. There are several signs for which I am unable to offer any explanation (e.g., no. 16), yet for which the phonetic value is reasonably certain. I did not guess the probable object source of no. 6 until after I had known its phonetic value for several years.

The extreme right-hand column shows the Maya word, as given in the Motul dictionary,[2] for the thing or condition postulated as the object

---

[1] Regularly but not always in the case of all these signs, for polyphony is a prevalent trait in Maya writing, as it is also in Sumerian and Akkadian (Babylonian) cuneiform. That is, various signs are polyphones, with two or more contrasting sets of sound values, besides the slightly differing values within a set, such as either *ha* or *h* with vowel lacking or indefinite, which slight differences are on another level than the polyphonic contrasts. The native reader, able to grasp words as wholes, is not confused by these polyphonic values; he knows from the other signs assembled with the one in question just which of the polyphonic values applies in a given case, just as the reader of English is not confused by the 'o' in 'women' or the 'olo' in 'colonel,' but is governed by the total collocation so that he reacts with fractions of utterance entirely unlike those regularly associated with the written forms o and olo. Polyphony is therefore the same type of thing as irregular spelling under an alphabetic system of writing. Thus the Maya sign no. 5 of Fig. 3 has also the value *la, l*, as in the writing of the word *lak'in, lik'in* 'east'; this value may very likely derive from the word *lalail* 'the largest, greatest, principal, chief'—a near-synonym of *ahaw*. Sign no. 15 occasionally has the value *č*, as in the writing of *čik'in* 'west'; this value probably derives from *čuk* 'catch or seize with the hand,' a near-synonym of *mač*.

[2] The Motul dictionary is an anonymous sixteenth century work ascribed to Fray Antonio de Ciudad Real, and is the most voluminous and authentic source of information on the Maya language at the time of the Conquest. Actually it is not only a dictionary but a grammar and a chrestomathy as well, for most of the word citations

source. It will be observed that the initial sound of this Maya name of the object (i.e., the first consonant and/or the first consonant and vowel) is the sound which the sign represents in writing, as shown in the left-hand column, except in the case of no. 1, in which the initial *h* is either lost or transposed, yielding *a* or *ah*. The Spanish entry under the English name of the object source is the way in which the Motul dictionary defines the Maya word in the extreme right-hand column.

Figure 3 then should be self-explanatory. The following supplementary remarks may be added: number 1 does not occur initially in a word. Primary word-initial *h* in Maya, in becoming secondarily word-internal, as when it begins the second member of a compound word, tends to be weakened or lost. This explains why a syllable originally denoting *ha* would denote *a* when used only to write noninitial fractions of words. Number 6 is especially interesting. Maya has simple, unanalyzable words for 'write' or 'book,' not connected with 'paint' or 'draw' as in Aztec and many other American languages. This fact, *ceteris paribus*, argues for the greater antiquity of writing in the Maya culture than in these other cultures. Maya missives and books (e.g., the codices) were written on an elongated strip of tissue which was then folded up, and, when tied or clasped, would have an appearance not unlike a modern letter sealed in its envelope, or like no. 6.[3] The nipple (*im*) sign for *i* appears in the codices usually with three nipples, which leads me to think that the teats of a deer or other animal may have been one of the

are accompanied by copious examples of phrases and sentences. The technique of stem composition in Maya of this period is beautifully brought out in these examples; the same is true of syntax. The Maya words in Fig. 3 are not cited in the conventional Maya orthography used in the Motul dictionary, but in the phonetic alphabet used by most present-day linguists for American Indian languages (the revised American Anthropological Association system), except that *ç* is used instead of *c* for the alveolar affricate (a sound like *ts*). The cedilla has been added to the *c* to avoid confusion with the *c* of Maya orthography which represents *k*. Symbol 22 is cited by Landa with the value *c*; it is unquestionable that he meant Spanish *ç* or the soft sound of *c*, as in the name of the letter "*ce*," which is very likely what he asked his Maya informant to write. This soft sound of *c* was close to *ts* in old Spanish, which is why it was equated to the Maya sign for *ts*, no. 22. The sounds *č* and *š* are English *ch* and *sh*, *k'* is a glottalized *k*; the language has a series of such glottalized sounds: *p', t', c', č', k'*. Through some curious omission, the Motul dictionary does not actually cite the word *ne*, 'tail,' but this is, of course, a well-known Maya word.

[3] As may be inferred from this, I regard the previous theories about what no. 6 represents, one of which calls it a kernel of maize (to which it has no resemblance), as fanciful. The fact that in some Maya pictures corn plants may sprout from characters of writing, and characters may take part in the scenes like persons or objects,

original forms; sometimes it appears with two; Landa shows it with two, and the sign of the day Ik (*ik'*) may be based on an original human breast form with only one. Number 8 probably represents a *kat*, an earthen, basketry, or wooden pan, tray, or low flat tub, often boat-shaped; it was also called a *ĉem* or 'boat' (see Motul, *chem licil ppo* and *chem che*), and conversely a boat may have been called a *kat*. The comblike lines may be the conventionalization of a fluted rim or of projecting basketry withes, or may represent people in a *kat* in the meaning 'boat.' Number 10 is an example of the many perspective drawings found in both Maya art and the writing symbols—a rounded, flattened pot, basket, or calabash with a *k'al*, a tied-on or clasped lid or cover. The Maya, as is well known, drew in perspective from very early times. Number 11 is a *k'uk'úm*, 'feather' or 'plume,' and in this word *k'úm* was probably felt to be the true initial form of the stem and *k'u-* a reduplication, which may not have been historically the case, but which would be felt analogically in a language like Maya in which initial reduplication is a derivational process in wide use. Nothing as yet is postulated as to the object source of 16, a profile head with a sort of parrotlike beak; a suggestion here would be the parrotlike bird called *moan* or *muan*. The sign corresponds to the consonantal sequence *mn*, with any or no vowel intervening, and as a day sign denotes the day Men. Number 23 looks very much like a form of no. 1, but it is always upright and placed in front of a sign cluster with its concave side

is secondary symbolism, not the original logic from which the character arose. All this elaborate secondary symbolism, perhaps religious and magical in large degree, has nothing whatever to do with the reading of the characters in their capacity of symbols of writing, any more than the elaborate symbolism and numerology that grew up around the Hebrew letters in rabbinical tradition affects the reading of the Hebrew text by one jot. This secondary symbolism may eventually become a matter of philo-logical literary study, wherein it will very likely prove important. At present, and from a linguistic standpoint, clearing away all this sort of symbolism is essential to understanding the proper symbolism and function of the Maya signs in writing. The use of no. 6 to denote the day Kan is a writing of the original name of the day Hu—i.e., 'lizard, iguana' (cf. Aztec Cuetzpalin, 'lizard,' for the same day). All the original names of the days, except for Ik, Cimi, Caban, and perhaps Manik, Cauac, and Eznab, and one or two more, became changed under the Maya culture after the establishment of the writing system. Some of the days continued to be represented by the initial letter or character of their original names, much as we write 'lb.' for 'libra,' but read it 'pound.' The voluminous speculations of Seler concerning the day symbols are to be taken with a great deal of caution, if they are not indeed stumbling blocks of the worst kind.

toward the cluster, while no. 1 is not placed in front of a cluster and is usually horizontal. Number 23 corresponds to initial *u* of a word or to *u* as a separate word or as a prefix.

Figure 4 shows the writing of six words occurring in the codices.[4] The sign clusters or glyphs of various animals, originally determined by Schellhas from their concurrence with pictures, have long been known.[5]

Figure 4.   Maya sign clusters representing words.

Number 1 is cited by Schellhas as the glyph meaning 'snake.' It will be noted that it consists of no. 8 of Figure 3, *ka*, and no. 17, *n*, and a third symbol. This third symbol and the iguana figure in the next glyph of Figure 4 are the only symbols cited in this paper which are not found in Figure 3. The first two symbols spell *kan*, which is the Maya word for 'snake.' The third symbol is probably derived from a picture of a

---

[4] In an unpublished paper read before the annual meeting of the American Anthropological Association at Washington, D. C., in December 1936, entitled "A comparative decipherment of forty-six Maya written words," I exhibited 46 word-writings similarly analyzed, including *hu* and *kumhu* of the present six.

[5] Paul Schellhas, *Göttergestalten der Mayahandschriften*, 1897.

rattlesnake's rattles, intended to evoke the linguistic response "snake," i.e., *kan*, and has itself the value *kan*. However, it is apparently insufficient by itself to write the word *kan*. It was not usual in the Maya system to write a word of one syllable simply by one sign having the value of that syllable, probably because that sign often was polyphonic, having other values. Instead, the Maya method was to suggest the syllable by a combination of signs that, to Maya speakers acquainted with the conventions of the writing, was probably unambiguous. This combination of signs could be made according to two principles: (1) synthetically, building the syllable from signs to be understood as fractions of the syllable, which together made the whole syllable; (2) by repeated affirmation, that is, by combining, in the sense of repeating, different ways of denoting the whole syllable. A word of one syllable, or often a syllable within a longer word, could be written by either method, or by both together, as in the case of this writing of the word *kan*. The signs *ka* and *n* build the word synthetically, the sign *kan* repeats it; we have double writing, but only single reading. It is as if the writing said "my first is *ka*, my second is *n*, my whole is one of the values of the snake-rattle sign, and so must be *kan*." The combination is, by sum of all its parts, *ka-n-kan*, but we may use the convention of transliteration *ka-n*^{kan} to show that the final *kan* is a doubling in the writing only, not in the reading.

Number 2, Figure 4, is the sign cluster meaning 'iguana,' or 'large lizard,' a meaning which is quite obvious, since it accompanies plain pictures of that animal, besides containing such a picture itself. But this one picture-like sign, no matter how much it may look like the animal, is not sufficient by itself to write the word meaning 'iguana.' The Maya system, as already noted, requires combination with at least one other sign before we can have a unit of writing, capable of standing alone. The exceptions to this rule form a very restricted list indeed, the most important ones being the 20-day signs, which are single elements enlarged to the size of a full cluster and capable of standing alone. The month glyphs and calendric and mathematical glyphs, in general, conform quite to the rule, being clusters of signs. Number 2 writes the one-syllable word *hu* 'iguana' entirely by the method of repeated affirmation, using the ordinary sign for *hu*, no. 6 of Figure 3, topped by an iguana figure, which of course has the linguistic value of the animal's name. Here the formula which we use in transliterating is *hu-hu*, to be read or pronounced, of course, as "*hu*."

Number 3 writes the word *kumhu*, the name of a Maya month, entirely by the synthetic method. It is the well-known glyph of this month Cumhu as found in the codices. It uses the feather sign *kum*, no. 11 of Figure 3, plus *hu*, no. 6; so we transliterate *kum-hu*. Some other words of the codices using the sign *kum*, no. 11 of Figure 3, are *kumah*, the stem "sit" with transitive suffix meaning 'seats' or 'carries seated,' and *kumaç*, another word meaning snake (cf. Quiche *kumaç* 'snake'). Although we are still somewhat in doubt concerning the values of the vowels in these words, the general phonetic contour is interestingly confirmed by the fact that the codices write *kumah* not only as *kum-ma* (with 11 and 15) but also as *kw-m-a*, while Landa cites a way of writing the month Cumhu which is the cluster of *kw-m-hw*; in both of which writings *kw* and *m* are signs not included in Figure 3 (but confirmed by other evidence) while *a* is 1 and *hw* is 5 of Figure 3.

Number 4 of Figure 4 occurs in texts of the Codex Tro-Cortesianus dealing with hunting and illustrated with hunting pictures. It is obviously a sign cluster or word referring to animals killed by spears or arrows, and the commentary in the Villacorta edition [6] of the Tro-Cortesianus calls it "signo de cacería por medio de flecha y lanza." It is a writing composed synthetically with doubling of one subsyllabic sign. At the top is the cup-and-loop sign *lu*, *lo*, no. 14 of Figure 3, written within the outlines of no. 15, *m*, *ma*, which is doubled, the lower member of the doubled pair enclosing the tail sign *n*, no. 17 of Figure 3. When we find doubled a sign which according to the total setup is probably to be interpreted as a syllabic confirmed by a subsyllabic, we may transliterate without the convention of writing a superscript, using instead a convention that permits of possible interpretation as a long consonant or vowel, e.g., in this case not *ma-ma* but *m-ma*. Number 4 is then transliterated *lu-m-ma-n* or *lo-m-ma-n*, which is a word meaning exactly what the accompaniment of pictured scenes tells us. It is the passive participial inflection in *-an* of the stem *lom*, which means a 'spearing or stabbing thrust or blow,' and by extension a 'spear,' while with the verbal inflection it denotes the occurrence of a spearing action. The Motul dictionary gives "*lom* : tiro de lanza, o dardo, y

[6] J. Antonio Villacorta C. and Carlos A. Villacorta, *Códices Mayas*, published in *Arqueología Guatemalteca*, 1932.

cosas assi, y estocada, o puñalada." This stem with the transitive verbal inflection is given by the Motul as "*lomah, ob* : fisgar, o harponear, dar estocada o puñalada, alancear y aguijonear," this citation being followed by that of the passive participial form, "*lomán* : cosa que esta assi fisgada." Hence this word *loman* written in the hieroglyphs of the Maya text means 'speared, stabbed; pierced, wounded or killed by a spear, arrow,' etc.

Number 5 of Figure 4 is synthetic with doubling of the inherent vowel of one sign. It is common in the hunting section of the Codex Tro-Cortesianus, and is obviously the word denoting catching of animals by a noose or lasso, or in a noose snare—a trap consisting of a noose set to spring by a stretched rope triggered and attached to a small bent-down tree so that, when the animal steps in the noose and releases the trigger, the tree springs back, drawing the slipknot of the noose and catching the animal. The glyph or sign cluster no. 5 accompanies pictures of this operation, e.g., Tro-Cortesianus 42c. Villacorta calls it "signo de cacería por trampa." It consists of the double loop or knot sign *l, le,* no. 13 of Figure 3, and the dot sign *e,* no. 3 of Figure 3, and is to be transliterated *le-e* and read *le* 'loop, noose, slipknot, noose trap or snare,' Motul "*le* : lazo para cazar y pescar, y pescar con lazo," with the verbal inflection, e.g., *leah* meaning 'catch or trap with noose snare,' for which the Motul gives the participial "*lean* : cosa enlazada o cogida en lazo." Here again we see the principle that a sign is inadequate by itself, in that no. 13, though itself derived from the picture of a slipknot or noose *le* and denoting the sound fraction *le,* is not sufficient alone to write the monosyllabic word having this sound, i.e., *le* 'noose,' but is subject to the rule that a sign must be combined with another and cannot stand alone. Here it has its inherent vowel reaffirmed by attachment of the sign *e.* Hence there is a mixture of the synthetic and the repeated-affirmation principles in sign clusters or glyphs of this type. We also find the verbally inflected form *leah* 'catch with noose,' written *le-e-a,* with no. 1 of Figure 3 for *a.* Cyrus Thomas correctly analyzed the *le-e* 'cluster,' I believe, though I worked it out without referring to his work. A number of Thomas' readings are undoubtedly correct.

In no. 6, Figure 4, we have one of the polysynthetic words common in Maya, in which two stems are compounded and suffixes attached. It is illustrated in Tro-Cortesianus, page 46, by three pictures showing vividly in successive stages of action a deer caught and jerked upward by the spring of the bent tree to which the noose of the trap is attached. It is written *le-e-sin-a* (or *-ah*), with signs 12, 3, 19, and 1 of Figure 3, and is to be read *lesinah*. This word is typical of a common kind of Maya compound, consisting of two stems with the verbal inflection suffixed after the second. The stems are *le*, already defined, and *sin* 'stretch or string tightly (as cloth, hides, or cords are stretched on a frame), draw taut, string with stretched cords, string up, string or rig a noose trap or the like to spring when released,' etc. The Motul gives "*zin* (i.e., *sin*) : estender paños o cueros y colgar estendiendo o tender desarrugando; armar lazos; armar arco o ballesta." Such a compound usually has the following type of meaning: designating the two stems as X and Y, a compound X-Y-*ah* or X-Y-*t-ah* [7] means do X by means of Y, transitively, or to an object. Thus, since *le-ah* means catch in a noose, we can form freely words such as *le-k'ab-ah* (or more modern *le-k'ab-t-ah*) 'catch in a noose by action of the hand' (*k'ab* 'hand'), *le-k'as-ah* 'catch in a noose by a tying action,' and so on. Our word *le-sin-ah* then means 'catch in a noose by the action *sin* or catch in a noose by tight stretching, catch by the spring of a tautly strung noose trap.' [8]

Now, having noted the reading of a few individual words, let us read a short sentence written in Maya hieroglyphs. Figure 5 shows page 38 of the Codex Tro-Cortesianus, and the sentence thereon to be examined in particular is that made by the four sign clusters or glyphs over the second seated figure in section *b*, the middle of the three horizontal divisions of the page. Figure 6 shows this sentence written on one line, analyzed, transliterated, and translated. As can easily be observed from Figure 5, the texts which comment on the pictures, or, to put it the other way, which are illustrated by the pictures, are placed over the pictures, reading from right to left across the width of the picture, and then on the line below similarly; or they run vertically downward in the cases where there are no pictures. This order is easily demonstrated from the

---

[7] The form with the suffix *-t-* before the suffix *-ah* is the common form in Maya of the Motul dictionary for binary compounds of this type.

[8] We find in the codices other compounds of this type, including some others with *sin* as second member; thus in the Tro-Cortesianus (e.g., 41*a*) the picture of a deer trussed up in a bundle, legs folded up, with cords lashed around it, is accompanied by the sign cluster *ma-sin-a* (with Landa's *ma* sign), to be read probably *massinah*, assimilated from *mačinah* (compound of stems *mač* and *sin*), meaning 'clasp together (like a clasped fist) by pulling and tension, by tight stringing, by tightly drawn cords.'

Figure 5. Page 38 of the Codex Tro-Cortesianus.

parallelism of the writing; we have here plainly a repetition of very similar short sentences or clauses. Thus, if we give a letter to each cluster or glyph which is the same, the middle-section text over the first or left-hand picture runs A–B, and then on the line below C–D, next to the right running straight downward we have A–B–E–F, then over the next picture A–B–C–D again, then downward again A–B–G–H. The texts of the top and bottom sections can be seen to run in the same manner, which indeed is general throughout the codices. The texts would seem to be in a style which is common enough in aboriginal American songs, chants, and ceremonies: sets of phrases containing a constant element repeated throughout a set, as when each line of a song stanza begins the same way but then introduces a certain difference. Thus the text which we have just examined consists of lines each beginning A–B and then becoming different. Navaho chants are of course typical cases of this sort of thing. In the top section, dealing, as the pictures show, with hunting by means of the spear, each clause begins with the word *loman* 'speared' that we have already studied. We shall not pause however to analyze this top section in detail, since the limits of this paper do not allow it.

The middle and bottom sections are very similar to each other, though not identical, and deal with drilling, as can be seen from the pictures. The pictures of the middle section show the using of the drill to make fire; the bottom set shows the drilling of an object which appears to be a stone. Each clause in each section begins with the word for drilling or drill, as is evident not only from comparison with these pictures, but also from one of the other Maya books, the Dresden Codex, in which the same sign cluster accompanies pictures of drilling. This cluster, A, occupies first position, which is the regular position of the predicating word of a clause in Maya of the sixteenth century (if not also today) as shown by the hundreds of short simple sentences in the Motul dictionary. This predicator need not be a formal verb in Maya grammar (though it most often is), but it is what corresponds to the predicate in an English translation. The final two words of each clause, C, D, ⋯ etc., are the well-known name glyphs of the Maya gods. They are the names of the persons shown in the pictures, as has long been known, and consequently they are undoubtedly the grammatical subjects of the clauses. The second cluster of each clause may be called B_1 in the middle section, B_2 in the bottom section, to indicate that it is the same throughout each section but differs between the two sections. By elimination and by position after the predicator, it should indicate the grammatical object and/or result of the verb action, which

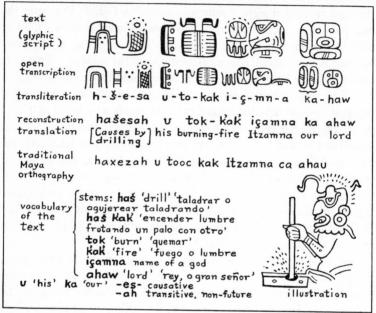

Figure 6. Analysis of a Maya sentence taken from page 38 of the Codex Tro-Cortesianus.

agrees with the fact that the drilling is pictured with different objects and results in the two sections. Thus we have, as a first schematization:

> A, predicator or verb (drilling)
> B_1, B_2, object and/or result (fire, stone)
> C, D, · · · etc., subject (names of gods or persons)

Figure 6 is a detailed exposition of the sentence over the second picture of the middle section, which shows the Roman-nosed god of the codices, or god D, making fire with a drill. The top line is a copy of the text, arranged from left to right on one line, instead of on two lines as in the original. This line, like the original text, is in glyphic script, the form of writing used in the codices. It closely resembles the monumental glyphic style of the stone inscriptions, but is less ornate and has more rounded outlines. In both these styles the signs in a cluster are gathered into a tight bunch or cartouche, in which they are grouped in two dimensions, and there is only a vestige of linear order in that the front or extreme left-hand part of a cluster never stands for the last part of a word, and similarly the rear or right-hand part never stands for the beginning of a word. The signs in a cluster are usually in contact and often fused together or enveloped in the same flowing outline; they may be attached to the top or bottom of a central sign, or they may be one within another; i.e., one sign may serve as the frame or ground of another. In short, the putting together of signs is more like a heraldic device than like our kind of writing.[9] But the reading of the signs is exactly as if they were written in linear order, although this order must be learned separately for each glyph and hence requires a separate and often prolonged study of each by the decipherer.

The second line from the top in Figure 6 shows the signs which compose each cluster regrouped in one-dimensional linear order. Such an arrangement I call open transcription or linear script, and there is some evidence that the Maya actually used such a form of script, though not in the inscriptions or in the codices that happen to have been preserved. Landa cites instances of the utterances *ma in k'ati* and *elele* written by a native informant in this manner,[10] the signs delineated consecutively from left to right and either close together or actually touching one another. It seems not unlikely that such a linear script may have been used by the later Maya for convenience in ordinary purposes, as the Egyptians used demotic, while the glyphic script would have been regarded as more hieratic and ornamental and used for important books,

[9] It should be pointed out that, even in our kind of writing, i.e., the alphabetic kind, linear order of signs is not quite absolute in many systems, which contain vestiges of an older two-dimensional way of grouping. Thus, in the writing of pointed Arabic, pointed Hebrew, and Pitman shorthand, the vowel points are grouped two-dimensionally with the consonantal signs, not written consecutively with them in the order of actual utterance. In the Devanagari alphabet the vowel signs are fused two-dimensionally with the consonant signs, and the vowel *i* to be uttered after a consonant is actually attached in front of that consonant. Our own '*wh*' is similarly written backward, being actually '*hw*'—a special cluster of signs that retains an unusual order of positions. Some monograms and modern advertising placards also use two-dimensional groupings of letters.

[10] Diego de Landa, *Relación de las cosas de Yucatán*. The first phrase means 'I do not want.' The second utterance is gibberish from the Maya standpoint, but, judging from the context, it evidently represents the informant's attempt to comply with a request to "write L-E, '*le*.'"

priestly writings, and inscriptions. Be that as it may, conversion of a passage of glyphic into open transcription is a device which is often helpful to the decipherer. It will be noted that all the signs in this passage are given in Figure 3, so that, from this line of open transcription, the whole utterance can be read off in rough outline, as shown in the third line or transliteration. Since many of the signs can be indefinite as to vocalic timbre, even when they imply a preferred inherent vowel, the vowels of the utterance are here and there doubtful, although the indication of definite vowels is generally much better than in Egyptian or unpointed Hebrew. To a certain extent, but by no means wholly, the transliteration of vowels is based on sixteenth century Maya, which can hardly have changed radically in this respect since the period of the codices, probably not very many centuries earlier; and it is also based partly on comparative evidence from other Mayan dialects, a field of research which must of course go hand in hand with scholarly and philological reading of the codices. But it must also be emphasized that the text itself contains unmistakable reference to many of its vowels; thus the signs *a*, *e*, *i*, *u* of Figure 3 are unambiguous in their indication of vowels, though the position of the vowel in the word may not always be clear. Thus we arrive at the transliteration, namely:

h-š-e-sa u-to-kak i-ç-mn-a k-ka-haw

The position of the *e* in the first word is not wholly clear, since this *e* is written inside both the *h* and the *s* signs; and another possible transliteration is *h-e-š-sa* or *he-e-š-sa*, to be read either *hešesah* or *heššah*, which would indicate that the stem which means 'drilling,' which is *haš* in sixteenth century Maya, was pronounced more nearly *heš* in the dialect of the codices. At present more evidence would be needed to confirm this, and the reading *hašesah* seems preferable, the vowel *a* not being indicated in the writing but a reasonable reconstruction from Maya linguistic evidence.

Under the transliteration is a reconstruction of the original sentence in the light of Maya linguistics, written in the usual Americanist phonetic system, and below the translation of this is a repetition of the reconstruction written in the traditional Maya orthography. This is included in order that Maya students may see the sentence written in the way most familiar to them, though the use of this traditional spelling for linguistic purposes is not to be recommended and imposes a handicap, indeed may breed quite misleading notions in the minds of students. Thus we have for the reconstruction:

Phonetic	*hašesah u-to · k-k'ak' içamna ka-ahaw*
Traditional	*haxezah u tooc kak Itzamna ca ahau*

Under the phonetic transcription is the literal translation: 'makes (or made) by drilling his burning-fire Itzamna our lord,' or in smoother English: 'Our lord Itzamna kindles (kindled) his fire with a drill.'

The first word is a derivative of the stem *haš* meaning 'twisting or rolling between the palms, drilling,' and with the verbal inflection, 'twist between the palms, work a drill, bore, drill.' The Motul has "*hax, ah, ab* (i.e. *haš, hašah, hašab*) : torcer con la palma o palmas de las manos y hazer tomiza, o cordel assi, y lo assi torcido" and again "*haxs* : taladrar o agujerar taladrando y la cosa taladrada o agujerada assi." This stem is the only word for drilling in Maya that I know of, so the case is particularly convincing. The word for 'a drill, the instrument,' is *hašab*; we do not have it in this codex, but rather the verbal inflection. The suffix *-es, -s* (followed by *-ah*) of the verbal inflection is causative, similar in meaning to the suffix *-bes; X-es-ah* means 'puts (put) it (grammatical object) into the condition X,' or else 'cause (caused) it to exist by the condition or action X, makes (made) it by X-ing, by doing X.' The second type of causative meaning is that which fits the present case. The suffix *-ah* denotes transitive action already accomplished, in contrast with *-ik*, transitive action not accomplished or not finished, either future or continuing in the present. Thus *hašesah* means 'makes (made) it by drilling.'

Makes what by drilling? According to our scheme above, that which is denoted by the next sign cluster, B_1. In the bottom section of the same page, the corresponding cluster B_2 denotes the stone or stone object being drilled. In that case 'makes by drilling' of course does not mean create the object wholly by drilling, but rather perform that step in the manufacture of the object that requires drilling. Hence in that case there is merely a subtle shade of difference between *hašesah* and *hašah* 'drills it.' To digress a little, cluster B_2 is probably to be read *e-i-l-l: e*, dots, here many instead of three, *i* of three nipples, and a form of double-loop *l* doubled by scratches (*lač*) between the loops. The word *eil* could mean 'edge tool,' i.e., 'weapon point, knife,' etc. Such points or knives were of course predominantly of stone among the Maya, and were no doubt sometimes drilled.

Returning to the middle-section text; here *hašesah* B_1 means 'makes B_1 by drilling,' actually in the sense of 'causes' or 'creates,' since B_1 evidently denotes 'fire.' This fits in well with the expression cited by the Motul for 'making fire with the firedrill': *hašah k'ak'* (*k'ak'* 'fire'), which uses the simpler or less inflected form *hašah* rather than *hašesah*. The Motul gives "*hax kak* (i.e., *haš-[ah] k'ak'*) : encender lumbre casando fuego frotando un palo con otro," also "*haxab kak* (*hašab k'ak'* 'drill for fire') : artificio o recaudo con que sacan fuego los indios."

The cluster B_1 is analyzed as *u-to-kak*, consisting of sign 23 of Figure 3, *u*; sign 21, *to*, *tu* (to be read here *to*); and 9 of Figure 3, which if it is a doubled and enlarged *ka* (no. 8) might be read *kaka*, *kak*, or simply *ka*. Here the reading *kak* fits exactly. The initial *u* here would denote the preposed third-person pronominal reference *u*. For our present purposes it is immaterial whether this be regarded as a prefix or a separate word always occurring immediately before nonpronominal stems. Owing wholly to the grammatical patterns of English (and other European languages), it must be translated as 'he (she, it, they)' if the following stem is translated as an English verb, but as 'his (her, its, their)' if that stem is translated as an English noun. From the Maya standpoint it denotes the same relationship at all times; Maya stems are neither nouns nor verbs in the English sense, but a single class delimited on a quite different basis from our parts of speech. The stem with which this *u* is in construction is what is written as *to-kak* in the rest of the cluster.

The writing *to-kak* however is only approximately phonetic, as with Maya writing in general; it suggests only in rough outline the sound of the utterance, from which suggestion the reader is expected to infer the right Maya word; the Maya application of phonetics in writing had progressed no farther than this, as we have already seen. Now the word that is apparently indicated is not what a modern Americanist phonetician understands by the transcription *tokak*, but rather what he would transcribe as *to·kk'ak'*. This is a compound word, *to·k-k'ak'*, consisting of the stems *to·k* 'burn, burning, ignition' (*o·* denotes long *o*) and *k'ak'* 'fire.' The Motul gives these as "*tooc* (i.e., *to·k*) : quemar, abrazar, y cosa quemada" and "*kak* (i.e., *k'ak'*) : fuego, o lumbre." Note that the Maya way of writing *to·kk'ak'* does not distinguish the glottalized palatal stop *k'* at the end of *k'ak'* from the corresponding unglottalized stop *k* at the end of *to·k*, nor does it distinguish the sequence of the two, *kk'* from either one singly nor the long vowel *o* from a short *o*. This is all part and parcel of the approximate and out-line-like character of the phoneticism, implicit rather than clearly conscious phoneticism, which Maya scribes employed. There is a phonemic difference between the simple and the glottalized stops in Maya, but it is a minimal difference. The writing used the same symbol for both a simple stop and the homorganic glottalized stop; instances of this are numerous. This does not mean that these were not distinct sounds in the Maya dialect of the codices. It is almost a certainty that they were distinct, just as they are in all modern dialects of Maya. They were not distinguished in writing probably in the same way that minimally differing phonemes (e.g., the long and short vowels of Latin) are often not distinguished in a writing system, because the native reader can always tell from the context which sound to supply. And this condition is no more than we meet, to varying degree, in all systems of writing other than those devised by linguistic scientists for the express purpose of an accuracy going beyond the needs of simple communication.

The expression *u-to·k-k'ak'* may be translated 'his burning fire,' or probably better 'his kindling fire, his igniting of fire.' It follows a type of Maya two-stem compound, probably the same type as already explained, though the idea of "by means of" here need not be injected into the translation. We now have attained to translation of the whole predicate: '(he) causes by drilling his ignition of fire'; and it is evident that this expression *hašesah u-to·k-k'ak* is but a more elaborate form of the *hašah k'ak'* cited by the Motul dictionary as the way of saying that one starts fire with a fire drill; it follows the same basic pattern.

I might here digress briefly, anticipating a misconceived objection that might be raised, to say that the sign cluster *to-kak* sometimes occurs in the codices where there is no pictured reference to fire, and seems in these cases to refer to an animal in a hunting scene. An instance of this is seen in Figure 5, top section, over the second picture, where occurs the cluster *to-kak-a*, with *-a* of no. 1, Figure 3, and without preceding *u-*, forming part of a sentence roughly analyzable as *loman u-NORTH tokaka X* 'speared (in) his north (is) (grammat. object)–X.' I shall suggest first, but not in seriousness, a type of explanation that overstresses the mentalistic approach. I shall suggest that the reason why this glyph accompanies both pictures of fire and pictures of a hunted animal is that it is a glyph which denotes sacrifice or a sacrifice: hence either a sacrificial fire or a sacrificial animal. Now apparently just this sort of explanation, with its thin veneer of ethnological allusion, sounds plausible to some minds that have engaged themselves with Maya hieroglyphs, and it is necessary to warn against it. This is the reason why no people but linguists should touch the hieroglyphs. In the present case of course, the explanation is an out-and-out concoction of my own, cooked up in a few seconds merely to illustrate a point. A trained linguist would, I believe, be inclined to ask: "Have you searched for an explanation in the configurations of utterances and in the data of the vocabulary, before adopting this quite speculative hypothesis?" The real reason no doubt is that, besides the stem *to·k* 'burn,' Maya has the similar sounding stem *tok* (with nonlong *o*) 'take away, take by force, capture, carry off,' etc. The Motul has "*toc, ah, ob* (i.e., *tok*) : quitar, tomar por fuerza, privar, arrebatar, robar y usurpar casas, y cosas muebles." The sign cluster *to-kak* in this case is not being used to write the compound word *to·k-k'ak'* but to write some similarly-sounding derivative or inflection of the stem *tok*, and the word probably means 'prey, animal taken or carried off, catch, game.' Possibly the word contains *tok* and the repetitive plural suffix *-ak*; hence '(successive) catches of game.' The context is enough to distinguish this word from the similarly-written word pertaining to fire.

The next sign cluster, *i-ç-mn-a*, writing the word *içamna* "Itzamna, name of the leading Maya god, the Roman-nosed god of the codices," is very important because it is the first proper name written in Maya hieroglyphs to be deciphered. Proper names and especially personal names have a peculiar convincingness in the decipherment of any script. They are ideal tools for decipherment when they can be had. When a decipherer can with the aid of his system spell out some well-known proper name which should occur in his text, he knows that he is on the right track. It will be remembered that it was the names of Ptolemy and Cleopatra in an inscription that gave Champollion his most effective clues, and similarly it was the names of Xerxes and Darius in the Behistun inscription that afforded Rawlinson his starting point for the decipherment of cuneiform. It has long been agreed that the Roman-nosed god of the codex pictures, or god D, corresponds in characters to the one traditionally known as Itzamna. His glyph is always written in this way. If we knew more of the ancient names of the gods, our progress in decipherment would be materially aided. Unfortunately the god Kukulcan, who appears so frequently in the codices, evidently is not called by that name in the codices, or else, if he is called by that name, it is written by a unitary word sign.

The next cluster, *k-ka-haw*, representing the pronunciation *kahaw*, is to be reconstructed *ka-ahaw* 'our lord, our master, our king.' This was the characteristic epithet of Itzamna as the Maya Zeus. In the Chilam Balam of Chumayel and also that of Tizimin, this god is referred to and called *Itzamna kavil*. Here *kavil* equals in the Americanist phonetic system, *k'awil*, from *kahawil* (glottalization arising from loss of -*ah*-) from *ka-ahawil*, which has the same meaning as *ka-ahaw*. Thus this decipherment may be likened to Rawlinson's recognition of 'king, great king, king of kings' after the name of Xerxes. The Motul defines *ahaw* as "*ahau* (*ahaw*) : rey o emperador, monarca, principe o gran señor." The preposed pronominal *ka* (traditional spelling *ca*) is the second-person plural governing the following word, the translation of the relationship being possessive when that word is translated as a noun, subject when it is translated by a verb. Here of course the translation is 'our.' The cluster *k-ka-haw* 'our lord' is an almost invariable accompaniment of the name Itzamna in the codices; rarely it is omitted, and rarely it occurs with the names of other gods. Occasionally also with names of gods we find the simple epithet *ahaw* 'lord,' written *a-hw*, with an *a* sign not listed in this paper but cited in slightly variant form by Landa, and with no. 6 of Figure 3 for *hw*. In accordance with the general principle of Maya writing that signs may not be used in isolation, except as day signs, the word *ahaw* is not written with sign 5 (*haw*) alone, except when it means the day Ahau.

Thus we arrive at our final translation: 'Our lord Itzamna kindles his fire by drilling.'

The importance of this decipherment and translation is quite independent of the interest or lack of interest of the subject matter. As far as concerns the information which this translation gives us about the Maya, or about its own subject matter, it is quite trivial; it is no more than we could have gathered from the pictures alone. Its importance is linguistic and philological—linguistic because it gives information about the structure of a language, as far as the writing can express it, at a certain period of past time; philological because it is precedent to the study of a literature and of culture as reflected in this literature, at a period of past time and in a historical context and perspective. From this one short sentence can be gathered a host of linguistic and philological data, only a small fraction of which has been discussed in this paper, data which can be tested and correlated, and employed heuristically in further investigations, of progressive difficulty. A very few of these further ramifications of this sentence are barely hinted at in the footnotes, which the exigencies of space have kept relatively brief. Each such footnote actually represents an extensive study. In this way the decipherment establishes itself upon a constantly growing enlacement of sentences, their translations controlled by sets of pictures, which sentences mutually give rise to a growing grammar, syntax, vocabulary, and sign list.

There are two main wrong ways of trying to read the Maya codices. One wrong way is to attempt a clean sweep of the job—to retire into seclusion and eventually emerge with a book—a book which "tells all," which reels off, interprets, explains, epitomizes, and comments on everything from page 1 of the Tro-Cortesianus to the last page of the Dresden. There have been several such books in the past hundred years. Usually such books proclaim the discovery of a key. This key is then applied at the author's sweet will, and the trick is turned as easily as a magician lifts a rabbit out of a hat. Often, moreover, such an author has exposed his slight acquaintance with the Maya language and with linguistic procedures in general. Historical writings are not to be read with keys; there is never any key but research. The amateur decipherer is prone to make a false analogy between straightforward writing and a cipher. Actually the very word "decipher" which I have employed so profusely in this essay, embodies a misconception. Why have I used it? I suppose because it is simple and vivid, it has been generally used for this sort of research, and I have succumbed to usage. But really one does not decipher a literature; one deciphers only a cipher. A cipher is a method of writing with deliberate intent to conceal the content from those who do not possess the key. It is deciphered with a key because it has first been enciphered with a key. A straightforward writing, not intended to conceal its tenor from all but a select few, is not really deciphered; it is analyzed and translated. The methods of such analysis and translation are quite different from the methods of message decoders; they are the methods of Champollion and Young with Egyptian, of Rawlinson and Grotefend with Babylonian, of Hrozny and Sturtevant with Hittite; they are the methods of linguistics and philology.

The other wrong way of attacking the linguistic portion of the Maya codices is the Sitzenfleisch approach. It concentrates for long periods upon isolated glyphs or words, having conveniently forgotten that such things as sentences exist. Suppose that, in this method, one succeeds in deciphering or partly deciphering the glyph of Itzamna. Then one next spends years scrutinizing every glyph of Itzamna in the literature, noting the most minute differences, to the pen quirk, and linking it up first with every scrap of information that can be gleaned about Itzamna, then with every god in the Middle American area that can be connected with Itzamna. The mere glyph disappears from view, having served as the springboard into a sea of mythology, religion, and folklore, from which one may perhaps emerge at last with a monograph entitled "The Concept of Itzamna." This method, through concentrating entirely on word study, wanders so far from the specific incidences of the word in the texts that it finally ceases to be linguistic altogether, and becomes something else. Words are nothing without sentences. What a word is depends on what it does: i.e., on its position and function in the sentence. This is even more important than how it is written. In Maya as in English there are many homonyms, and also words which though not homonyms are written alike, as in English are 'lead' (the metal) and 'lead' (go in front). Hence the determination of the sounds of signs and of their glyphic combinations is only half the battle.

There is only one road to decipherment of the Maya hieroglyphs and reading of the Maya literature. It is through a growing concatenation of sentences, proceeding from the less to the more difficult, beginning with sentences whose meaning can be understood from pictures, with the linguistic interest and linguistic findings kept constantly foremost, and conclusions relative to subject matter resolutely submerged. The linguistic findings must eventually bear the scrutiny of, and become the ground of, collaboration for various linguistic scholars. One man cannot be the medium for interpreting a literature; such a task requires the mutual contributions of many scholars who are able to proceed in general agreement as to basic principles. Linguistic principles alone carry the conviction necessary to such scientific agreement.

As the research progresses and expands and grows more sure, it becomes able to read with some confidence sentences which lack pictures to control the translation. We shall thus begin to read cautiously portions of the inscriptions, and the long pictureless texts of the Peresianus codex whose meaning is now utterly mysterious. As the major linguistic difficulties are conquered, the study becomes more and more philological; that is to say, subject matter, cultural data, and history play an increasing role—it becomes a matter not only of reading but also of understanding as much as possible the allusions, the references, the nonlinguistic contexts, the cultural patterns which are seen by glimpses, as it were, through the bare words and grammar of the translations. This is philology. But as the base of philology we must have linguistics. Only in this way can we ever hope to understand the history and culture of the Maya.

LINGUISTIC FACTORS

IN THE TERMINOLOGY

OF HOPI ARCHITECTURE *

The common material of Hopi buildings is stone. Adobe, the usual
building material of the Rio Grande country, is rarely used. The
stone is quarried and roughly dressed by the Hopi themselves, and set
up without mortar. Walls are stone, roofs and floors above ground are
tamped earth or clay several inches thick on a layer of close-set poles laid
across cylindrical timbers or beams ledged in the walls. Interior surfaces
of walls and ceilings are usually finished with a clay plaster or stucco,
and then whitewashed with a fine white clay; exteriors are sometimes
stuccoed, usually left in bare masonry. One-story buildings are the most
frequent, but two-story ones are not uncommon, and in Walpi even
occasional third stories are to be seen. Stairways and ladders, both of
which are used, are external to the buildings. The pit house or kiva,
used for ceremonial purposes, is essentially similar except that it is buried
and wholly or partially hollowed out of the ground, its upper portion
projecting like a well-curb and bearing a roof with a hatchway for the
entrance ladder.

Hopi has a fairly considerable number of terms for what might be
called structural elements or component parts of a building, including
essential appurtenances to a building such as ladders, stairs, and windows.

* Reprinted from *Int. J. Amer. Linguistics*, 19:141–145 (1953). This article was
prepared by Whorf for presentation to the New York and Yale informal linguistic
group at its meeting on February 25, 1940. The manuscript was among the papers
left by Whorf to George L. Trager. It was checked by Edward A. Kennard.

Such terms are grammatically all nouns. The following is a representative list; it follows the order of construction, from the foundations up.

kiŋa 'foundation,' or 'foundations'; *te'kʷa* 'an erection of masonry,' not a part of a finished building, 'unfinished wall, unroofed wall, or standing portion of a ruin'; *tekʷánmère* 'encircling or enclosing wall'; *te·wi* 'ledge, shelf, or setback,' applied both to a natural ledge and to the architectural form; *tekʷni* 'wall,' chiefly a roofed wall, but also applied to a finished stone fence or rampart; *ʔe'ci* 'partition,' or 'closure' of any kind; *ʔeʔécpi, ʔecpi* 'door,' i.e. closing piece or door proper; *hóciwa* 'door opening, doorway'; *poksö* 'vent hole, unglazed window, chimney'; *panávca* 'piece of glass, glazed window'; *nayáve* 'adobe brick'; *palwi, pálwicôqa* 'plastering clay,' used as stucco whitewash, and 'floor clay'; *ki·qôlö* 'lowest story of a building of more than one story, or a sunken room like a basement; story with a floor above it'; *ké·vèla, ké·vèɭpi* 'ceiling'; *wúna* piece of timber of any kind, 'board, plank, post, log, pole,' whether placed in structure or not; *lèstàvi* 'beam or joist of roof or upper floor, timber or log' for this purpose, usually when in place in the structure; *kiqálmö* 'eaves,' or 'cornice'; *kí·ʔàmi* 'roof' (not however the term in such expressions as 'on the roof'); *kiska* 'tunnel or covered way, roofed passage.'

Of these 19 terms, which are some of the most common ones, 8 are unanalyzable stems, or in a few cases partially and conjecturally analyzable; the other 11 are transparent derivatives or compounds.

Terms of this class, all denoting structural elements or parts, are nouns, having the noun declension of two cases, nominative and objective, and a set of construct-state or possessed forms. They all denote three-dimensional solids in the geometrical sense, solid and rigid masses, or definitely bounded areas on or perforations through such solids.

As we look over the grammatical class of nouns we are struck by the absence of terms for interior three-dimensional spaces, such as our words 'room, chamber, hall, passage = interior passage, cell, crypt, cellar, attic, loft, vault, storeroom,' etc., in spite of the fact that Hopi buildings are frequently divided into several rooms, sometimes specialized for different occupancies. We should never notice this state of affairs unless we approached it from the grammatical viewpoint first, for, if we simply ask the informant for the word for 'room' we shall certainly get a reply— a word which to him is the equivalent and translation of our word 'room.' Nevertheless, this word, and a few other words used to denote interior spaces, on examination will be found to have different grammatical or paradigmatic properties from the words for architectural elements or structural members which we have just noted. They do not seem to be nouns in the strict sense at least. The word for 'room' $\partial \acute{a}' p \grave{a} v \varepsilon \partial$, has no nominative or objective case and no construct state; one cannot say, based on this stem, 'my room,' whereas one CAN say 'my door' or 'my ceiling' even though these expressions have no socially functioning meaning, for Hopi society does not reveal any individual proprietorship or retainership of rooms, doors, OR ceilings. Here we see the difference between a purely linguistic or formulaic meaning, which COULD be said but probably would not be said, like 'my ceiling,' and the case of a cultural and practically recognizable meaning which also coincides with linguistic meaning, like 'my house.' On the contrary, an expression formally equivalent to English 'my room' DOES NOT EXIST, or have even a formulaic meaning; there is a gap here in the language as compared to ours. If the Hopi should borrow from us the custom of having individual "own" rooms, or should rent individual rooms when they visited other Hopi villages, they would STILL be unable to say 'my room.' What they would probably do would be to coin a new expression for this need. There are many ways they could do this. They could say for instance 'my ceiling,' 'my door,' or 'my floor,' and in time the word 'ceiling,' 'door,' or 'floor,' as the case might be, would acquire the extended meaning of an individual person's own room, like French *foyer* 'hearth' meaning one's home. This slight digression from the main topic will serve to illustrate the conservativism of grammatical patterns and their resistance to change as compared to simple lexical items.

Returning to the word for 'room' $\partial \acute{a}' p \grave{a} v \varepsilon \partial$, let us examine its case properties. Though it has not the noun cases nominative and objective, it has the cases locative, illative, and ablative $\partial \acute{a}' p \grave{a} v \varepsilon \partial$, $\partial \acute{a}' p \grave{a} m i q$, $\partial \acute{a}' p \grave{a} \eta k$, case-relations which are found among pronouns, along with a number of others of similar nature called the locational cases. But pronouns have the nominative and objective cases also, as well as other peculiar properties all their own. It will be found that $\partial \acute{a}' p \grave{a} v \varepsilon \partial$ belongs to a part of speech called LOCATORS, which include such words as 'here, there, above, below, in front, in back, north, south, east, west,' and a good many others, among them the Hopi geographical names, such as Oraibi, Walpi, Shipaulovi. These all have a paradigm of locational cases, and every form ends in suffix; there is no bare-stem form such as exists in nouns and therein forms the nominative. In saying 'north' it is necessary to say 'in the north, from the north, to the north,' etc. These are forms that all belong in the predicate, while something else serves as the subject, or else there is no subject. In other words they are adverbial forms. The word translated 'room' means 'in a house, room, or other enclosed chamber' or, more precisely, 'in an architectural interior,' or 'into' such an interior, or 'from' such an interior, etc., according to the case suffix. The *-vε?* suffix in *?á'pàvε?* is the locative. There is also a quasilocative suffix *-vi* or *-pi* which cannot be applied to the stem *?á'pa-*, nor to most of these locationals, but can be applied to geographical place names and one or two other special words for 'room.'

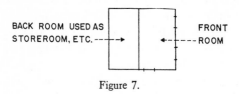

Figure 7.

Its locative sense is so weak that it can be used as a nominative or objective noun, though this use is rare. The chief other word for interior space in a building is locative *yé·mòkvi*, illative *yé·mòk*, often translated 'the other room' or 'the next room'—but it is also used equivalent to 'back room, closet, recess, spare room, storeroom.' Perhaps the closest semantic effect in English would be 'inner room,' though this must be construed 'inner' in the sense of the Hopi illative, which would include 'further room' or 'adjoining room.' It is any chamber one goes INTO from another interior which is the point of reference. One of the most common room plans of a Hopi house is shown in Figure 7.

This is in line with the way Hopi and, in fact, most or all Uto-Aztecan languages represent location in space, or regions of space. They are not set up as entities that can function in a sentence like terms for people, animals, or masses of matter having characteristic form, or, again, human groups and human relations, but are treated as PURELY RELATIONAL CONCEPTS, of an adverbial type. Thus hollow spaces like room, chamber, hall, are not really NAMED as objects are, but are rather LOCATED; i.e. positions of other things are specified so as to show their location in such hollow spaces. Contrasted with the considerable number of terms for solid architectural members, there seems at first a remarkable paucity of terms for architectural HOLLOW SPACES, with only two stems of any practical importance. At first one might be led to ascribe this to something culturally peculiar in Hopi architecture—their concepts of building construction are limited and one-sided as a given cultural fact, we might suppose. On more intimate knowledge of the language we see that it has nothing to do with the architecture that there is this paucity of terms where we have a rich array of terms; it is a matter of the structure of the language. It is not the two stems that determine paucity or richness of expression, but the large array of suffixes with locational case-endings which may be used on these stems, because they belong to

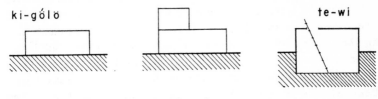

Figure 8.

the locator group. In the locator group the number of initial stems is not an important criterion of vocabulary richness; it is rather the profusion of suffixes, which in this group are in effect noninitial stems.

Now there is still a third class of architectural terms to be considered—terms for different types of buildings. There are certainly different structural types of building among the Hopi. The three main types may be illustrated by diagrams (Figure 8).

These buildings are put to various specialized uses. Most are dwellings, but the so-called piki-houses are used only as bakeries for baking piki or Hopi corn wafers; others are used only for storehouses, the kivas only for ceremonies. Since white influence there are buildings occupied solely as stores, churches, and schools. Now we, and many peoples much less sophisticated architecturally than the Hopi, have a vocabulary of different terms for buildings: we have the terms 'house, building, cottage, castle, fort, temple, church, chapel, palace, theater, school, store, inn, hotel, barn, shed, garage, stable, hut, shack, shanty, prison, jail, tower, station, depot' and so on. Many of the terms denote occupancy-types; others structural types. It might be noted, from a detached viewpoint, that this English list is quite a miscellany and has practically no system to it. However, it seems to us the NATURAL THING, for a people who have a building technology at least as diversified as the Hopi.

Yet the fact is that, except for a few marginal terms of extremely restricted application (below), the Hopi language has only one word for a building; and it may be said, without any qualifications, that the language has no architectural terminology that classifies buildings into types—in spite of the fact that it does have a considerable architectural terminology serving another purpose. There is only the word *ki·he* 'house' (as usually translated), which really means 'building' of any kind. This word is a noun, but the only noun of its kind in the language. This word 'house,' though not compounds ending in '-house,' can serve as base or initial stem for suffixing the vocabulary of locational suffixes terminating in locational case endings, as if it were a pronoun or a locator. Certain other nouns can take a few of these suffixes, but 'house' is the only one that can take the entire set. In this respect it is like a place pronoun, but it is not a pronoun, for it has the construct state forms which only nouns have, so that one can say 'my house,' 'your house,' etc.

The marginal cases which might possibly be considered terms for building other than *ki·he* may be cited, and it will be seen that these hardly denote true buildings in the usual sense: *mecávki* 'tent,' lit. 'cloth house'—a foreign object to the Hopi, and denoted by a compound of 'house'; *té·tèska* 'shrine'—a small, crude enclosure of stones, covered over and located outdoors; *kiska* 'tunnel'—also a covered outdoor passage with walls and roof, usually connecting different buildings.

One reason for the great paucity of Hopi building terms is that the Hopi either do not use occupancy terms as synonymous with the term for the building housing the occupancy, or, if they do this, they have begun to do it only recently, and few terms of this sort have accumulated. They do not have, at least not firmly rooted, the pattern which is so natural to us, in which 'a church,' i.e. an institution, is a term that merges quite imperceptibly into 'a church' meaning a type of building used as a meeting place for this institution, with the distinction hardly felt until attention is called to it; or in which 'a school,' the institution, is hardly distinguished from 'a school,' i.e. a schoolhouse, or 'garage' denoting a kind of occupancy from 'garage' the building housing this occupancy, or 'hospital' the occupancy from 'hospital' the building, or 'the theater' in the sense of 'the dramatic art' from 'the theater,' a building. The Hopi language does not have this imperceptible fusion, but rather a distinction between the two. The occupancy and the spot of ground or floor on which the occupancy occurs is called simply 'the building,' a *ki·he*. This is not a matter of stylistics, for it is not variable by the artistic modulations of the speaker, but of linguistics, for it is a form which the native speaker must follow willy-nilly, just as much as he must follow matters of grammar. The occupancy of a piki-house is called by a term which means 'place where the griddle is set up,' but it would be called that if set up outdoors, and there is no term for the piki-house itself, except in English, although the piki-house is a rather distinct architectural type.

The fact that occupancy terms can be used in conjunction with the separate and uncombined word 'building,' with its array of inflected forms, to specify all sorts of places both outside and inside of given buildings, makes up for the lack of building terms, so far as fluency of expression goes. However, it seems rather queer that there should be no terms for such distinctly different shapes of buildings as e.g. the one-story building, the two-story setback building, and the kiva; this fact has to be recorded as a peculiar datum of the language not explainable either from other patterns in the language or from anything in the architecture or anything else in the culture.

It seems especially queer from the standpoint of our ways of thinking that there should be no name for the kiva, that structure so highly typical of pueblo culture and so intimately connected with their religion.

Many people know that our word kiva is taken from Hopi, but they think that it is the Hopi word for a kiva, which it is not.

TERMINOLOGY OF HOPI BUILDING CONSTRUCTION

Unanalyzable stems: *ʔá·pa-* 'interior,' *ʔá·pàveʔ* 'at the inside'; *ʔé·ci* 'door,' *ʔé·cpi*, *ʔéʔe·cpi* 'at the door'; *ʔéci* 'closure, partition'; *sa·qa* 'ladder'; *té·kwa* 'something built of stones, but not finished building, erection of stones, unfinished wall, standing portion of a ruin'; *té·wi* 'ledge, shelf' (natural or architectural); *wéna* 'a timber, board, plank.'

ki·he 'building, house.'

Compounds with *-ki*: occupancy terms: *hé·yaNki* 'store, trading post'; *té·teqàyki* 'school.'

Locator suffixes: *kíco²o-* 'roof,' *kicó²òvi* 'from the roof,' *kicó²òmiq* 'to the roof'; *yé·mok* 'into another enclosure, room, closet,' etc., *yé·mokvì* 'far inside.'

Compounds and miscellaneous architectural terms: *kiŋa, ki·het ŋa²at* 'foundation (root of the house)'; *kiska* 'tunnel, covered way'; *kí·coki* 'village'; *kí·sonvi* 'plaza'; *hóciwa* 'opening, doorway'; *kɛ́·vɛla* 'ceiling'; *kiqálmo* 'eaves, cornice'; *kí·qölô* 'lowest story of a house, cave'; *lɛ́stavi* 'viga, beam, roof support'; *mecávki* 'tent'; *nayávɛ* 'adobe'; *pálwicôqa* 'plastering clay'; *panávca* 'window, glass, mirror'; *poksö* 'vent hole, chimney, window hole'; *tekʷni* 'roofed wall, stone fence'; *tekʷánmère* 'enclosing wall, corral.'

SCIENCE AND LINGUISTICS *

E very normal person in the world, past infancy in years, can and does
talk. By virtue of that fact, every person—civilized or uncivilized—
carries through life certain naïve but deeply rooted ideas about talking
and its relation to thinking. Because of their firm connection with
speech habits that have become unconscious and automatic, these
notions tend to be rather intolerant of opposition. They are by no
means entirely personal and haphazard; their basis is definitely systematic, so that we are justified in calling them a system of natural logic—
a term that seems to me preferable to the term common sense, often
used for the same thing.

According to natural logic, the fact that every person has talked
fluently since infancy makes every man his own authority on the process
by which he formulates and communicates. He has merely to consult
a common substratum of logic or reason which he and everyone else are
supposed to possess. Natural logic says that talking is merely an incidental process concerned strictly with communication, not with formulation of ideas. Talking, or the use of language, is supposed only to
"express" what is essentially already formulated nonlinguistically. Formulation is an independent process, called thought or thinking, and is
supposed to be largely indifferent to the nature of particular languages.
Languages have grammars, which are assumed to be merely norms of
conventional and social correctness, but the use of language is supposed

* Reprinted from *Technol. Rev.*, 42:229–231, 247–248, no. 6 (April 1940).

to be guided not so much by them as by correct, rational, or intelligent THINKING.

Thought, in this view, does not depend on grammar but on laws of logic or reason which are supposed to be the same for all observers of the universe—to represent a rationale in the universe that can be "found" independently by all intelligent observers, whether they speak Chinese

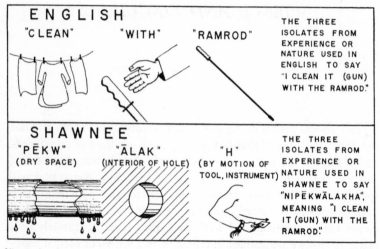

Figure 9. Languages dissect nature differently. The different isolates of meaning (thoughts) used by English and Shawnee in reporting the same experience, that of cleaning a gun by running the ramrod through it. The pronouns 'I' and 'it' are not shown by symbols, as they have the same meaning in each language. In Shawnee ni- equals 'I'; -a equals 'it.'

or Choctaw. In our own culture, the formulations of mathematics and of formal logic have acquired the reputation of dealing with this order of things: i.e., with the realm and laws of pure thought. Natural logic holds that different languages are essentially parallel methods for expressing this one-and-the-same rationale of thought and, hence, differ really in but minor ways which may seem important only because they are seen at close range. It holds that mathematics, symbolic logic, philosophy, and so on are systems contrasted with language which deal directly with this realm of thought, not that they are themselves specialized extensions of language. The attitude of natural logic is well shown in an old quip about a German grammarian who devoted his whole life to the study of the dative case. From the point of view of natural logic, the dative case and grammar in general are an extremely minor issue. A different attitude is said to have been held by the ancient Arabians: Two princes, so the story goes, quarreled over the honor of putting on the shoes of the most learned grammarian of the realm; whereupon their father, the caliph, is said to have remarked that it was the glory of his kingdom that great grammarians were honored even above kings.

The familiar saying that the exception proves the rule contains a good deal of wisdom, though from the standpoint of formal logic it became an absurdity as soon as "prove" no longer meant "put on trial." The old saw began to be profound psychology from the time it ceased to have standing in logic. What it might well suggest to us today is that, if a rule has absolutely no exceptions, it is not recognized as a rule or as anything else; it is then part of the background of experience of which we tend to remain unconscious. Never having experienced anything in contrast to it, we cannot isolate it and formulate it as a rule until we so enlarge our experience and expand our base of reference that we encounter an interruption of its regularity. The situation is somewhat analogous to that of not missing the water till the well runs dry, or not realizing that we need air till we are choking.

For instance, if a race of people had the physiological defect of being able to see only the color blue, they would hardly be able to formulate the rule that they saw only blue. The term blue would convey no meaning to them, their language would lack color terms, and their words denoting their various sensations of blue would answer to, and translate, our words "light, dark, white, black," and so on, not our word "blue." In order to formulate the rule or norm of seeing only blue, they would need exceptional moments in which they saw other colors. The phenomenon of gravitation forms a rule without exceptions; needless to say, the untutored person is utterly unaware of any law of gravitation, for it would never enter his head to conceive of a universe in which bodies behaved otherwise than they do at the earth's surface. Like the color blue with our hypothetical race, the law of gravitation is a part of the untutored individual's background, not something he isolates from that background. The law could not be formulated until bodies that always fell were seen in terms of a wider astronomical world in which bodies moved in orbits or went this way and that.

Similarly, whenever we turn our heads, the image of the scene passes across our retinas exactly as it would if the scene turned around us. But this effect is background, and we do not recognize it; we do not see a room turn around us but are conscious only of having turned our heads in a stationary room. If we observe critically while turning the head or eyes quickly, we shall see, no motion it is true, yet a blurring of the

Figure 10. Languages classify items of experience differently. The class corresponding to one word and one thought in language A may be regarded by language B as two or more classes corresponding to two or more words and thoughts.

scene between two clear views. Normally we are quite unconscious of this continual blurring but seem to be looking about in an unblurred world. Whenever we walk past a tree or house, its image on the retina changes just as if the tree or house were turning on an axis; yet we do not see trees or houses turn as we travel about at ordinary speeds. Sometimes ill-fitting glasses will reveal queer movements in the scene as we look about, but normally we do not see the relative motion of the environment when we move; our psychic makeup is somehow adjusted to disregard whole realms of phenomena that are so all-pervasive as to be irrelevant to our daily lives and needs.

Natural logic contains two fallacies: First, it does not see that the phenomena of a language are to its own speakers largely of a background character and so are outside the critical consciousness and control of the speaker who is expounding natural logic. Hence, when anyone, as a natural logician, is talking about reason, logic, and the laws of correct thinking, he is apt to be simply marching in step with purely grammatical facts that have somewhat of a background character in his own language or family of languages but are by no means universal in all languages and in no sense a common substratum of reason. Second, natural logic confuses agreement about subject matter, attained through use of language, with knowledge of the linguistic process by which agreement is attained: i.e., with the province of the despised (and to its notion superfluous) grammarian. Two fluent speakers, of English let us say, quickly reach a point of assent about the subject matter of their speech; they agree about what their language refers to. One of them, A, can give directions that will be carried out by the other, B, to A's complete satisfaction. Because they thus understand each other so perfectly, A and B, as natural logicians, suppose they must of course know how it is all done. They think, e.g., that it is simply a matter of choosing words to express thoughts. If you ask A to explain how he got B's agreement so readily, he will simply repeat to you, with more or less elaboration or abbreviation, what he said to B. He has no notion of the process involved. The amazingly complex system of linguistic patterns and classifications, which A and B must have in common before they can adjust to each other at all, is all background to A and B.

These background phenomena are the province of the grammarian—or of the linguist, to give him his more modern name as a scientist. The word linguist in common, and especially newspaper, parlance means something entirely different, namely, a person who can quickly attain agreement about subject matter with different people speaking a number of different languages. Such a person is better termed a polyglot or a multilingual. Scientific linguists have long understood that ability to speak a language fluently does not necessarily confer a linguistic knowledge of it, i.e., understanding of its background phenomena and its systematic processes and structure, any more than ability to play a good game of billiards confers or requires any knowledge of the laws of mechanics that operate upon the billiard table.

The situation here is not unlike that in any other field of science. All real scientists have their eyes primarily on background phenomena that cut very little ice, as such, in our daily lives; and yet their studies have a way of bringing out a close relation between these unsuspected realms of fact and such decidedly foreground activities as transporting goods, preparing food, treating the sick, or growing potatoes, which in time may become very much modified, simply because of pure scientific investigation in no way concerned with these brute matters themselves. Linguistics presents a quite similar case; the background phenomena with which it deals are involved in all our foreground activities of talking and of reaching agreement, in all reasoning and arguing of cases, in all law, arbitration, conciliation, contracts, treaties, public opinion, weighing of scientific theories, formulation of scientific results. Whenever agreement or assent is arrived at in human affairs, and whether or not mathematics or other specialized symbolisms are made part of the procedure, THIS AGREEMENT IS REACHED BY LINGUISTIC PROCESSES, OR ELSE IT IS NOT REACHED.

As we have seen, an overt knowledge of the linguistic processes by which agreement is attained is not necessary to reaching some sort of agreement, but it is certainly no bar thereto; the more complicated and difficult the matter, the more such knowledge is a distinct aid, till the point may be reached—I suspect the modern world has about arrived at it—when the knowledge becomes not only an aid but a necessity. The situation may be likened to that of navigation. Every boat that sails is in the lap of planetary forces; yet a boy can pilot his small craft around a harbor without benefit of geography, astronomy, mathematics, or international politics. To the captain of an ocean liner, however, some knowledge of all these subjects is essential.

When linguists became able to examine critically and scientifically a large number of languages of widely different patterns, their base of reference was expanded; they experienced an interruption of phenomena hitherto held universal, and a whole new order of significances came into their ken. It was found that the background linguistic system (in other words, the grammar) of each language is not merely a reproducing instrument for voicing ideas but rather is itself the shaper of ideas, the program and guide for the individual's mental activity, for his analysis of impressions, for his synthesis of his mental stock in trade. Formulation of ideas is not an independent process, strictly rational in the old sense, but is part of a particular grammar, and differs, from slightly to

greatly, between different grammars. We dissect nature along lines laid
down by our native languages. The categories and types that we isolate
from the world of phenomena we do not find there because they stare
every observer in the face; on the contrary, the world is presented in a

OBJECTIVE FIELD	SPEAKER (SENDER)	HEARER (RECEIVER)	HANDLING OF TOPIC, RUNNING OF THIRD PERSON
SITUATION 1 a.			ENGLISH... "HE IS RUNNING" HOPI... "WARI" (RUNNING. STATEMENT OF FACT)
SITUATION 1 b. OBJECTIVE FIELD BLANK DEVOID OF RUNNING			ENGLISH..."HE RAN" HOPI... "WARI" (RUNNING, STATEMENT OF FACT)
SITUATION 2			ENGLISH..."HE IS RUNNING" HOPI ... "WARI" (RUNNING, STATEMENT OF FACT)
SITUATION 3 OBJECTIVE FIELD BLANK			ENGLISH..."HE RAN" HOPI ... "ERA WARI" (RUNNING, STATEMENT OF FACT FROM MEMORY)
SITUATION 4 OBJECTIVE FIELD BLANK			ENGLISH..."HE WILL RUN" HOPI ... "WARIKNI" (RUNNING, STATEMENT OF EXPECTATION)
SITUATION 5 OBJECTIVE FIELD BLANK			ENGLISH..."HE RUNS" (E.G. ON THE TRACK TEAM) HOPI ... "WARIKNGWE" (RUNNING, STATEMENT OF LAW)

Figure 11. Contrast between a "temporal" language (English) and a "timeless"
language (Hopi). What are to English differences of time are to Hopi differences
in the kind of validity.

kaleidoscopic flux of impressions which has to be organized by our
minds—and this means largely by the linguistic systems in our minds.
We cut nature up, organize it into concepts, and ascribe significances
as we do, largely because we are parties to an agreement to organize it
in this way—an agreement that holds throughout our speech community
and is codified in the patterns of our language. The agreement is, of
course, an implicit and unstated one, BUT ITS TERMS ARE ABSOLUTELY

OBLIGATORY; we cannot talk at all except by subscribing to the organization and classification of data which the agreement decrees.

This fact is very significant for modern science, for it means that no individual is free to describe nature with absolute impartiality but is constrained to certain modes of interpretation even while he thinks himself most free. The person most nearly free in such respects would be a linguist familiar with very many widely different linguistic systems. As yet no linguist is in any such position. We are thus introduced to a new principle of relativity, which holds that all observers are not led by the same physical evidence to the same picture of the universe, unless their linguistic backgrounds are similar, or can in some way be calibrated.

This rather startling conclusion is not so apparent if we compare only our modern European languages, with perhaps Latin and Greek thrown in for good measure. Among these tongues there is a unanimity of major pattern which at first seems to bear out natural logic. But this unanimity exists only because these tongues are all Indo-European dialects cut to the same basic plan, being historically transmitted from what was long ago one speech community; because the modern dialects have long shared in building up a common culture; and because much of this culture, on the more intellectual side, is derived from the linguistic backgrounds of Latin and Greek. Thus this group of languages satisfies the special case of the clause beginning "unless" in the statement of the linguistic relativity principle at the end of the preceding paragraph. From this condition follows the unanimity of description of the world in the community of modern scientists. But it must be emphasized that "all modern Indo-European-speaking observers" is not the same thing as "all observers." That modern Chinese or Turkish scientists describe the world in the same terms as Western scientists means, of course, only that they have taken over bodily the entire Western system of rationalizations, not that they have corroborated that system from their native posts of observation.

When Semitic, Chinese, Tibetan, or African languages are contrasted with our own, the divergence in analysis of the world becomes more apparent; and, when we bring in the native languages of the Americas, where speech communities for many millenniums have gone their ways independently of each other and of the Old World, the fact that languages dissect nature in many different ways becomes patent. The relativity of all conceptual systems, ours included, and their dependence upon language stand revealed. That American Indians speaking only their native tongues are never called upon to act as scientific observers is in no wise to the point. To exclude the evidence which their languages offer as to what the human mind can do is like expecting botanists to study nothing but food plants and hothouse roses and then tell us what the plant world is like!

Let us consider a few examples. In English we divide most of our words into two classes, which have different grammatical and logical properties. Class 1 we call nouns, e.g., 'house, man'; class 2, verbs, e.g., 'hit, run.' Many words of one class can act secondarily as of the other class, e.g., 'a hit, a run,' or 'to man (the boat),' but, on the primary level, the division between the classes is absolute. Our language thus gives us a bipolar division of nature. But nature herself is not thus polarized. If it be said that 'strike, turn, run,' are verbs because they denote temporary or short-lasting events, i.e., actions, why then is 'fist' a noun? It also is a temporary event. Why are 'lightning, spark, wave, eddy, pulsation, flame, storm, phase, cycle, spasm, noise, emotion' nouns? They are temporary events. If 'man' and 'house' are nouns because they are long-lasting and stable events, i.e., things, what then are 'keep, adhere, extend, project, continue, persist, grow, dwell,' and so on doing among the verbs? If it be objected that 'possess, adhere' are verbs because they are stable relationships rather than stable percepts, why then should 'equilibrium, pressure, current, peace, group, nation, society, tribe, sister,' or any kinship term be among the nouns? It will be found that an "event" to us means "what our language classes as a verb" or something analogized therefrom. And it will be found that it is not possible to define 'event, thing, object, relationship,' and so on, from nature, but that to define them always involves a circuitous return to the grammatical categories of the definer's language.

In the Hopi language, 'lightning, wave, flame, meteor, puff of smoke, pulsation' are verbs—events of necessarily brief duration cannot be anything but verbs. 'Cloud' and 'storm' are at about the lower limit of duration for nouns. Hopi, you see, actually has a classification of events (or linguistic isolates) by duration type, something strange to our modes of thought. On the other hand, in Nootka, a language of Vancouver Island, all words seem to us to be verbs, but really there are no classes 1 and 2; we have, as it were, a monistic view of nature that gives us only one class of word for all kinds of events. 'A house occurs' or 'it houses' is the way of saying 'house,' exactly like 'a flame occurs' or 'it burns.' These terms seem to us like verbs because they are inflected for durational and temporal nuances, so that the suffixes of the word for house event make it mean long-lasting house, temporary house, future house, house that used to be, what started out to be a house, and so on.

Hopi has one noun that covers every thing or being that flies, with the exception of birds, which class is denoted by another noun. The former noun may be said to denote the class $(FC–B)$—flying class minus bird. The Hopi actually call insect, airplane, and aviator all by the same word, and feel no difficulty about it. The situation, of course, decides any possible confusion among very disparate members of a broad linguistic class, such as this class $(FC–B)$. This class seems to us too large and inclusive, but so would our class 'snow' to an Eskimo. We have the same word for falling snow, snow on the ground, snow packed hard like ice, slushy snow, wind-driven flying snow—whatever the situation may be. To an Eskimo, this all-inclusive word would be almost unthinkable; he would say that falling snow, slushy snow, and so on, are sensuously and operationally different, different things to contend with; he uses different words for them and for other kinds of snow. The Aztecs go even farther than we in the opposite direction, with 'cold,' 'ice,' and 'snow' all represented by the same basic word with different terminations; 'ice' is the noun form; 'cold,' the adjectival form; and for 'snow,' "ice mist."

What surprises most is to find that various grand generalizations of the Western world, such as time, velocity, and matter, are not essential to the construction of a consistent picture of the universe. The psychic experiences that we class under these headings are, of course, not destroyed; rather, categories derived from other kinds of experiences take over the rulership of the cosmology and seem to function just as well. Hopi may be called a timeless language. It recognizes psychological time, which is much like Bergson's "duration," but this "time" is quite unlike the mathematical time, T, used by our physicists. Among the peculiar properties of Hopi time are that it varies with each observer, does not permit of simultaneity, and has zero dimensions; i.e., it cannot be given a number greater than one. The Hopi do not say, "I stayed five days," but "I left on the fifth day." A word referring to this kind of time, like the word day, can have no plural. The puzzle picture (Fig.

11, page 213) will give mental exercise to anyone who would like to figure out how the Hopi verb gets along without tenses. Actually, the only
practical use of our tenses, in one-verb sentences, is to distinguish among
five typical situations, which are symbolized in the picture. The timeless Hopi verb does not distinguish between the present, past, and future
of the event itself but must always indicate what type of validity the
SPEAKER intends the statement to have: (a) report of an event (situations
1, 2, 3 in the picture); (b) expectation of an event (situation 4); (c) generalization or law about events (situation 5). Situation 1, where the
speaker and listener are in contact with the same objective field, is divided by our language into the two conditions, 1*a* and 1*b*, which it calls
present and past, respectively. This division is unnecessary for a language which assures one that the statement is a report.

Hopi grammar, by means of its forms called aspects and modes, also
makes it easy to distinguish among momentary, continued, and repeated
occurrences, and to indicate the actual sequence of reported events.
Thus the universe can be described without recourse to a concept of
dimensional time. How would a physics constructed along these lines
work, with no T (time) in its equations? Perfectly, as far as I can see,
though of course it would require different ideology and perhaps different mathematics. Of course V (velocity) would have to go too. The
Hopi language has no word really equivalent to our 'speed' or 'rapid.'
What translates these terms is usually a word meaning intense or very,
accompanying any verb of motion. Here is a clue to the nature of our
new physics. We may have to introduce a new term I, intensity. Every
thing and event will have an I, whether we regard the thing or event as
moving or as just enduring or being. Perhaps the I of an electric charge
will turn out to be its voltage, or potential. We shall use clocks to
measure some intensities, or, rather, some RELATIVE intensities, for the
absolute intensity of anything will be meaningless. Our old friend acceleration will still be there but doubtless under a new name. We shall
perhaps call it V, meaning not velocity but variation. Perhaps all
growths and accumulations will be regarded as V's. We should not
have the concept of rate in the temporal sense, since, like velocity, rate
introduces a mathematical and linguistic time. Of course we know that
all measurements are ratios, but the measurements of intensities made
by comparison with the standard intensity of a clock or a planet we do

not treat as ratios, any more than we so treat a distance made by comparison with a yardstick.

A scientist from another culture that used time and velocity would have great difficulty in getting us to understand these concepts. We should talk about the intensity of a chemical reaction; he would speak of its velocity or its rate, which words we should at first think were simply words for intensity in his language. Likewise, he at first would think that intensity was simply our own word for velocity. At first we should agree, later we should begin to disagree, and it might dawn upon both sides that different systems of rationalization were being used. He would find it very hard to make us understand what he really meant by velocity of a chemical reaction. We should have no words that would fit. He would try to explain it by likening it to a running horse, to the difference between a good horse and a lazy horse. We should try to show him, with a superior laugh, that his analogy also was a matter of different intensities, aside from which there was little similarity between a horse and a chemical reaction in a beaker. We should point out that a running horse is moving relative to the ground, whereas the material in the beaker is at rest.

One significant contribution to science from the linguistic point of view may be the greater development of our sense of perspective. We shall no longer be able to see a few recent dialects of the Indo-European family, and the rationalizing techniques elaborated from their patterns, as the apex of the evolution of the human mind, nor their present wide spread as due to any survival from fitness or to anything but a few events of history—events that could be called fortunate only from the parochial point of view of the favored parties. They, and our own thought processes with them, can no longer be envisioned as spanning the gamut of reason and knowledge but only as one constellation in a galactic expanse. A fair realization of the incredible degree of diversity of linguistic system that ranges over the globe leaves one with an inescapable feeling that the human spirit is inconceivably old; that the few thousand years of history covered by our written records are no more than the thickness of a pencil mark on the scale that measures our past experience on this planet; that the events of these recent millenniums spell nothing in any evolutionary wise, that the race has taken no sudden spurt, achieved no commanding synthesis during recent millenniums, but has only played a little with a few of the linguistic formulations and views of nature bequeathed from an inexpressibly longer past. Yet neither this feeling nor the sense of precarious dependence of all we know upon linguistic tools which themselves are largely unknown need be discouraging to science but should, rather, foster that humility which accompanies the true scientific spirit, and thus forbid that arrogance of the mind which hinders real scientific curiosity and detachment.

LINGUISTICS AS

AN EXACT SCIENCE *

The revolutionary changes that have occurred since 1890 in the world
of science—especially in physics but also in chemistry, biology, and
the sciences of man—have been due not so much to new facts as to new
ways of thinking about facts. The new facts themselves of course have
been many and weighty; but, more important still, the realms of research
where they appear—relativity, quantum theory, electronics, catalysis,
colloid chemistry, theory of the gene, Gestalt psychology, psychoanalysis,
unbiased cultural anthropology, and so on—have been marked to an
unprecedented degree by radically new concepts, by a failure to fit the
world view that passed unchallenged in the great classical period of
science, and by a groping for explanations, reconciliations, and restate-
ments.

I say new ways of THINKING about facts, but a more nearly accurate
statement would say new ways of TALKING about facts. It is this USE OF
LANGUAGE UPON DATA that is central to scientific progress. Of course,
we have to free ourselves from that vague innuendo of inferiority which
clings about the word 'talk,' as in the phrase 'just talk'; that false opposition which the English-speaking world likes to fancy between talk
and action. There is no need to apologize for speech, the most human
of all actions. The beasts may think, but they do not talk. 'Talk'
OUGHT TO BE a more noble and dignified word than 'think.' Also we
must face the fact that science begins and ends in talk; this is the re-

* Reprinted from *Technol. Rev.*, 43:61–63, 80–83 (December 1940).

verse of anything ignoble. Such words as 'analyze, compare, deduce, reason, infer, postulate, theorize, test, demonstrate' mean that, whenever a scientist does something, he talks about this thing that he does. As Leonard Bloomfield has shown, scientific research begins with a set of sentences which point the way to certain observations and experiments, the results of which do not become fully scientific until they have been turned back into language, yielding again a set of sentences which then become the basis of further exploration into the unknown. This scientific use of language is subject to the principles or the laws of the science that studies all speech—linguistics.

As I was concerned to point out in a previous article, "Science and linguistics," in the *Review* for April, we all hold an illusion about talking, an illusion that talking is quite untrammeled and spontaneous and merely "expresses" whatever we wish to have it express. This illusory appearance results from the fact that the obligatory phenomena within the apparently free flow of talk are so completely autocratic that speaker and listener are bound unconsciously as though in the grip of a law of nature. The phenomena of language are background phenomena, of which the talkers are unaware or, at the most, very dimly aware—as they are of the motes of dust in the air of a room, though the linguistic phenomena govern the talkers more as gravitation than as dust would. These automatic, involuntary patterns of language are not the same for all men but are specific for each language and constitute the formalized side of the language, or its "grammar"—a term that includes much more than the grammar we learned in the textbooks of our school days.

From this fact proceeds what I have called the "linguistic relativity principle," which means, in informal terms, that users of markedly different grammars are pointed by their grammars toward different types of observations and different evaluations of externally similar acts of observation, and hence are not equivalent as observers but must arrive at somewhat different views of the world. (A more formal statement of this point appears in my article of last April.) From each such unformulated and naïve world view, an explicit scientific world view may arise by a higher specialization of the same basic grammatical patterns that fathered the naïve and implicit view. Thus the world view of modern science arises by higher specialization of the basic grammar of the Western Indo-European languages. Science of course was not CAUSED by this grammar; it was simply colored by it. It appeared in this group of languages because of a train of historical events that stimulated commerce, measurement, manufacture, and technical invention in a quarter of the world where these languages were dominant.

The participants in a given world view are not aware of the idiomatic nature of the channels in which their talking and thinking run, and are perfectly satisfied with them, regarding them as logical inevitables. But take an outsider, a person accustomed to widely different language and culture, or even a scientist of a later era using somewhat different language of the same basic type, and not all that seems logical and inevitable to the participants in the given world view seems so to him. The reasons that officially pass current may strike him as consisting chiefly of highly idiomatic "façons de parler." Consider the answers that were at one time given even by learned men to questions about nature: Why does water rise in a pump? Because nature abhors a vacuum. Why does water quench fire? Because water is wet or because the fiery principle and the watery principle are antithetical. Why do flames rise? Because of the lightness of the element fire. Why can one lift a stone with a leather sucker? Because the suction draws the stone up. Why does a moth fly toward a light? Because the moth is curious or because light attracts it. If once these sentences seemed satisfying logic, but today seem idiosyncrasies of a peculiar jargon, the change did not come about because science has discovered new facts. Science has adopted new linguistic formulations of the old facts, and, now that we have become at home in the new dialect, certain traits of the old one are no longer binding upon us.

We moderns are not yet in a position to poke fun at the wiseacres of old who explained various properties of water by its wetness. The terminology which we apply to language and cultural phenomena is often of a piece with the wetness of water and nature's abhorrence of a vacuum. The researches of linguists into the ways of languages many and diverse are needed if we are to think straight and escape the errors which unconscious acceptance of our language background otherwise engenders. An increasing contribution from linguistics to the general philosophy of science is demanded by the new ways of thinking implied by those new realms of science cited at the beginning of this essay. It is needed for science's next great march into the unknown.

The situation is not likely to be aided by the philosophical and mathematical analyst who may try to exploit the field of higher linguistic symbolism with little knowledge of linguistics itself. Unfortunately the essays of most modern writers in this field suffer from this lack of apprenticeship training. To strive at higher mathematical formulas for linguistic meaning while knowing nothing correctly of the shirt-sleeve rudiments of language is to court disaster. Physics does not begin with atomic structures and cosmic rays, but with motions of ordinary gross physical objects and symbolic (mathematical) expressions for these movements. Linguistics likewise does not begin with meaning nor with the

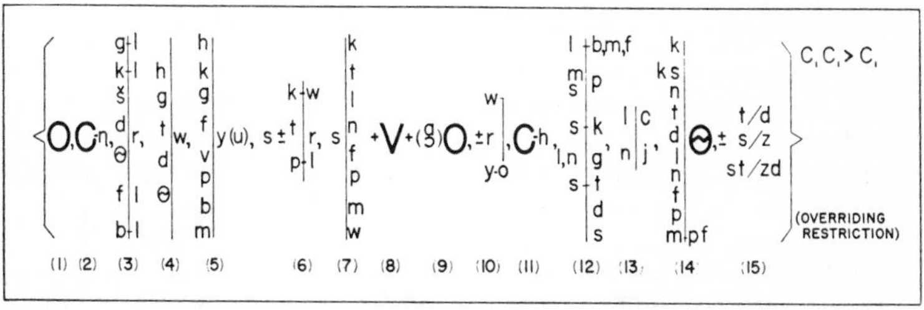

Figure 12. Structural formula of the monosyllabic word in English (standard mid-western American). The formula can be simplified by special symbols for certain groups of letters, but this simplification would make it harder to explain. The simplest possible formula for a monosyllabic word is $C + V$, and some languages actually conform to this. Polynesian has the next most simple formula, $O, C + V$. Contrast this with the intricacy of English word structure, as shown above.

structure of logical propositions, but with the obligatory patterns made by the gross audible sounds of a given language and with certain symbolic expressions of its own for these patterns. Out of these relatively simple terms dealing with gross sound patterning are evolved the higher analytical procedures of the science, just as out of the simple experiments and mathematics concerning falling and sliding blocks of wood is evolved all the higher mathematics of physics up into quantum theory. Even the facts of sound patterning are none too simple. But they illustrate the unconscious, obligatory, background phenomena of talking as nothing else can.

For instance, the structural formula for words of one syllable in the English language (Fig. 12) looks rather complicated; yet for a linguistic pattern it is rather simple. In the English-speaking world, every child between the ages of two and five is engaged in learning the pattern expressed by this formula, among many other formulas. By the time the child is six, the formula has become ingrained and automatic; even the little nonsense words the child makes up conform to it, exploring its possibilities but venturing not a jot beyond them. At an early age the formula becomes for the child what it is for the adult; no sequence of sounds that deviates from it can even be articulated without the greatest difficulty. New words like "blurb," nonsense words like Lewis

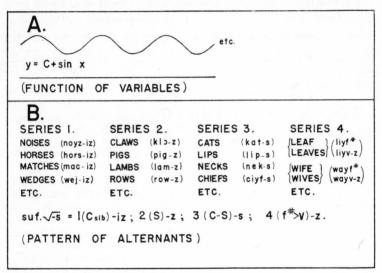

A.

$y = C + \sin x$

(FUNCTION OF VARIABLES)

B.

SERIES 1.	SERIES 2.	SERIES 3.	SERIES 4.
NOISES (noyz-iz)	CLAWS (klɔ-z)	CATS (kat-s)	{LEAF } {LEAVES} {liyf# } {liyv-z}
HORSES (hors-iz)	PIGS (pig-z)	LIPS (lip-s)	
MATCHES (mac-iz)	LAMBS (lam-z)	NECKS (nek-s)	{WIFE } {WIVES} {wayf# } {wayv-z}
WEDGES (wej-iz)	ROWS (row-z)	CHIEFS (ciyf-s)	
ETC.	ETC.	ETC.	ETC.

$\text{suf.}\sqrt{-s} = 1(C_{sib})\text{-iz} ; \ 2(S)\text{-z} ; \ 3(C\text{-}S)\text{-s} ; \ 4(f\#{>}v)\text{-z}.$

(PATTERN OF ALTERNANTS)

Figure 13. Variables and alternants: *A* shows by graph and by mathematical formula (equation) an interrelation of variables. *B* illustrates by extensible examples and by a pattern formula an interrelation of alternants. The formula means that the English suffix which is theoretically ("by root," ∨) a final 's' is actualized in any given case by one of four alternants: after a sibilant-ending consonant, by '-iz'; after any sonant (vowel or consonant), by '-z,' after any voiceless (nonsonant) consonant by '-s'; except that, after the special alternant 'f♯,' it is actualized by '-z,' the 'f♯' alternating to 'v.'

Carroll's "mome raths," combinations intended to suggest languages of savages or animal cries, like "glub" and "squonk"—all come out of the mold of this formula. When the youth begins to learn a foreign language, he unconsciously tries to construct the syllables according to this formula. Of course it won't work; the foreign words are built to a formula of their own. Usually the student has a terrible time. Not even knowing that a formula is back of all the trouble, he thinks his difficulty is his own fault. The frustrations and inhibitions thus set up at the start constantly block his attempts to use foreign tongues. Or else he even HEARS by the formula, so that the English combinations that he makes sound to him like real French, for instance. Then he suffers less inhibition and may become what is called a "fluent" speaker of French—bad French!

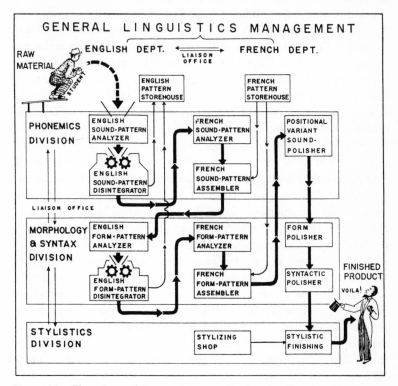

Figure 14. Flow sheet of improved process for learning French without tears. Guaranteed: no bottlenecks in production.

If, however, he is so fortunate as to have his elementary French taught by a theoretic linguist, he first has the patterns of the English formula explained in such a way that they become semiconscious, with the result that they lose the binding power over him which custom has given them, though they remain automatic as far as English is concerned. Then he acquires the French patterns without inner opposition, and the time for attaining command of the language is cut to a fraction (see Fig. 14).

To be sure, probably no elementary French is ever taught in this way—at least not in public institutions. Years of time and millions of dollars' worth of wasted educational effort could be saved by the adoption of such methods, but men with the grounding in theoretic linguistics are as yet far too few and are chiefly in the higher institutions.

Let us examine the formula for the English monosyllabic word (Fig. 12). It looks mathematical, but it isn't. It is an expression of pattern symbolics, an analytical method that grows out of linguistics and bears to linguistics a relation not unlike that of higher mathematics to physics. With such pattern formulas, various operations can be performed, just as mathematical expressions can be added, multiplied, and otherwise operated with; only the operations here are not addition, multiplication, and so on, but are meanings that apply to linguistic contexts. From these operations, conclusions can be drawn and experimental attacks directed intelligently at the really crucial points in the welter of data presented by the language under investigation. Usually the linguist does not need to manipulate the formulas on paper but simply performs the symbolic operations in his mind and then says: "The paradigm of class A verbs can't have been reported right by the previous investigator"; or "Well, well, this language must have alternating stresses, though I couldn't hear them at first"; or "Funny, but *d* and *l* must be variants of the same sound in this language," and so on. Then he investigates by experimenting on a native informant and finds that the conclusion is justified. Pattern-symbolic expressions are exact, as mathematics is, but are not quantitative. They do not refer ultimately to number and dimension, as mathematics does, but to pattern and structure. Nor are they to be confused with theory of groups or with symbolic logic, though they may be in some ways akin.

Returning to the formula, the simplest part of it is the eighth term (the terms are numbered underneath), consisting of a V between plus signs. This means that every English word contains a vowel (not true of all languages). As the V is unqualified by other symbols, any one of the English vowels can occur in the monosyllabic word (not true of all syllables of the polysyllabic English word). Next we turn to the first term, which is a zero and which means that the vowel may be preceded by nothing; the word may begin with a vowel—a structure impossible in many languages. The commas between the terms mean "or." The second term is C minus a long-tailed *n*. This means that a word can begin with any single English consonant except one—the one linguists designate by a long-tailed *n*, which is the sound we commonly write *ng*, as in "hang." This *ng* sound is common at the ends of English words but never occurs at the beginnings. In many languages, such as Hopi, Eskimo, or Samoan, it is a common beginning for a word. Our patterns set up a terrific resistance to articulation of these foreign words beginning with *ng*, but as soon as the mechanism of producing *ng* has been explained and we learn that our inability has been due to a habitual pattern, we can place the *ng* wherever we will and can pronounce these words with the greatest of ease. The letters in the formula thus are not always equivalent to the letters by which we express our words in ordinary spelling but are unequivocal symbols such as a linguist would assign to the sounds in a regular and scientific system of spelling.

According to the third term, which consists of two columns, the word can begin with any consonant of the first column followed by *r*, or with *g, k, f*, or *b* followed by *l*. The *s* with a wedge over it means *sh*. Thus we have 'shred,' but not *shled*. The formula represents the fact that *shled* is un-English, that it will suggest a Chinese pronunciation of 'shred' or a German's of 'sled' (*sl* is permitted by term 7). The Greek theta means *th*; so we have 'thread' but not *thled*, which latter suggests either a Chinese saying 'thread' or a child lisping 'sled.' But why aren't *tr, pr*, and *pl* in this third term? Because they can be preceded by *s* and so belong in term 6. The fourth term similarly means that the word can begin with a consonant of the first column followed by *w*. *Hw* does not occur in all dialects of English; in ordinary spelling it is written backwards, *wh*. If the dialect does not have *hw*, it pronounces the spelled *wh* simply as *w*. *Thw* occurs in a few words, like 'thwack' and 'thwart,' and *gw*, oddly enough, only in proper names, like 'Gwen' or 'Gwynn.' *Kw*, ordinarily spelled *qu*, can have *s* before it and therefore belongs in term 6.

The fifth term indicates that the word may begin with one of the first-column consonants followed by *y*, but only when the vowel of the word is *u*; thus we have words like 'hue' (*hyuw*), 'cue, few, muse.' Some dialects have also *tyu, dyu*, and *nyu* (e.g., in 'tune,' 'due,' and 'new'), but I have set up the formula for the typical dialects of the northern United States, which have simple *tu, du, nu* in these words. The sixth term indicates pairs that can commence a word either alone or preceded by *s*, that is, *k, t*, or *p* followed by *r*, also *kw* and *pl* (think of 'train, strain;

crew, screw; quash, squash; play, splay'). The seventh term, which means the word can begin with *s* followed by any one of the consonants of the second column, completes the parts of the word that can precede its vowel.

The terms beyond the eighth show what comes after the vowel. This portion is rather more complex than the beginning of the word, and it would take too long to explain everything in detail. The general principles of the symbolism will be clear from the preceding explanations. The ninth term, with its zero, denotes that a vowel can end the word if the vowel is *a*—which means (1) the vowel of the article 'a' and the exclamation 'huh?' and (2) the vowel of 'pa, ma,' and the exclamations 'ah!' and 'bah!'—or the vowel can end the word if it is the *aw* sound, as in 'paw, thaw.' In some dialects (eastern New England, southern United States, South British) the vowel ending occurs in words which are SPELLED with *ar*, like 'car, star' (*ka, sta,* in these dialects), but in most of the United States dialects and in those of Ireland and Scotland these words end in an actual *r*. In eastern New England and South British dialects, but not in southern United States, these words cause a linking *r* to appear before a vowel beginning a following word. Thus for 'far off' your Southerner says *fa of*; your Bostonian and your Britisher say *fa rof,* with a liquid initial *r*; but most of the United States says *far of,* with a rolled-back *r*. For some dialects, term 9 would be different, showing another possible final vowel, namely, the peculiar sound which the Middle Westerner may notice in the Bostonian's pronunciation of 'fur, cur' (*fə, kə*) and no doubt may find very queer. This funny sound is common in Welsh, Gaelic, Turkish, Ute, and Hopi, but I am sure Boston did not get it from any of these sources.

Can one-syllable words end in *e, i, o,* or *u*? No, not in English. The words so spelled end in a consonant sound, *y* or *w*. Thus, 'I,' when expressed in formula pattern, is *ay*, 'we' is *wiy*, 'you' is *yuw*, 'how' is *haw*, and so on. A comparison of the Spanish *no* with the English 'No!' shows that, whereas the Spanish word actually ends with its *o* sound trailing in the air, the English equivalent closes upon a *w* sound. The patterns to which we are habituated compel us to close upon a consonant after most vowels. Hence when we learn Spanish, instead of saying *como no,* we are apt to say *kowmow now*; instead of *si,* we say our own word 'see' (*siy*). In French, instead of *si beau,* we are apt to say 'see bow.'

Term 10 means that *r, w,* or *y* may be interpolated at this point except when the interpolation would result in joining *w* and *y* with each other. Term 11 means that the word may end in any single English consonant except *h*; this exception is most unlike some languages, e.g., Sanskrit, Arabic, Navaho, and Maya, in which many words end in *h*. The reader can figure out terms 12, 13, and 14 if he has stuck so far. A small *c* means *ch* as in 'child'; *j* is as in 'joy.' Term 13, which contains these letters, expresses the possibility of words like 'gulch, bulge, lunch, lounge.' Term 14 represents the pattern of words like 'health, width, eighth' (*eytθ*), 'sixth, xth' (*eksθ*). Although we can say 'nth' power or 'fth' power, it takes effort to say the unpermitted 'sth' power or 'hth' power. 'Hth' would be symbolized **eycθ*, the star meaning that the form does not occur. Term 14, however, allows both *mθ* and *mpf*, the latter in words like 'humph' or the recent 'oomph' (*umpf*). The elements of term 15 may be added after anything—the *t* and *s* forms after voiceless sounds, the *d* and *z* after voiced sounds. Thus, 'towns' is *tawnz*, with *wnz* attained by term 10 plus 11 plus 15; whereas 'bounce' is *bawns*, with *wns* by 10 plus 12. Some of the combinations resulting in this way are common; others are very rare but still are possible English forms. If Charlie McCarthy should pipe up in his coy way, "Thou oomphst, dost thou not?"; or a Shakespearean actor should thunder out, "Thou triumphst!" the reason would be that the formula yields that weird sputter *mpfst* by term 14 plus term 15. Neither Mr. Bergen nor Mr. Shakespeare has any power to vary the formula.

The overriding factor applicable to the whole expression is a prohibition of doubling. Notwithstanding whatever the formula says, the same two consonants cannot be juxtaposed. While by term 15 we can add *t* to 'flip' and get 'flipt (flipped),' we can't add *t* to 'hit' and get *hitt*. Instead, at the point in the patterns where *hitt* might be expected, we find simply 'hit (I hit it yesterday, I flipt it yesterday).' Some languages, such as Arabic, have words like *hitt*, *fadd*, and so on, with both paired consonants distinct. The Creek Indian language permits three, e.g. *nnn*.

The way the patterns summarized in this formula control the forms of English words is really extraordinary. A new monosyllable turned out, say, by Walter Winchell or by a plugging adman concocting a name for a new breakfast mush, is struck from this mold as surely as if I pulled the lever and the stamp came down on his brain. Thus linguistics, like the physical sciences, confers the power of prediction. I can predict, within limits, what Winchell will or won't do. He may coin a word *thrub,* but he will not coin a word *srub,* for the formula cannot produce a *sr.* A different formula indicates that, if Winchell invents any word beginning with *th,* like *thell* or *therg,* the *th* will have the sound it has in 'thin,' not the sound it has in 'this' or 'there.' Winchell will not invent a word beginning with this latter sound.

We can wheeze forth the harshest successions of consonants if they are only according to the patterns producing the formula. We easily say 'thirds' and 'sixths,' though 'sixths' has the very rough sequence of four consonants, *ksθs.* But the simpler *sisths* is against the patterns and so is harder to say. 'Glimpst (glimpsed)' has *gl* by term 3, *i* by 8, *mpst* by 12 plus 15. But *dlinpfk* is eliminated on several counts: Term 3 allows for no *dl,* and by no possible combination of terms can one get *npfk.* Yet the linguist can say *dlinpfk* as easily as he can say 'glimpsed.' The formula allows for no final *mb;* so we do not say 'lamb' as it is spelled, but as *lam.* 'Land,' quite parallel but allowed by the formula, trips off our tongues as spelled. It is not hard to see why the "explanation," still found in some serious textbooks, that a language does this or that "for the sake of euphony" is on a par with nature's reputed abhorrence of a vacuum.

The exactness of this formula, typical of hundreds of others, shows that, while linguistic formulations are not those of mathematics, they are nevertheless precise. We might bear in mind that this formula, compared with the formulation of some of the English (or other) grammatical patterns that deal with meaning, would appear like a simple sum in addition compared with a page of calculus. It is usually more convenient to treat very complex patterns by successive paragraphs of precise sentences and simpler formulas, so arranged that each additional paragraph presupposes the previous ones, than to try to embrace all in one very complex formula.

Linguistics is also an experimental science. Its data result from long series of observations under controlled conditions, which, as they are systematically altered, call out definite, different responses. The experiments are directed by the theoretic body of knowledge, just as with physics or chemistry. They usually do not require mechanical apparatus. In place of apparatus, linguistics uses and develops TECHNIQUES. Experimental need not mean quantitative. Measuring, weighing, and pointer-reading devices are seldom needed in linguistics, for quantity and number play little part in the realm of pattern, where there are no variables but, instead, abrupt alternations from one configuration to another. The mathematical sciences require exact measurement, but what linguistics requires is, rather, exact "patternment"—an exactness of relation irrespective of dimensions. Quantity, dimension, magnitude are metaphors since they do not properly belong in this spaceless, relational world. I might use this simile: Exact measurement of lines and angles will be needed to draw exact squares or other regular polygons, but measurement, however precise, will not help us to draw an exact circle. Yet it is necessary only to discover the principle of the compass to reach by a leap the ability to draw perfect circles. Similarly, linguistics has developed techniques which, like compasses, enable it without any true measurement at all to specify EXACTLY the patterns with which it is concerned. Or I might perhaps liken the case to the state of affairs within the atom, where also entities appear to alternate from configuration to configuration rather than to move in terms of measurable positions. As alternants, quantum phenomena must be treated by a method of analysis that substitutes a point in a pattern under a set of conditions for a point in a pattern under another set of conditions—a method similar to that used in analysis of linguistic phenomena.

Physics and chemistry, dealing with inanimate matter, require chiefly inanimate apparatus and substances for their experiments. As conducted today upon a large scale, they require highly wrought physical equipment at every step, immense investments in physical plant. Their experiments are costly to conduct, both absolutely and relatively to the number of scientists. Experimental biology uses much inanimate apparatus, too, but its fundamental apparatus is its experimental animals and plants and their food, housing, and growth facilities. These also are expensive in the quantities needed. No one grudges the expense, either here or in the physical sciences, so long as an increase in human knowledge and welfare is promised.

The apparatus of linguistics is much less expensive than that of these sciences, but it, too, costs money. The experimental linguist, like the biologist, uses and must have experimental animals. Only, his "animals" are human. They are his informants and must be paid for working with him. Sometimes he must make trips to Indian reservations or African villages where his informants live; at other times it is more economical to transport them to him. They provide the field for experimental investigation. They are apparatus, not teachers. It is as important to study in this way languages of Indians, Africans, and other aborigines as it is to study the English dialects of Brooklyn, Boston, Richmond, or London.

While informants are the basic apparatus, the linguist can improve and speed up his work with the aid of mechanical tools, just as the biologist studies his animals and plants with the aid of microscopes, X-ray machines, and other costly instruments. The linguist is aided by judicious use of good phonographic reproducing devices. Much could also be done with the help of business machines.

Although linguistics is a very old science, its modern experimental phase, which stresses the analysis of unwritten speech, could be called one of the newest. So far as our knowledge goes, the science of linguistics was founded, or put on its present basis, by one Panini in India several centuries before Christ. Its earliest form anticipated its most recent one. Panini was highly algebraic, i.e., pattern-symbolic, in his treatment; he used formulas in a very modern way for expressing the obligatory patterns of Sanskrit. It was the Greeks who debased the science. They showed how infinitely inferior they were to the Hindus as scientific thinkers, and the effect of their muddling lasted two thousand years. Modern scientific linguistics dates from the rediscovery of Panini by the Western world in the early nineteenth century.

Yet linguistics is still in its infancy so far as concerns wherewithal for its needed equipment, its supply of informants, and the minimum of tools, books, and the like. Money for mechanical aids, such as I referred to above, is at present only a happy dream. Perhaps this condition results from lack of the publicity the other sciences receive and, after all, fairly earn. We all know now that the forces studied by physics, chemistry, and biology are powerful and important. People generally do not yet know that the forces studied by linguistics are powerful and important, that its principles control every sort of agreement and understanding among human beings, and that sooner or later it will have to sit as judge while the other sciences bring their results to its court to inquire into what they mean. When this time comes, there will be great and well-equipped laboratories of linguistics as there are of other exact sciences.

LANGUAGES AND LOGIC *

In English, the sentences 'I pull the branch aside' and 'I have an extra toe on my foot' have little similarity. Leaving out the subject pronoun and the sign of the present tense, which are common features from requirements of English syntax, we may say that no-similarity exists. Common, and even scientific, parlance would say that the sentences are unlike because they are talking about things which are intrinsically unlike. So Mr. Everyman, the natural logician, would be inclined to argue. Formal logic of an older type would perhaps agree with him.

If, moreover, we appeal to an impartial scientific English-speaking observer, asking him to make direct observations upon cases of the two phenomena to see if they may not have some element of similarity which we have overlooked, he will be more than likely to confirm the dicta of Mr. Everyman and the logician. The observer whom we have asked to make the test may not see quite eye to eye with the old-school logician and would not be disappointed to find him wrong. Still he is compelled sadly to confess failure. "I wish I could oblige you," he says, "but try as I may, I cannot detect any similarity between these phenomena."

By this time our stubborn streak is aroused; we wonder if a being from Mars would also see no resemblance. But now a linguist points out that it is not necessary to go as far as Mars. We have not yet scouted around this earth to see if its many languages all classify these phenomena as disparately as our speech does. We find that in Shawnee

* Reprinted from *Technol. Rev.*, 43:250–252, 266, 268, 272 (April 1941).

these two statements are, respectively, *ni-l'θawa-'ko-n-a* and *ni-l'θawa-'ko-θite* (the θ here denotes *th* as in 'thin' and the apostrophe denotes a breath-catch). The sentences are closely similar; in fact, they differ only at the tail end. In Shawnee, moreover, the beginning of a construction is generally the important and emphatic part. Both sentences start with *ni-* ('I'), which is a mere prefix. Then comes the really im-

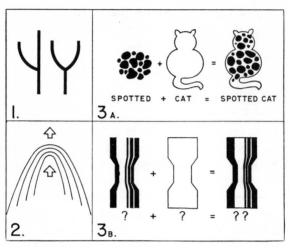

Figure 15. Suggested above are certain linguistic concepts which, as explained in the text, are not easily definable.

portant key word, *l'θawa*, a common Shawnee term, denoting a forked outline, like Fig. 15, no. 1. The next element, *-'ko*, we cannot be sure of, but it agrees in form with a variant of the suffix *-a'kw* or *-a'ko*, denoting tree, bush, tree part, branch, or anything of that general shape. In the first sentence, *-n-* means 'by hand action' and may be either a causation of the basic condition (forked outline) manually, an increase of it, or both. The final *-a* means that the subject ('I') does this action to an appropriate object. Hence the first sentence means 'I pull it (something like branch of tree) more open or apart where it forks.' In the other sentence, the suffix *-θite* means 'pertaining to the toes,' and the absence of further suffixes means that the subject manifests the condition in his own person. Therefore the sentence can mean only 'I have an extra toe forking out like a branch from a normal toe.'

Shawnee logicians and observers would class the two phenomena as intrinsically similar. Our own observer, to whom we tell all this, focuses his instruments again upon the two phenomena and to his joy sees at once a manifest resemblance. Figure 16 illustrates a similar situation: 'I push his head back' and 'I drop it in water and it floats,' though very dissimilar sentences in English, are similar in Shawnee. The point of

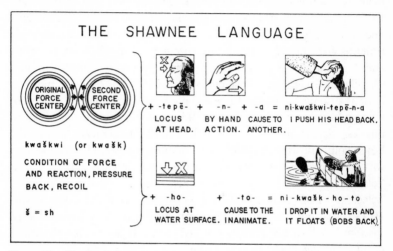

Figure 16. The English sentences 'I push his head back' and 'I drop it in water and it floats' are unlike. But in Shawnee the corresponding statements are closely similar, emphasizing the fact that analysis of nature and classification of events as like or in the same category (logic) are governed by grammar.

view of linguistic relativity changes Mr. Everyman's dictum: Instead of saying, "Sentences are unlike because they tell about unlike facts," he now reasons: "Facts are unlike to speakers whose language background provides for unlike formulation of them."

Conversely, the English sentences, 'The boat is grounded on the beach' and 'The boat is manned by picked men,' seem to us to be rather similar. Each is about a boat; each tells the relation of the boat to other objects—or that's OUR story. The linguist would point out the parallelism in grammatical pattern thus: "The boat is $x$ed preposition y." The logician might turn the linguist's analysis into "A is in the state x in relation to y," and then perhaps into $fA = xRy$. Such symbolic methods lead to fruitful techniques of rational ordering, stimulate our thinking, and bring valuable insight. Yet we should realize that the similarities and contrasts in the original sentences, subsumed under the foregoing formula, are dependent on the choice of mother tongue and that the properties of the tongue are eventually reflected as peculiarities of structure in the fabric of logic or mathematics which we rear.

In the Nootka language of Vancouver Island, the first "boat" statement is *tlih-is-ma;* the second, *lash-tskwiq-ista-ma.* The first is thus I-II-*ma;* the second, III-IV-V-*ma;* and they are quite unlike, for the final *-ma* is only the sign of the third-person indicative. Neither sentence contains any unit of meaning akin to our word 'boat' or even 'canoe.' Part I, in the first sentence, means 'moving pointwise,' or moving in a way like the suggestion of the outline in Fig. 15, no. 2; hence 'traveling in or as a canoe,' or an event like one position of such motion. It is not a name for what we should call a "thing," but is more like a vector in physics. Part II means 'on the beach'; hence I-II-*ma* means 'it is on the beach pointwise as an event of canoe motion,' and would normally refer to a boat that has come to land. In the other sentence, part III means 'select, pick,' and IV means 'remainder, result,' so that III-IV means 'selected.' Part V means 'in a canoe (boat) as crew.' The whole, III-IV-V-*ma,* means either 'they are in the boat as a crew of picked men' or 'the boat has a crew of picked men.' It means that the whole event involving picked ones and boat's crew is in process.

As a hang-over from my education in chemical engineering, I relish an occasional chemical simile. Perhaps readers will catch what I mean when I say that the way the constituents are put together in these sentences of Shawnee and Nootka suggests a chemical compound, whereas their combination in English is more like a mechanical mixture. A mixture, like the mountaineer's potlicker, can be assembled out of almost anything and does not make any sweeping transformation of the overt appearance of the material. A chemical compound, on the other hand, can be put together only out of mutually suited ingredients, and the result may be not merely soup but a crop of crystals or a cloud of smoke. Likewise the typical Shawnee or Nootka combinations appear to work with a vocabulary of terms chosen with a view not so much to the utility of their immediate references as to the ability of the terms to combine suggestively with each other in manifold ways that elicit novel and useful images. This principle of terminology and way of analyzing events would seem to be unknown to the tongues with which we are familiar.

It is the analysis of nature down to a basic vocabulary capable of this sort of evocative recombination which is most distinctive of polysynthetic languages, like Nootka and Shawnee. Their characteristic quality is not, as some linguists have thought, a matter of the tightness or indissolubility of the combinations. The Shawnee term *l'θawa* could probably be said alone but would then mean 'it (or something) is forked,' a statement which gives little hint of the novel meanings that arise out of its combinations—at least to our minds or our type of logic. Shawnee and Nootka do not use the chemical type of synthesis exclusively. They make large use of a more external kind of syntax, which, however, has no basic structural priority. Even our own Indo-European tongues are not wholly devoid of the chemical method, but they seldom make sentences by it, afford little inkling of its possibilities, and give structural priority to another method. It was quite natural, then, that Aristotle should found our traditional logic wholly on this other method.

Let me make another analogy, not with chemistry but with art—art of the pictorial sort. We look at a good still-life painting and seem to see a lustrous porcelain bowl and a downy peach. Yet an analysis that screened out the totality of the picture—as if we were to go over it carefully, looking through a hole cut in a card—would reveal only oddly shaped patches of paint and would not evoke the bowl and fruit. The synthesis presented by the painting is perhaps akin to the chemical type of syntax, and it may point to psychological fundamentals that enter into both art and language. Now the mechanical method in art and language might be typified by no. 3A in Fig. 15. The first element, a field of spots, corresponds to the adjective 'spotted,' the second corresponds to the noun 'cat.' By putting them together, we get 'spotted cat.' Contrast the technique in Fig. 15, no. 3B. Here the figure corresponding to 'cat' has only vague meaning by itself—"chevron-like," we might say—while the first element is even vaguer. But, combined, these evoke a cylindrical object, like a shaft casting.

The thing common to both techniques is a systematic synthetic use of pattern, and this is also common to all language techniques. I have put question marks below the elements in Fig. 15, no. 3B, to point out the difficulty of a parallel in English speech and the fact that the method probably has no standing in traditional logic. Yet examination of other languages and the possibility of new types of logic that has been advanced by modern logicians themselves suggest that this matter may be significant for modern science. New types of logic may help us eventually to understand how it is that electrons, the velocity of light, and other components of the subject matter of physics appear to behave illogically, or that phenomena which flout the sturdy common sense of yesteryear can nevertheless be true. Modern thinkers have long since pointed out that the so-called mechanistic way of thinking has come to an impasse before the great frontier problems of science. To rid ourselves of this way of thinking is exceedingly difficult when we have no linguistic experience of any other and when even our most advanced logicians and mathematicians do not provide any other—and obviously they cannot without the linguistic experience. For the mechanistic way of thinking is perhaps just a type of syntax natural to Mr. Everyman's daily use of the western Indo-European languages, rigidified and intensified by Aristotle and the latter's medieval and modern followers.

As I said in an article, "Science and linguistics," in the *Review* for April 1940, the effortlessness of speech and the subconscious way we picked up that activity in early childhood lead us to regard talking and thinking as wholly straightforward and transparent. We naturally feel that they embody self-evident laws of thought, the same for all men. We know all the answers! But, when scrutinized, they become dusty answers. We use speech for reaching agreements about subject matter: I say, "Please shut the door," and my hearer and I agree that 'the door' refers to a certain part of our environment and that I want a certain result produced. Our explanations of how we reached this understanding, though quite satisfactory on the everyday social plane, are merely more agreements (statements) about the same subject matter (door, and so on), more and more amplified by statements about the social and personal needs that impel us to communicate. There are here no laws of thought. Yet the structural regularities of our sentences enable us to sense that laws are SOMEWHERE in the background. Clearly, explanations of understanding such as "And so I ups and says to him, says I; see here, why don't you . . . !" evade the true process by which 'he' and 'I' are in communication. Likewise psychological-social descriptions of the social and emotional needs that impel people to communicate with their fellows tend to be learned versions of the same method and, while interesting, still evade the question. In similar case is evasion of the question by skipping from the speech sentence, via physiology and "stimuli" to the social situation.

The WHY of understanding may remain for a long time mysterious; but the HOW or logic of understanding—its background of laws or regularities—is discoverable. It is the grammatical background of our mother tongue, which includes not only our way of constructing propositions but the way we dissect nature and break up the flux of experience into objects and entities to construct propositions about. This fact is important for science, because it means that science CAN have a rational or logical basis even though it be a relativistic one and not Mr. Everyman's natural logic. Although it may vary with each tongue, and a planetary mapping of the dimensions of such variation may be necessitated, it is, nevertheless, a basis of logic with discoverable laws. Science is not compelled to see its thinking and reasoning procedures turned into processes merely subservient to social adjustments and emotional drives.

Moreover, the tremendous importance of language cannot, in my opinion, be taken to mean necessarily that nothing is back of it of the nature of what has traditionally been called "mind." My own studies suggest, to me, that language, for all its kingly role, is in some sense a superficial embroidery upon deeper processes of consciousness, which are necessary before any communication, signaling, or symbolism whatsoever can occur, and which also can, at a pinch, effect communication (though not true AGREEMENT) without language's and without symbolism's aid. I mean "superficial" in the sense that all processes of chemistry, for example, can be said to be superficial upon the deeper layer of physical existence, which we know variously as intra-atomic, electronic, or subelectronic. No one would take this statement to mean that chemistry is UNIMPORTANT—indeed the whole point is that the more superficial can mean the more important, in a definite operative sense. It may even be in the cards that there is no such thing as "Language" (with a capital L) at all! The statement that "thinking is a matter of LANGUAGE" is an incorrect generalization of the more nearly correct idea that "thinking is a matter of different tongues." The different tongues are the real phenomena and may generalize down not to any such universal as "Language," but to something better—called "sublinguistic" or "superlinguistic"—and NOT ALTOGETHER unlike, even if much unlike, what we now call "mental." This generalization would not diminish, but would rather increase, the importance of intertongue study for investigation of this realm of truth.

Botanists and zoologists, in order to understand the world of living species, found it necessary to describe the species in every part of the globe and to add a time perspective by including the fossils. Then they found it necessary to compare and contrast the species, to work out families and classes, evolutionary descent, morphology, and taxonomy. In linguistic science a similar attempt is under way. The far-off event toward which this attempt moves is a new technology of language and thought. Much progress has been made in classifying the languages of earth into genetic families, each having descent from a single precursor, and in tracing such developments through time. The result is called "comparative linguistics." Of even greater importance for the future technology of thought is what might be called "contrastive linguistics." This plots the outstanding differences among tongues—in grammar, logic, and general analysis of experience.

As I said in the April 1940 *Review*, segmentation of nature is an aspect of grammar—one as yet little studied by grammarians. We cut up and organize the spread and flow of events as we do, largely because, through our mother tongue, we are parties to an agreement to do so, not because nature itself is segmented in exactly that way for all to see. Languages differ not only in how they build their sentences but also in how they break down nature to secure the elements to put in those sentences. This breakdown gives units of the lexicon. "Word" is not a very good "word" for them; "lexeme" has been suggested, and "term" will do for the present. By these more or less distinct terms we ascribe a semifictitious isolation to parts of experience. English terms, like 'sky, hill, swamp,' persuade us to regard some elusive aspect of nature's endless variety as a distinct THING, almost like a table or chair. Thus English and similar tongues lead us to think of the universe as a collection of rather distinct objects and events corresponding to words. Indeed this is the implicit picture of classical physics and astronomy—that the universe is essentially a collection of detached objects of different sizes.

The examples used by older logicians in dealing with this point are usually unfortunately chosen. They tend to pick out tables and chairs and apples on tables as test objects to demonstrate the object-like nature of reality and its one-to-one correspondence with logic. Man's artifacts and the agricultural products he severs from living plants have a unique degree of isolation; we may expect that languages will have fairly isolated terms for them. The real question is: What do different languages do, not with these artificially isolated objects but with the flowing face of nature in its motion, color, and changing form; with clouds, beaches, and yonder flight of birds? For, as goes our segmentation of the face of nature, so goes our physics of the Cosmos.

Here we find differences in segmentation and selection of basic terms. We might isolate something in nature by saying 'It is a dripping spring.' Apache erects the statement on a verb *ga*: 'be white (including clear, uncolored, and so on).' With a prefix *nō-* the meaning of downward motion enters: 'whiteness moves downward.' Then *tó*, meaning both 'water' and 'spring' is prefixed. The result corresponds to our 'dripping spring,' but synthetically it is 'as water, or springs, whiteness moves downward.' How utterly unlike our way of thinking! The same verb, *ga*, with a prefix that means 'a place manifests the condition' becomes *gohlga*: 'the place is white, clear; a clearing, a plain.' These examples show that some languages have means of expression—chemical combination, as I called it—in which the separate terms are not so separate as in English but flow together into plastic synthetic creations. Hence such languages, which do not paint the separate-object picture of the universe to the same degree as English and its sister tongues, point toward possible new types of logic and possible new cosmical pictures.

The Indo-European languages and many others give great prominence to a type of sentence having two parts, each part built around a class of word—substantives and verbs—which those languages treat differently in grammar. As I showed in the April 1940 *Review*, this distinction is not drawn from nature; it is just a result of the fact that every tongue must have some kind of structure, and those tongues have made a go of exploiting this kind. The Greeks, especially Aristotle, built up this contrast and made it a law of reason. Since then, the contrast has been stated in logic in many different ways: subject and predicate, actor and action, things and relations between things, objects and their attributes, quantities and operations. And, pursuant again to grammar, the notion became ingrained that one of these classes of entities can exist in its own right but that the verb class cannot exist without an entity of the other class, the "thing" class, as a peg to hang on. "Embodiment is necessary," the watchword of this ideology, is seldom STRONGLY questioned. Yet the whole trend of modern physics, with its emphasis on "the field," is an implicit questioning of the ideology. This contrast crops out in our mathematics as two kinds of symbols—the kind like 1,

2, 3, x, y, z and the kind like $+$, $-$, $\div$, $\sqrt{}$, log $-$, though, in view of 0, ½, ¾, π, and others, perhaps no strict two-group classification holds. The two-group notion, however, is always present at the back of the thinking, although often not overtly expressed.

Our Indian languages show that with a suitable grammar we may have intelligent sentences that cannot be broken into subjects and predicates. Any attempted breakup is a breakup of some English translation or paraphrase of the sentence, not of the Indian sentence itself. We might as well try to decompose a certain synthetic resin into Celluloid and whiting because the resin can be imitated with Celluloid and whiting. The Algonkian language family, to which Shawnee belongs, does use a type of sentence like our subject and predicate but also gives prominence to the type shown by our examples in the text and in Fig. 15. To be sure, *ni-* is represented by a subject in the translation but means 'my' as well as 'I,' and the sentence could be translated thus: 'My hand is pulling the branch aside.' Or *ni-* might be absent; if so, we should be apt to manufacture a subject, like 'he, it, somebody,' or we could pick out for our English subject an idea corresponding to any one of the Shawnee elements.

When we come to Nootka, the sentence without subject or predicate is the only type. The term "predication" is used, but it means "sentence." Nootka has no parts of speech; the simplest utterance is a sentence, treating of some event or event-complex. Long sentences are sentences of sentences (complex sentences), not just sentences of words. In Fig. 17 we have a simple, not a complex, Nootka sentence. The translation, 'he invites people to a feast,' splits into subject and predicate. Not so the native sentence. It begins with the event of 'boiling or cooking,' *tl'imsh*; then comes *-ya* ('result') = 'cooked'; then *-'is* 'eating' = 'eating cooked food'; then *-ita* ('those who do') = 'eaters of cooked food'; then *-'itl* ('going for'); then *-ma*, sign of third-person indicative, giving *tl'imshya'isita'itlma*, which answers to the crude paraphrase, 'he, or somebody, goes for (invites) eaters of cooked food.'

The English technique of talking depends on the contrast of two artificial classes, substantives and verbs, and on the bipartitioned ideology of nature, already discussed. Our normal sentence, unless imperative, must have some substantive before its verb, a requirement that corresponds to the philosophical and also naïve notion of an actor who produces an action. This last might not have been so if English had

had thousands of verbs like 'hold,' denoting positions. But most of our verbs follow a type of segmentation that isolates from nature what we call "actions," that is, moving outlines.

Following majority rule, we therefore read action into every sentence, even into 'I hold it.' A moment's reflection will show that 'hold' is no action but a state of relative positions. Yet we think of it and even see it as an action because language formulates it in the same way as it

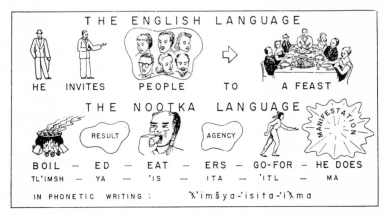

Figure 17. Here are shown the different ways in which English and Nootka formulate the same event. The English sentence is divisible into subject and predicate; the Nootka sentence is not, yet it is complete and logical. Furthermore, the Nootka sentence is just one word, consisting of the root *tl'imsh* with five suffixes.

formulates more numerous expressions, like 'I strike it,' which deal with movements and changes.

We are constantly reading into nature fictional acting entities, simply because our verbs must have substantives in front of them. We have to say 'It flashed' or 'A light flashed,' setting up an actor, 'it' or 'light,' to perform what we call an action, "to flash." Yet the flashing and the light are one and the same! The Hopi language reports the flash with a simple verb, *rehpi*: 'flash (occurred).' There is no division into subject and predicate, not even a suffix like *-t* of Latin *tona-t* 'it thunders.' Hopi can and does have verbs without subjects, a fact which may give that tongue potentialities, probably never to be developed, as a logical system for understanding some aspects of the universe. Undoubtedly modern science, strongly reflecting western Indo-European tongues, often does as we all do, sees actions and forces where it sometimes might be better to see states. On the other hand, 'state' is a noun, and as such it enjoys the superior prestige traditionally attaching to the subject or thing class; therefore science is exceedingly ready to speak of states if permitted to manipulate the concept like a noun. Perhaps, in place of the 'states' of an atom or a dividing cell, it would be better if we could manipulate as readily a more verblike concept but without the concealed premises of actor and action.

I can sympathize with those who say, "Put it into plain, simple English," especially when they protest against the empty formalism of loading discourse with pseudolearned words. But to restrict thinking to the patterns merely of English, and especially to those patterns which represent the acme of plainness in English, is to lose a power of thought which, once lost, can never be regained. It is the "plainest" English which contains the greatest number of unconscious assumptions about nature. This is the trouble with schemes like Basic English, in which an eviscerated British English, with its concealed premises working harder than ever, is to be fobbed off on an unsuspecting world as the substance of pure Reason itself. We handle even our plain English with much greater effect if we direct it from the vantage point of a multilingual awareness. For this reason I believe that those who envision a future world speaking only one tongue, whether English, German, Russian, or any other, hold a misguided ideal and would do the evolution of the human mind the greatest disservice. Western culture has made, through language, a provisional analysis of reality and, without correctives, holds resolutely to that analysis as final. The only correctives lie in all those other tongues which by aeons of independent evolution have arrived at different, but equally logical, provisional analyses.

In a valuable paper, "Modern logic and the task of the natural sciences," Harold N. Lee says: "Those sciences whose data are subject to quantitative measurement have been most successfully developed because we know so little about order systems other than those exemplified in mathematics. We can say with certainty, however, that there are other kinds, for the advance of logic in the last half century has clearly indicated it. We may look for advances in many lines in sciences at present well founded if the advance of logic furnishes adequate knowledge of other order types. We may also look for many subjects of inquiry whose methods are not strictly scientific at the present time to become so when new order systems are available." [1]   To which may be added that an important field for the working out of new order systems, akin to, yet not identical with, present mathematics, lies in more penetrating investigation than has yet been made of languages remote in type from our own.

[1] *Sigma Xi Quart.*, 28:125 (Autumn 1940).

LANGUAGE, MIND,

AND REALITY*

I

It needs but half an eye to see in these latter days that science, the Grand Revelator of modern Western culture, has reached, without having intended to, a frontier. Either it must bury its dead, close its ranks, and go forward into a landscape of increasing strangeness, replete with things shocking to a culture-trammeled understanding, or it must become, in Claude Houghton's expressive phrase, the plagiarist of its own past. The frontier was foreseen in principle very long ago, and given a name that has descended to our day clouded with myth. That name is Babel. For science's long and heroic effort to be strictly factual has at last brought it into entanglement with the unsuspected facts of the linguistic order. These facts the older classical science had never admitted, confronted, or understood as facts. Instead they had entered its house by the back door and had been taken for the substance of Reason itself.

What we call "scientific thought" is a specialization of the western Indo-European type of language, which has developed not only a set of different dialectics, but actually a set of different dialects. THESE DIALECTS ARE NOW BECOMING MUTUALLY UNINTELLIGIBLE. The term 'space,' for instance, does not and CANNOT mean the same thing to a psychologist as to a physicist. Even if psychologists should firmly resolve, come

* Reprinted by permission of the Theosophical Society from *Theosophist* (Madras, India), January and April issues, 1942.

hell or high water, to use "space" only with the physicist's meaning, they could not do so, any more than Englishmen could use in English the word 'sentiment' in the meanings which the similarly spelled but functionally different French utterance *le sentiment* has in its native French.

Now this does not simply breed confusions of mere detail that an expert translator could perhaps resolve. It does something much more perplexing. Every language and every well-knit technical sublanguage incorporates certain points of view and certain patterned resistances to widely divergent points of view. This is especially so if language is not surveyed as a planetary phenomenon, but is as usual taken for granted, and the local, parochial species of it used by the individual thinker is taken to be its full sum. These resistances not only isolate artificially the particular sciences from each other; they also restrain the scientific spirit as a whole from taking the next great step in development—a step which entails viewpoints unprecedented in science and a complete severance from traditions. For certain linguistic patterns rigidified in the dialectics of the sciences—often also embedded in the matrix of European culture from which those sciences have sprung, and long worshipped as pure Reason *per se*—have been worked to death. Even science senses that they are somehow out of focus for observing what may be very significant aspects of reality, upon the due observation of which all further progress in understanding the universe may hinge.

Thus one of the important coming steps for Western knowledge is a re-examination of the linguistic backgrounds of its thinking, and for that matter of all thinking. My purpose in developing this subject before a Theosophical audience is not to confirm or affirm any Theosophical doctrines. It is rather that, of all groups of people with whom I have come in contact, Theosophical people seem the most capable of becoming excited about ideas—new ideas. And my task is to explain an idea to all those who, if Western culture survives the present welter of barbarism, may be pushed by events to leadership in reorganizing the whole human future.

This idea is one too drastic to be penned up in a catch phrase. I would rather leave it unnamed. It is the view that a noumenal world— a world of hyperspace, of higher dimensions—awaits discovery by all the sciences, which it will unite and unify, awaits discovery under its first aspect of a realm of PATTERNED RELATIONS, inconceivably manifold

and yet bearing a recognizable affinity to the rich and systematic organization of LANGUAGE, including *au fond* mathematics and music, which
are ultimately of the same kindred as language. The idea is older than
Plato, and at the same time as new as our most revolutionary thinkers.
It is implied in Whitehead's world of prehensive aspects, and in relativity physics with its four-dimensional continuum and its Riemann-
Christoffel tensor that sums up the PROPERTIES OF THE WORLD at any
point-moment; while one of the most thought-provoking of all modern
presentations, and I think the most original, is the *Tertium Organum* of
Ouspensky. All that I have to say on the subject that may be new is
of the PREMONITION IN LANGUAGE of the unknown, vaster world—that
world of which the physical is but a surface or skin, and yet which we
ARE IN, and BELONG TO. For the approach to reality through mathematics, which modern knowledge is beginning to make, is merely the
approach through one special case of this relation to language.

This view implies that what I have called patterns are basic in a really
cosmic sense, and that patterns form wholes, akin to the Gestalten of
psychology, which are embraced in larger wholes in continual progression. Thus the cosmic picture has a serial or hierarchical character, that
of a progression of planes or levels. Lacking recognition of such serial
order, different sciences chop segments, as it were, out of the world,
segments which perhaps cut across the direction of the natural levels,
or stop short when, upon reaching a major change of level, the phenomena become of quite different type, or pass out of the ken of the
older observational methods.

But in the science of linguistics, the facts of the linguistic domain
compel recognition of serial planes, each explicitly given by an order of
patterning observed. It is as if, looking at a wall covered with fine
tracery of lacelike design, we found that this tracery served as the ground
for a bolder pattern, yet still delicate, of tiny flowers, and that upon
becoming aware of this floral expanse we saw that multitudes of gaps
in it made another pattern like scrollwork, and that groups of scrolls
made letters, the letters if followed in a proper sequence made words,
the words were aligned in columns which listed and classified entities,
and so on in continual cross-patterning until we found this wall to be—
a great book of wisdom!

First, the plane "below" the strictly linguistic phenomena is a physical,
acoustic one, phenomena wrought of sound waves; then comes a level

of patterning in rippling muscles and speech organs, the physiological-phonetic plane; then the phonemic plane, patterning that makes a systematic set of consonants, vowels, accents, tones, etc. for each language; then the morphophonemic plane in which the "phonemes" of the previous level appear combined into "morphemes" (words and sub-words like suffixes, etc.); then the plane of morphology; then that of the intricate, largely unconscious patterning that goes by the meaningless name of syntax; then on to further planes still, the full import of which may some day strike and stagger us.

Speech is the best show man puts on. It is his own "act" on the stage of evolution, in which he comes before the cosmic backdrop and really "does his stuff." But we suspect the watching Gods perceive that the order in which his amazing set of tricks builds up to a great climax has been stolen—from the Universe!

The idea, entirely unfamiliar to the modern world, that nature and language are inwardly akin, was for ages well known to various high cultures whose historical continuity on the earth has been enormously longer than that of Western European culture. In India, one aspect of it has been the idea of the MANTRAM and of a MANTRIC ART. On the simplest cultural level, a mantram is merely an incantation of primitive magic, such as the crudest cultures have. In the high culture it may have a different, a very intellectual meaning, dealing with the inner affinity of language and the cosmic order. At a still higher level, it becomes "Mantra Yoga." Therein the mantram becomes a manifold of conscious patterns, contrived to assist the consciousness into the noumenal pattern world—whereupon it is "in the driver's seat." It can then SET the human organism to transmit, control, and amplify a thousandfold forces which that organism normally transmits only at un-observably low intensities.

Somewhat analogously, the mathematical formula that enables a physicist to adjust some coils of wire, tinfoil plates, diaphragms, and other quite inert and innocent gadgets into a configuration in which they can project music to a far country puts the physicist's consciousness on to a level strange to the untrained man, and makes feasible an adjustment of matter to a very strategic configuration, one which makes possible an unusual manifestation of force. Other formulas make possible the strategic arrangement of magnets and wires in the powerhouse so that, when the magnets (or rather the field of subtle forces, in and around the magnets) are set in motion, force is manifested in the way we call an electric current. We do not think of the designing of a radio station or a power plant as a linguistic process, but it is one nonetheless. The necessary mathematics is a linguistic apparatus, and, without its correct specification of essential patterning, the assembled gadgets would be out of proportion and adjustment, and would remain inert. But the mathematics used in such a case is a SPECIALIZED formula-language, contrived for making available a specialized type of force manifestation through metallic bodies only, namely, ELECTRICITY as we today define what we call by that name. The mantric formula-language is specialized in a different way, in order to make available a different type of force manifestation, by repatterning states in the nervous system and glands—or again rather in the subtle "electronic" or "etheric" forces in and around those physical bodies. Those parts of the organism, until such strategic patterning has been effected, are merely "innocent gadgets," as incapable of dynamic power as loose magnets and loose wires, but IN THE PROPER PATTERN they are something else again—not to be understood from the properties of the unpatterned parts, and able to amplify and activate latent forces.

In this way I would link the subtle Eastern ideas of the mantric and yogic use of language with the configurative or pattern aspect which is so basic in language. But this brings me to the most important part of my discussion. We must find out more about language! Already we know enough about it to know it is not what the great majority of men, lay or scientific, think it is. The fact that we talk almost effortlessly, unaware of the exceedingly complex mechanism we are using, creates an illusion. We think we know how it is done, that there is no mystery; we have all the answers. Alas, what wrong answers! It is like the way a man's uncorrected sense impressions give him a picture of the universe that is simple, sensible, and satisfying, but very wide of the truth.

Consider how the world appears to any man, however wise and experienced in human life, who has never heard one word of what science has discovered about the Cosmos. To him the earth is flat; the sun and moon are shining objects of small size that pop up daily above an eastern rim, move through the upper air, and sink below a western edge; obviously they spend the night somewhere underground. The sky is an inverted bowl made of some blue material. The stars, tiny and rather near objects, seem as if they might be alive, for they "come out" from the sky at evening like rabbits or rattlesnakes from their burrows, and slip back again at dawn. "Solar system" has no meaning to him, and the concept of a "law of gravitation" is quite unintelligible—nay, even nonsensical. For him bodies do not fall because of a law of gravitation, but rather "because there is nothing to hold them up"—i.e., because he cannot imagine their doing anything else. He cannot conceive space without an "up" and "down" or even without an "east" and "west" in it. For him the blood does not circulate; nor does the heart pump blood; he thinks it is a place where love, kindness, and thoughts are kept. Cooling is not a removal of heat but an addition of "cold"; leaves are green not from the chemical substance chlorophyll in them, but from the "greenness" in them. It will be impossible to reason him out of these beliefs. He will assert them as plain, hard-headed common sense; which means that they satisfy him because they are completely adequate as a SYSTEM OF COMMUNICATION between him and his fellow men. That is, they are adequate LINGUISTICALLY to his social needs, and will remain so until an additional group of needs is felt and is worked out in language.

But as this man is in conception of the physical universe, of whose scope and order he has not the faintest inkling, so all of us, from rude savage to learned scholar, are in conception of language. Only the science of linguistics has begun to penetrate a little into this realm, its findings still largely unknown to the other disciplines. Natural man, whether simpleton or scientist, knows no more of the linguistic forces that bear upon him than the savage knows of gravitational forces. He supposes that talking is an activity in which he is free and untrammeled. He finds it a simple, transparent activity, for which he has the necessary explanations. But these explanations turn out to be nothing but statements of the NEEDS THAT IMPEL HIM TO COMMUNICATE. They are not germane to the process by which he communicates. Thus he will say that he thinks something, and supplies words for the thoughts "as they come." But his explanation of why he should have such and such thoughts before he came to utter them again turns out to be merely the story of his social needs at that moment. It is a dusty answer that throws no light. But then he supposes that there need be no light thrown on this talking process, since he can manipulate it anyhow quite well for his social needs. Thus he implies, wrongly, that thinking is an

OBVIOUS, straightforward activity, the same for all rational beings, of which language is the straightforward expression.

Actually, thinking is most mysterious, and by far the greatest light upon it that we have is thrown by the study of language. This study shows that the forms of a person's thoughts are controlled by inexorable laws of pattern of which he is unconscious. These patterns are the unperceived intricate systematizations of his own language—shown readily enough by a candid comparison and contrast with other languages, especially those of a different linguistic family. His thinking itself is in a language—in English, in Sanskrit, in Chinese.[1] And every language is a vast pattern-system, different from others, in which are culturally ordained the forms and categories by which the personality not only communicates, but also analyzes nature, notices or neglects types of relationship and phenomena, channels his reasoning, and builds the house of his consciousness.

This doctrine is new to Western science, but it stands on unimpeachable evidence. Moreover, it is known, or something like it is known, to the philosophies of India and to modern Theosophy. This is masked by the fact that the philosophical Sanskrit terms do not supply the exact equivalent of my term "language" in the broad sense of the linguistic order. The linguistic order embraces all symbolism, all symbolic processes, all processes of reference and of logic. Terms like *Nāma* refer rather to subgrades of this order—the lexical level, the phonetic level. The nearest equivalent is probably *Manas*, to which our vague word 'mind' hardly does justice. *Manas* in a broad sense is a major hierarchical grade in the world-structure—a "manasic plane" as it is indeed explicitly called. Here again "mental plane" is apt to be misleading to an English-speaking person. English "mental" is an unfortunate word, a word whose function in our culture is often only to stand in lieu of an intelligent explanation, and which connotes rather a foggy limbo than a cosmic structural order characterized by patterning. Sometimes *Manas*

[1] To anticipate the text, "thinking in a language" does not necessarily have to use WORDS. An uncultivated Choctaw can as easily as the most skilled litterateur contrast the tenses or the genders of two experiences, though he has never heard of any WORDS like "tense" or "gender" for such contrasts. Much thinking never brings in words at all, but manipulates whole paradigms, word-classes, and such grammatical orders "behind" or "above" the focus of personal consciousness.

is used to mean, however, simply the personal psyche; this according to Mr. Fritz Kunz is the case in the famous saying of *The Voice of the Silence:* "The mind is the great slayer of the real."

It is said that in the plane of *Manas* there are two great levels, called the *Rūpa* and *Arūpa* levels. The lower is the realm of "name and form," *Nāma* and *Rūpa.* Here "form" means organization in space ("our" three-dimensional space). This is far from being coextensive with pattern in a universal sense. And *Nāma*, 'name,' is not language or the linguistic order, but only one level in it, the level of the process of "lexation" or of giving words (names) to parts of the whole manifold of experience, parts which are thereby made to stand out in a semi-fictitious isolation. Thus a word like 'sky,' which in English can be treated like 'board' (the sky, a sky, skies, some skies, piece of sky, etc.), leads us to think of a mere optical apparition in ways appropriate only to relatively isolated solid bodies. 'Hill' and 'swamp' persuade us to regard local variations in altitude or soil composition of the ground as distinct THINGS almost like tables and chairs. Each language performs this artificial chopping up of the continuous spread and flow of existence in a different way. Words and speech are not the same thing. As we shall see, the patterns of sentence structure that guide words are more important than the words.

Thus the level of *Rūpa* and *Nāma*—shape-segmentation and vocabulary—is part of the linguistic order, but a somewhat rudimentary and not self-sufficient part. It depends upon a higher level of organization, the level at which its COMBINATORY SCHEME appears. This is the *Arūpa* level—the pattern world par excellence. *Arūpa*, 'formless,' does not mean without linguistic form or organization, but without reference to spatial, visual shape, marking out in space, which as we saw with 'hill' and 'swamp' is an important feature of reference on the lexical level. *Arūpa* is a realm of patterns that can be "actualized" in space and time in the materials of lower planes, but are themselves indifferent to space and time. Such patterns are not like the meanings of words, but they are somewhat like the way meaning appears in sentences. They are not like individual sentences but like SCHEMES of sentences and designs of sentence structure. Our personal conscious "minds" can understand such patterns in a limited way by using mathematical or grammatical FORMULAS into which words, values, quantities, etc., can be substituted. A rather simple instance will be given presently.

It is within the possibilities of the "culture of consciousness" that the *Arūpa* level of the "mental" plane may be contacted directly in an expansion of consciousness. In Ouspensky's book, *A New Model of the Universe*, there are arresting glimpses of extraordinary mental states which that philosopher attained—adumbrations only, for these completely "nonlexical" vistas cannot be well put into words. He speaks of realms of "moving hieroglyphs" composed entirely of "mathematical relations," and of the expansion and ramification of such a "hieroglyph" till it covered a whole aspect of the universe. Ouspensky's mathematical predilections and his study of such things as non-Euclidean geometries, hyperspace, and the relation between time and consciousness may have led him to stress mathematical analogies. Mathematics is a special kind of language, expanded out of special sentences containing the numeral words, 1, 2, 3, 4, . . . x, y, z, etc. But every other type of sentence of every language is also the potential nucleus of a far-reaching system. To very few is it granted to attain such consciousness as a durable state; yet many mathematicians and scientific linguists must have had the experience of "seeing," in one fugitive flash, a whole system of relationships never before suspected of forming a unity. The harmony and scientific beauty in the whole vast system momently overwhelms one in a flood of aesthetic delight. To "see," for instance, how all the English elementary sounds ("phonemes") and their groupings are coordinated by an intricate yet systematic law into all possible forms of English monosyllabic words, meaningful or nonsensical, existent or still unthought of, excluding all other forms as inevitably as the chemical formula of a solution precludes all but certain shapes of crystals from emerging—this might be a distinct experience.

To show the full formula for this law or pattern—a so-called "morphophonemic structural formula"—I should need a large piece of paper. I can however set up a condensed form of it as [2]

$$O, C - ng, C_1C_2, C_3C_4, \text{etc.} \ldots$$
$$s \pm C_mC_n + V + (V_1) \ O, \pm (r, w, y);$$
$$C - h, C'_1C'_2, C'_3C'_4, \text{etc.} \ldots$$
$$C'_mC'_n \pm (t/d, s/z, st/zd).$$

[2] The full formula from which this is abbreviated is printed and explained in my paper "Linguistics as an exact science" in *Technol. Rev.*, December 1940, Massachusetts Institute of Technology, Cambridge, Mass. (p. 223 in this volume).

This formula requires that the English words be symbolized or "spelt" according to standard phonemic spelling of the type described by Leonard Bloomfield in his book *Language*. In this system the diphthongal vowels must be represented by a pure vowel (V) followed by *w* or *y* from the term (r, w, y), so that 'note' is symbolized *nowt* (or *newt*, depending on the dialect), 'date' is *deyt*, 'ice' is *ays*. That this is correct analysis on the physical or acoustic level is shown by the fact that, if we reverse a phonographic recording of 'ice' we get a sound like *sya*, and, if we say *sya* properly into the phonograph and reverse it, the machine will say 'ice.' For English this analysis happens to be exact also on the structural level two stages above the acoustic one, for the *ys* of *ays* (ice) is seen to be on the same line of pattern as the *ls* or *els* (else), the *ns* of *sins* (since) the *ts* of *hats*, etc.—it is part of a general architectonic scheme of having two consonants together.

Now, by reading the commas in the formula as "or," we see that the formula is equivalent to a large series of subsidiary formulas. One of the simplest of these is $O + V + C - h$ (see how it is contained in the big formula) which means that the word can begin without a consonant and with any one vowel, followed by any one consonant except *h*—giving us words like 'at, or, if.' Changing the first term to the next symbol in the big formula, we get $C - ng + V + C - h$, which means that the word, ending as before, can begin with any single English consonant except the *ng* sound as in 'sing' (this sound ought to be written with ONE symbol, but, in deference to the printer, I shall employ the usual digraph). This pattern gives us the long array of words like 'hat, bed, dog, man,' and permits us to coin new ones like 'tig, nem, zib'—but not, be it noted, *ngib* or *zih*.

So far the patterns are simple. From now on they become intricate! The formula in this abbreviated form needs along with it a series of lists of assorted consonants, like so many laundry lists, each list being represented by one of the symbols C_1, C_2, etc. The formula C_1C_2 means that you can begin the word with any consonant out of list C_1 and follow it with any from list C_2, which happens to contain only *r* and *l*. Since C_1 contains *p*, *b*, *f*, for instance, we can have words like 'pray, play, brew, blew, free, flee,' and the nonsensical 'frig, blosh,' etc. But suppose we want a word beginning with *sr*, *zr*, *tl*, or *dl*. We go to our list C_1, but to our surprise there is no *s*, *z*, *t*, or *d*, on it. We appear to be stumped! We pick up our other lists, but are no better off. There is no way of combining our lists according to the formula to get these initial combinations. Evidently there just aren't any such English words; and what is more, any budding Lewis Carrolls or Edward Lears will somehow mysteriously refuse to coin such words. This shows that word-coining is no act of unfettered imagination, even in the wildest flights of nonsense, but a strict use of already patterned materials. If asked to invent forms not already prefigured in the patternment of his language, the speaker is negative in the same manner as if asked to make fried eggs without the eggs!

Thus the formula sums up every combination that English one-syllable words or wordlike forms have, and bars out every one they do not and cannot have. Contained in it is the *mpst* of 'glimpsed,' the *ksths* of 'sixths,' the *ftht* of 'he fifthed it,' the *nchst* of the queer but possible 'thou *munchst* it greedily,' and multitudes of other "rugged sounds which to our mouths grow sleek," but which would have "made Quintilian stare and gasp." At the same time the formula BARS OUT numerous smooth but to us difficult (because unpatterned) combinations, like *litk*, *fpat*, *nwelng*, *dzogb*, and a myriad more, all possible and easy to some languages, but not to English.

It will be evident that implicit in our one-syllable words is an undreamed-of complexity of organization, and that the old gag, "say it in words of one syllable," as a metaphor of simplicity, is from the standpoint of a more penetrative insight the most arrant nonsense! Yet to such insight this old cliché bears unconscious witness to the truth that those who easily and fluently use the intricate systems of language are utterly blind and deaf to the very existence of those systems, until the latter have been, not without some difficulty, pointed out.

And the adage "as above, so below" applies strongly here. As below, on the phonological plane of language, significant behavior is ruled by pattern from outside the focus of personal consciousness, so is it on the higher planes of language that we call expression of the thought. As we shall see in Part II, thinking also follows a network of tracks laid down in the given language, an organization which may concentrate systematically upon certain phases of reality, certain aspects of intelligence, and may systematically discard others featured by other languages. The individual is utterly unaware of this organization and is constrained completely within its unbreakable bonds.

II

We saw in Part I that, in linguistic and mental phenomena, significant behavior (or what is the same, both behavior and significance, so far as interlinked) are ruled by a specific system or organization, a "geometry" of form principles characteristic of each language. This organization is imposed from outside the narrow circle of the personal consciousness, making of that consciousness a mere puppet whose linguistic maneuverings are held in unsensed and unbreakable bonds of pattern. It is as if the personal mind, which selects words but is largely oblivious to pattern, were in the grip of a higher, far more intellectual mind which has very little notion of houses and beds and soup kettles, but can systematize and mathematize on a scale and scope that no mathematician of the schools ever remotely approached.

And now appears a great fact of human brotherhood—that human beings are all alike in this respect. So far as we can judge from the systematics of language, the higher mind or "unconscious" of a Papuan headhunter can mathematize quite as well as that of Einstein; and conversely, scientist and yokel, scholar and tribesman, all use their personal consciousness in the same dim-witted sort of way, and get into similar kinds of logical impasse. They are as unaware of the beautiful and inexorable systems that control them as a cowherd is of cosmic rays. Their understanding of the processes involved in their talk and ratiocination is a purely superficial, pragmatic one, comparable to little Sue Smith's understanding of the radio, which she turns on in such a way as to evoke a bedtime story. Men even show a strong disposition to make a virtue of this ignorance, to condemn efforts at a better understanding of the mind's workings as "impractical," or as "theories" if the condemner happens to be a yokel, or as "metaphysics" or "mysticism" or "epistemology" if he happens to be wearing the traditionally correct turnout of a scientist. Western culture in particular reserves for the investigators of language its most grudging meed of recognition and its meagerest rewards, even though it has to counter the natural human tendency to find language, mysterious as it is, the most fascinating of subjects—one about which men love to talk and speculate unscientifically, to discuss endlessly the meaning of words, or the odd speech of the man from Boston as it appears to the man of Oshkosh, or vice versa.

The higher mind would seem to be able to do any kind of purely intellectual feat, but not to "be conscious" on the personal level. That is, it does not focus on practical affairs and on the personal ego in its personal, immediate environment. Certain dreams and exceptional mental states may lead us to suppose it to be conscious on its own plane, and occasionally its consciousness may "come through" to the personality; but, barring techniques like Yoga, it ordinarily makes no nexus with the personal consciousness. We could call it a higher ego, bearing in mind a distinctive trait, appearing through every language, and its one striking resemblance to the personal self; namely, that it organizes its systems around a nucleus of three or more pronominal "person" categories, centered upon one we call the first-person singular. It can function in any linguistic system—a child can learn any language with the same readiness, from Chinese, with its separately toned and stressed monosyllables, to Nootka of Vancouver Island, with its frequent one-word sentences such as *mamamamamahln'iqk'okmaqama*— 'they each did so because of their characteristic of resembling white people.' [3]

Because of the systematic, configurative nature of higher mind, the "patternment" aspect of language always overrides and controls the "lexation" (*Nāma*) or name-giving aspect. Hence the meanings of specific words are less important than we fondly fancy. Sentences, not words, are the essence of speech, just as equations and functions, and not bare numbers, are the real meat of mathematics. We are all mistaken in our common belief that any word has an "exact meaning." We have seen that the higher mind deals in symbols that have no fixed reference to anything, but are like blank checks, to be filled in as required, that stand for "any value" of a given variable, like the C's and V's in the formula cited in Part I, or the x, y, z of algebra. There is a queer Western notion that the ancients who invented algebra made a great discovery, though the human unconscious has been doing the same sort of thing for eons! For the same reason the ancient Mayas or the ancient Hindus, in their staggering cycles upon cycles of astronomical

[3] This word and sentence contains only one *Nāma* or lexation, *mamahl* or 'white-race person.' The rest is all grammatical pattern which can refer to anything. The Nootka stem or *Nāma* for 'doll' with the same operations done upon it would mean 'they each did so because of their doll-like-ness.'

numbers, were simply being human. We should not however make the mistake of thinking that words, even as used by the lower personal mind, represent the opposite pole from these variable symbols, that a word DOES have an exact meaning, stands for a given thing, is only ONE value of a variable.

Even the lower mind has caught something of the algebraic nature of language; so that words are in between the variable symbols of pure patternment (*Arūpa*) and true fixed quantities. That part of meaning which is in words, and which we may call "reference," is only relatively fixed. Reference of words is at the mercy of the sentences and grammatical patterns in which they occur. And it is surprising to what a minimal amount this element of reference may be reduced. The sentence "I went all the way down there just in order to see Jack" contains only one fixed concrete reference: namely, "Jack." The rest is pattern attached to nothing specifically; even "see" obviously does not mean what one might suppose, namely, to receive a visual image.

Or, again, in word reference we deal with size by breaking it into size classes—small, medium, large, immense, etc.—but size objectively is not divided into classes, but is a pure continuum of relativity. Yet we think of size constantly as a set of classes because language has segmented and named the experience in this way. Number words may refer not to number as counted, but to number classes with elastic boundaries. Thus English 'few' adjusts its range according to the size, importance or rarity of the reference. A 'few' kings, battleships, or diamonds might be only three or four, a 'few' peas, raindrops, or tea leaves might be thirty or forty.

You may say, "Yes, of course this is true of words like large, small, and the like; they are obviously relative terms, but words like dog, tree, house, are different—each names a specific thing." Not so; these terms are in the same boat as 'large' and 'small.' The word 'Fido' said by a certain person at a certain time may refer to a specific thing, but the word 'dog' refers to a class with elastic limits. The limits of such classes are different in different languages. You might think that 'tree' means the same thing, everywhere and to everybody. Not at all. The Polish word that means 'tree' also includes the meaning 'wood.' The context or sentence pattern determines what sort of object the Polish word (or any word, in any language) refers to. In Hopi, an American Indian language of Arizona, the word for 'dog,' *pohko*, includes pet animal or domestic animal of any kind. Thus 'pet eagle' in Hopi is literally 'eagle-dog'; and having thus fixed the context a Hopi might next refer to the same eagle as so-and-so's *pohko*.

But lest this be dismissed as the vagary of a "primitive" language (no language is "primitive"), let us take another peep at our own beloved English. Take the word "hand." In 'his hand' it refers to a location on the human body, in 'hour hand' to a strikingly dissimilar object, in 'all hands on deck' to another reference, in 'a good hand at gardening' to another, in 'he held a good hand (at cards)' to another, whereas in 'he got the upper hand' it refers to nothing but is dissolved into a pattern of orientation. Or consider the word 'bar' in the phrases: 'iron bar, bar to progress, he should be behind bars, studied for the bar, let down all the bars, bar of music, sand bar, candy bar, mosquito bar, bar sinister, bar none, ordered drinks at the bar'!

But, you may say, these are popular idioms, not scientific and logical use of language. Oh, indeed? "Electrical" is supposed to be a scientific word. Do you know what its referent is? Do you know that the "electrical" in "electrical apparatus" is not the same "electrical" as the one in "electrical expert"? In the first it refers to a current of electricity in the apparatus, but in the second it does not refer to a current of electricity in the expert. When a word like "group" can refer either to a sequence of phases in time or a pile of articles on the floor, its element of reference is minor. Referents of scientific words are often conveniently vague, markedly under the sway of the patterns in which they occur. It is very suggestive that this trait, so far from being a hallmark of Babbittry, is most marked in intellectual talk, and—*mirabile dictu*—in the language of poetry and love! And this needs must be so, for science, poetry, and love are alike in being "flights" above and away from the slave-world of literal reference and humdrum prosaic details, attempts to widen the petty narrowness of the personal self's outlook, liftings toward *Arūpa*, toward that world of infinite harmony, sympathy and order, of unchanging truths and eternal things. And while all words are pitiful enough in their mere "letter that killeth," it is certain that scientific terms like 'force, average, sex, allergic, biological' are not less pitiful, and in their own way no more certain in reference than 'sweet, gorgeous, rapture, enchantment, heart and soul, star dust.' You have probably heard of 'star dust'—what is it? Is it a multitude of stars, a sparkling powder, the soil of the planet Mars, the Milky Way, a state of daydreaming, poetic fancy, pyrophoric iron, a spiral nebula, a suburb of Pittsburgh, or a popular song? You don't know, and neither does anybody. The word—for it is one LEXATION, not two—has no reference of its own. Some words are like that.[4] As we have seen, reference is the lesser part of meaning, patternment the greater. Science, the quest for truth, is a sort of divine madness like love. And music—is it not in the same category? Music is a quasilanguage based entirely on patternment, without having developed lexation.

Sometimes the sway of pattern over reference produces amusing results, when a pattern engenders meanings utterly extraneous to the original lexation reference. The lower mind is thrown into bewilderment, cannot grasp that compelling formulas are at work upon it, and resorts wildly and with glad relief to its favorite obvious type of explanation, even "seeing things" and "hearing things" that help out such explanation. The word 'asparagus,' under the stress of purely phonetic English patterns of the type illustrated in the formula cited in Part I, rearranges to 'sparagras'; and then since 'sparrer' is a dialectical form of 'sparrow,' we find 'sparrow grass' and then religiously accepted accounts of the relation of sparrows to this 'grass.' 'Cole slaw' came from German *Kohlsalat*, 'cabbage salad,' but the stress of the pattern tending to revamp it into 'cold slaw' has in some regions produced a new lexation 'slaw,' and a new dish 'hot slaw'! Children of course are constantly repatterning, but the pressure of adult example eventually brings their language back to the norm; they learn that Mississippi is not Mrs. Sippy, and the equator is not a menagerie lion but an imaginary line. Sometimes the adult community does not possess the special knowledge needed for correction. In parts of New England, Persian cats of a certain type are called Coon cats, and this name has bred the notion that they are a hybrid between the cat and the 'coon' (raccoon). This is often firmly believed by persons ignorant of biology, since the stress of the linguistic pattern (animal-name 1 modifying animal-name 2) causes them to "see" (or as the psychologists say "project") objective raccoon quality as located on the body of the cat—they point to its bushy tail, long hair, and so on. I knew of an actual case, a woman who owned

[4] Compare 'kith' and 'throe,' which give no meaning, and a bewildering effect, without the patterns 'kith and kin' and 'in throes of.'

a fine "Coon cat," and who would protest to her friend: "Why, just LOOK at him—his tail, his funny eyes—can't you see it?" "Don't be silly!" quoth her more sophisticated friend. "Think of your natural history! Coons cannot breed with cats; they belong to a different family." But the lady was so sure that she called on an eminent zoologist to confirm her. He is said to have remarked, with unwavering diplomacy, "If you like to think so, just think so." "He was even more cruel than you!" she snapped at her friend, and remained convinced that her pet was the outcome of an encounter between a philandering raccoon and a wayward cat! In just such ways on a vaster scale is woven the web of Māyā, illusion begotten of intrenched selfhood. I am told that Coon cats received their name from one Captain Coon, who brought the first of these Persian cats to the State of Maine in his ship.

In more subtle matters we all, unknowingly, project the linguistic relationships of a particular language upon the universe, and SEE them there, as the good lady SAW a linguistic relation (Coon = raccoon) made visible in her cat. We say 'see that wave'—the same pattern as 'see that house.' But without the projection of language no one ever saw a single wave. We see a surface in everchanging undulating motions. Some languages cannot say 'a wave'; they are closer to reality in this respect. Hopi say *walalata*, 'plural waving occurs,' and can call attention to one place in the waving just as we can. But, since actually a wave cannot exist by itself, the form that corresponds to our singular, *wala*, is not the equivalent of English 'a wave,' but means 'a slosh occurs,' as when a vessel of liquid is suddenly jarred.

English pattern treats 'I hold it' exactly like 'I strike it,' 'I tear it,' and myriads of other propositions that refer to actions effecting changes in matter. Yet 'hold' in plain fact is no action, but a state of relative positions. But we think of it, even see it, as an action, because language sets up the proposition in the same way as it sets up a much more common class of propositions dealing with movements and changes. We ASCRIBE action to what we call "hold" because the formula, substantive + verb = actor + his action, is fundamental in our sentences. Thus we are compelled in many cases to read into nature fictitious acting-entities simply because our sentence patterns require our verbs, when not imperative, to have substantives before them. We are obliged to say 'it flashed' or 'a light flashed,' setting up an actor IT, or A LIGHT, to perform what we call an action, FLASH. But the flashing and the light are the same; there is no thing which does something, and no doing. Hopi says only *rehpi*. Hopi can have verbs without subjects, and this gives to that language power as a logical system for understanding certain aspects of the cosmos. Scientific language, being founded on western Indo-European and not on Hopi, does as we do, sees sometimes actions and forces where there may be only states. For do you not conceive it possible that scientists as well as ladies with cats all unknowingly project the linguistic patterns of a particular type of language upon the universe, and SEE them there, rendered visible on the very face of nature? A change in language can transform our appreciation of the Cosmos.

All this is typical of the way the lower personal mind, caught in a vaster world inscrutable to its methods, uses its strange gift of language to weave the web of Māyā or illusion, to make a provisional analysis of reality and then regard it as final. Western culture has gone farthest here, farthest in determined thoroughness of provisional analysis, and farthest in determination to regard it as final. The commitment to illusion has been sealed in western Indo-European language, and the road out of illusion for the West lies through a wider understanding of language than western Indo-European alone can give. This is the "Mantra Yoga" of the Western consciousness, the next great step, which it is now ready to take. It is probably the most suitable way for Western man to begin that "culture of consciousness" which will lead him to a great illumination.

Again, through this sort of understanding of language is achieved a great phase of human brotherhood. For the scientific understanding of very diverse languages—not necessarily to speak them, but to analyze their structure—is a lesson in brotherhood which is brotherhood in the universal human principle—the brotherhood of the "Sons of Manas." It causes us to transcend the boundaries of local cultures, nationalities, physical peculiarities dubbed "race," and to find that in their linguistic systems, though these systems differ widely, yet in the order, harmony, and beauty of the systems, and in their respective subtleties and penetrating analysis of reality, all men are equal. This fact is independent of the state of evolution as regards material culture, savagery, civilization, moral or ethical development, etc., a thing most surprising to the cultured European, a thing shocking to him, indeed a bitter pill! But it is true; the crudest savage may unconsciously manipulate with effortless ease a linguistic system so intricate, manifoldly systematized, and intellectually difficult that it requires the lifetime study of our greatest scholars to describe its workings. The manasic plane and the "higher ego" have been given to all, and the evolution of human language was complete, and spread in its proud completeness up and down the earth, in a time far anterior to the oldest ruin that molders in the soil today.

Linguistic knowledge entails understanding many different beautiful systems of logical analysis. Through it, the world as seen from the diverse viewpoints of other social groups, that we have thought of as alien, becomes intelligible in new terms. Alienness turns into a new and often clarifying way of looking at things. Consider Japanese. The view of the Japanese that we get outwardly from their governmental policy seems anything but conducive to brotherhood. But to approach the Japanese through an aesthetic and scientific appreciation of their language transforms the picture. THAT is to realize kinship on the cosmopolitan levels of the spirit. One lovely pattern of this language is that its sentence may have two differently ranked subjects. We are familiar with the idea of two ranks of OBJECTS for our verbs, an immediate and a more remote goal, or direct and indirect object as they are commonly called. We have probably never thought of the possibilities of a similar idea applied to SUBJECTS. This idea is put to work in Japanese. The two subjects—call them subject 1 and subject 2—are marked by the particles *wa* and *ga*, and a diagram might show them with a line drawn from each subject word, the two lines converging upon the same predication, whereas our English sentence could have only one subject with one line to the predicate. An example would be the way of saying "Japan is mountainous": "Japan$_1$ mountain$_2$ (are) many"; [5] or: "Japan, in regard to its mountains are many." "John is long-legged" would be "John$_1$ leg$_2$ (are) long." This pattern gives great conciseness at the same time with great precision. Instead of the vagueness of our "mountainous," the Japanese can, with equal compactness of formulation, distinguish "mountainous" meaning that mountains not always high are abundant, from "mountainous" meaning that mountains not abundant relative to the whole area are high. We see how the logical uses of this pattern would give to Japanese great power in

---

[5] "Are" is in parentheses because "be many" is expressed by a single verblike word. The Japanese ordinarily does not use a plural.

concise scientific operations with ideas, could this power be properly developed.

The moment we begin scientific, unbiased RESEARCH into language we find, in people and cultures with the most unprepossessing exteriors, beautiful, effective, and scientific devices of expression unknown to western Indo-European tongues or mentalities. The Algonkian languages are spoken by very simple people, hunting and fishing Indians, but they are marvels of analysis and synthesis. One piece of grammatical finesse peculiar to them is called the obviative. This means that their pronouns have four persons instead of three, or from our standpoint two third persons. This aids in compact description of complicated situations, for which we should have to resort to cumbersome phraseology. Let us symbolize their third and fourth persons by attaching the numerals 3 and 4 to our written words. The Algonkians might tell the story of William Tell like this: "William Tell called his$_3$ son and told him$_4$ to bring him$_3$ his$_3$ bow and arrow, which$_4$ he$_4$ then brought to him$_3$. He$_3$ had him$_4$ stand still and placed an apple on his$_4$ head, then took his$_3$ bow and arrow and told him$_4$ not to fear. Then he$_3$ shot it$_4$ off his$_4$ head without hurting him$_4$." Such a device would greatly help in specifying our complex legal situations, getting rid of "the party of the first part" and "the aforesaid John Doe shall, on his part, etc."

Chichewa, a language related to Zulu, spoken by a tribe of unlettered Negroes in East Africa, has two past tenses, one for past events with present result or influence, one for past without present influence. A past as recorded in external situations is distinguished from a past recorded only in the psyche or memory; a new view of TIME opens before us. Let 1 represent the former and 2 the latter; then ponder these Chichewa nuances: I came$_1$ here; I went$_2$ there; he was$_2$ sick; he died$_1$; Christ died$_2$ on the cross; God created$_1$ the world. "I ate$_1$" means I am not hungry; "I ate$_2$" means I am hungry. If you were offered food and said: "No, I have eaten$_1$," it would be all right, but if you used the other past tense you would be uttering an insult. A Theosophical speaker of Chichewa might use tense 1 in speaking of the past involution of Monads, which has enabled the world to be in its present state, while he might use tense 2 for, say, long-past planetary systems now disintegrated and their evolution done. If he were talking about Reincarnation, he would use 2 for events of a past incarnation simply in their own frame of reference, but he would use 1 in referring to or implying their "Karma." It may be that these primitive folk are equipped with a language which, if they were to become philosophers or mathematicians, could make them our foremost thinkers upon TIME.

Or take the Coeur d'Alene language, spoken by the small Indian tribe of that name in Idaho. Instead of our simple concept of "cause," founded on our simple "makes it (him) do so," the Coeur d'Alene grammar requires its speakers to discriminate (which of course they do automatically) among three causal processes, denoted by three causal verb-forms: (1) growth, or maturation of an inherent cause, (2) addition or accretion from without, (3) secondary addition i.e., of something affected by process 2. Thus, to say "it has been made sweet" they would use form 1 for a plum sweetened by ripening, form 2 for a cup of coffee sweetened by dissolving sugar in it, and form 3 for griddle cakes sweetened by syrup made by dissolving sugar. If, given a more sophisticated culture, their thinkers erected these now unconscious discriminations into a theory of triadic causality, fitted to scientific observations, they might thereby produce a valuable intellectual tool for science. WE could imitate artificially such a theory, perhaps, but we could NOT apply it, for WE are not habituated to making such distinctions with effortless ease in daily life. Concepts have a basis in daily talk before scientific workers will attempt to use them in the laboratory. Even relativity has such a basis in the western Indo-European languages (and others)—the fact that these languages use many space words and patterns for dealing with time.

Language has further significance in other psychological factors on a different level from modern linguistic approach but of importance in music, poetry, literary style, and Eastern mantram. What I have been speaking of thus far concerns the plane of Manas in the more philosophical sense, the "higher unconscious" or the "soul" (in the sense as used by Jung). What I am about to speak of concerns the "psyche" (in the sense as used by Freud), the "lower" unconscious, the Manas which is especially the "slayer of the real," the plane of Kāma, of emotion or rather feeling (*Gefühl*). In a serial relation containing the levels of Nāma-Rūpa and Arūpa, this level of the unconscious psyche is on the other side of Nāma-Rūpa from Arūpa, and Nāma or lexation mediates in a sense between these extremes. Hence the psyche is the psychological correlative of the phonemic level in language, related to it not structurally as is Nāma or lexation, not by using it as building blocks, as word-making uses the phonemes (vowels, consonants, accents, etc.), but related as the feeling-content of the phonemes. There is a universal, *Gefühl*-type way of linking experiences, which shows up in laboratory experiments and appears to be independent of language—basically alike for all persons.

Without a serial or hierarchical order in the universe it would have to be said that these psychological experiments and linguistic experiments contradict each other. In the psychological experiments human subjects seem to associate the experiences of bright, cold, sharp, hard, high, light (in weight), quick, high-pitched, narrow, and so on in a long series, with each other; and conversely the experiences of dark, warm, yielding, soft, blunt, low, heavy, slow, low-pitched, wide, etc., in another long series. This occurs whether the WORDS for such associated experiences resemble or not, but the ordinary person is likely to NOTICE a relation to words only when it is a relation of likeness to such a series in the vowels or consonants of the words, and when it is a relation of contrast or conflict it is passed unnoticed. The noticing of the relation of likeness is an element in sensitiveness to literary style or to what is often rather inaccurately called the "music" of words. The noticing of the relation of conflict is much more difficult, much more a freeing oneself from illusion, and though quite "unpoetical" it is really a movement toward Higher Manas, toward a higher symmetry than that of physical sound.

What is significant for our thesis is that language, through lexation, has made the speaker more acutely conscious of certain dim psychic sensations; it has actually produced awareness on lower planes than its own: a power of the nature of magic. There is a yogic mastery in the power of language to remain independent of lower-psyche facts, to override them, now point them up, now toss them out of the picture, to mold the nuances of words to its own rule, whether the psychic ring of the sounds fits or not. If the sounds fit, the psychic quality of the sounds is increased, and this can be noticed by the layman. If the sounds do not fit, the psychic quality changes to accord with the linguistic meaning, no matter how incongruous with the sounds, and this is not noticed by the layman.

Thus the vowels *a* (as in 'father'), *o*, *u*, are associated in the laboratory tests with the dark-warm-soft series, and *e* (English *a* in 'date'), *i* (English *e* in 'be') with the bright-cold-sharp set. Consonants also are associated about as one might expect from ordinary naïve feeling in the matter. What happens is that, when a word has an acoustic similarity to its own meaning, we can notice it, as in English 'soft' and German *sanft*. But, when the opposite occurs, nobody notices it. Thus German *zart* (*tsart*) 'tender' has such a "sharp" sound, in spite of its *a*, that to a person who does not know German it calls up the bright-sharp meanings, but to a German it "sounds" soft—and probably warm, dark, etc., also. An even better case is DEEP. Its acoustic association should be like that of PEEP or of such nonsense words as VEEP, TREEP, QUEEP, etc., i.e., as bright, sharp, quick. But its linguistic meaning in the English language happens to refer to the wrong sort of experience for such an association. This fact completely overrides its objective sound, causing it to "sound" subjectively quite as dark, warm, heavy, soft, etc., as though its sounds really were of that type. It takes illusion-freeing, if unpoetic, linguistic analysis to discover this clash between two "musics," one more mental and one more psychic, in the word. Manas is able to disregard properties of the psychic plane, just as it can disregard whether an equational *x* refers to automobiles or sheep. It can project parts of its own patterns upon experience in such a way that they distort, and promote illusion, or again in such a way that they illuminate, and build up scientific theories and tools of research.

Yoga is defined by Patanjali as the complete cessation of the activity of the versatile psychic nature.[6] We have seen that this activity consists largely of personal-social reactions along unperceived tracks of pattern laid down from the Arūpa level functioning above or behind the focus of personal consciousness. The reason why the Arūpa level is beyond the ken of the consciousness is not because it is essentially different (as if it were, e.g., a passive network) but because the personality does focus, from evolution and habit, upon the aforesaid versatile activity. The stilling of this activity and the coming to rest of this focus, though difficult and requiring prolonged training, is by reliable accounts

---

[6] Bragdon's paraphrase of the Yoga Sūtras, *An Introduction to Yoga*, Claude Bragdon, New York, 1933.

from widely diverse sources, both Eastern and Western, a tremendous expansion, brightening and clarifying of consciousness, in which the intellect functions with undreamed-of rapidity and sureness. The scientific study of languages and linguistic principles is at least a partial raising of the intellect toward this level. In the understanding of a large linguistic pattern there is involved a partial shift of focus away from the versatile psychic activity. Such understandings have even a therapeutic value. Many neuroses are simply the compulsive working over and over of word systems, from which the patient can be freed by showing him the process and pattern.

All this leads back to the idea touched upon in part I of this essay, that the types of patterned relationship found in language may be but the wavering and distorted, pale, substanceless reflection of a CAUSAL WORLD. Just as language consists of discrete lexation-segmentation (Nāma-Rūpa) and ordered patternment, of which the latter has the more background character, less obvious but more infrangible and universal, so the physical world may be an aggregate of quasidiscrete entities (atoms, crystals, living organisms, planets, stars, etc.) not fully understandable as such, but rather emergent from a field of causes that is itself a manifold of pattern and order. It is upon the bars of the fence, beyond which it would meet these CHARACTERS OF THE FIELD, that science is now poised. As physics explores into the intra-atomic phenomena, the discrete physical forms and forces are more and more dissolved into relations of pure patternment. The PLACE of an apparent entity, an electron for example, becomes indefinite, interrupted; the entity appears and disappears from one structural position to another structural position, like a phoneme or any other patterned linguistic entity, and may be said to be NOWHERE in between the positions. Its locus, first thought of and analyzed as a continuous variable, becomes on closer scrutiny a mere alternation; situations "actualize" it, structure beyond the probe of the measuring rod governs it; three-dimensional shape there is none, instead—"Arūpa."

Science cannot yet understand the transcendental logic of such a state of affairs, for it has not yet freed itself from the illusory necessities of common logic which are only at bottom necessities of grammatical pattern in Western Aryan grammar; necessities for substances which are only necessities for substantives in certain sentence positions, necessities for forces, attractions, etc. which are only necessities for verbs in certain other positions, and so on. Science, if it survives the impending darkness, will next take up the consideration of linguistic principles and divest itself of these illusory linguistic necessities, too long held to be the substance of Reason itself.

BIBLIOGRAPHY

A. PUBLISHED WRITINGS OF BENJAMIN LEE WHORF

Date
of
Composition

1925   "Purpose vs. evolution." Letter to the editors of the *New Republic*, issue of December 19, 1925.

1927   ["On the connection of ideas."] Printed for the first time in this volume, pp. 35–39.

1928   "Toltec history." Twenty-Third International Congress of Americanists, New York, 1928: *Abstracts of Papers*, no. 109.

1928   "Aztec linguistics." Twenty-Third International Congress of Americanists, New York, 1928: *Abstracts of Papers*, no. 116.

1928   "An Aztec account of the period of the Toltec decline." *Proceedings of the Twenty-Third International Congress of Americanists*, New York, 1928, pp. 122–129.

1929   "The reign of Huemac." *American Anthropologist*, 31:667–684 (1929).

1931   "A central Mexican inscription combining Mexican and Maya day signs." *American Anthropologist*, 34:296–302 (1932).

1933   "The Maya manuscript in Dresden." *Art and Archaeology*, 34:270 (1933).

1933   *The phonetic value of certain characters in Maya writing.* Cambridge, Mass.: Harvard University Press, 1933 (*Papers of the Peabody Museum*, vol. XIII, no. 2). With an introduction by Alfred M. Tozzer. xii, 48 pp.

1935   Review of A. L. Kroeber, *Uto-Aztecan languages of Mexico*. *American Anthropologist*, 37:343–345 (1935).

1935   "The comparative linguistics of Uto-Aztecan." *American Anthropologist*, 37:600–608 (1935).

1935   "Maya writing and its decipherment." *Maya Research*, 2:367–382 (1935).

271

Date
of
Composition

1936   Appendix to J. Alden Mason, "The classification of the Sonoran
            languages," pp. 197–198 in Robert H. Lowie (editor), *Essays
            in anthropology in honor of Alfred Louis Kroeber.* Berkeley:
            University of California Press, 1936.

1936   Notes on the "Glossary," pp. 1198–1326 in Elsie Clews Parsons,
            Hopi Journal of Alexander M. Stephens, Part 2. New York:
            Columbia University Press, 1936 (*Columbia Contributions to
            Anthropology,* 23).

1936   "The punctual and segmentative aspects of verbs in Hopi."
            Language, 12:127–131 (1936).

1936   "Notes on the Tübatulabal language." *American Anthropolo-
            gist,* 38:341–344 (1936).

1936   "Loan-words in ancient Mexico." *Philological and Documentary
            Studies* (*Middle American Research Institute, Tulane Univer-
            sity of Louisiana*), 1:1–17 (1943). Also *Studies in Linguistics,*
            5:49–64 (1947).

1936(?)   "An American Indian model of the universe." *International
            Journal of American Linguistics,* 16:67–72 (1950).
            [Reprinted in *Etc., a Review of General Semantics,* 8:27–33
            (1950); also in *Collected papers on metalinguistics,* Foreign
            Service Institute, Department of State, Washington, D. C.,
            1952.]

1936(?)   "A linguistic consideration of thinking in primitive communi-
            ties." Printed for the first time in this volume, pp. 65–86.

1937   "The origin of Aztec TL." *American Anthropologist,* 39:265–
            274 (1937).

1937   (with George L. Trager) "The relationship of Uto-Aztecan and
            Tanoan." *American Anthropologist,* 39:609–624 (1937).

1937   "Grammatical categories." *Language,* 21:1–11 (1945).

1937   ["Discussion of Hopi linguistics."] Printed for the first time in
            this volume, pp. 102–111.

1938   "Some verbal categories of Hopi." *Language,* 14:275–286
            (1938)

1938   Review of K. T. Preuss and Ernst Mengin, *Die Mexikanische
            Bilderhandschrift Historia Tolteca-Chichimeca: die Manu-
            scripte 46–58bis der Nationalbibliothek in Paris,* Teil I, *Die
            Bilderschrift nebst Übersetzung* (Berlin, 1937). *American An-
            thropologist,* 40:729–730 (1938).

1938   "Language: plan and conception of arrangement." Printed for
            the first time in this volume, pp. 125–133.

1939   "The relation of habitual thought and behavior to language."
            Pp. 75–93 in Leslie Spier (editor), *Language, culture, and per-*

Date
of
Composition

sonality (Menasha, Wis.: Sapir Memorial Publication Fund, 1941).

[Reprinted in *Collected papers on metalinguistics*, Foreign Service Institute, Department of State, Washington, D. C., 1952.]

1939 "The Hopi Language, Toreva dialect." Pp. 158–183 in Harry Hoijer (editor), *Linguistic structures of native America* (New York: Viking Fund, 1946).

1939 "The Milpa Alta dialect of Aztec, with notes on the Classical and the Tepoztlán dialects." Pp. 367–397 in Harry Hoijer (editor), *Linguistic structures of native America* (New York: Viking Fund, 1946).

1939 "Gestalt technique of stem composition in Shawnee." Appendix, pp. 393–406, to C. F. Voegelin, *Shawnee stems and the Jacob P. Dunn Miami Dictionary.* Indianapolis: Indiana Historical Society, 1940 (*Prehistory Research Series*, vol. I, no. 9, April 1940).

1940 "Blazing icicles." [Article on fire prevention] Hartford, Conn.: Hartford Fire Insurance Company, n.d. [Reprinted from the *Hartford Agent.*]

1940 "Decipherment of the linguistic portion of the Maya hieroglyphs," pp. 479–502 in *The Smithsonian report for 1941,* Publication 3669 (Washington: U. S. Government Printing Office, 1942). [Also in Spanish, "Interpretacion de la parte lingüistica de los geroglificos Maya." *Tzunpame, Órgano de Publicidad del Museo Nacional y Auexos (San Salvador),* 5:50–73 (August 1945), and *Suplemento* (Figures 1–4).]

1940 "Phonemic analysis of the English of eastern Massachusetts." *Studies in Linguistics,* 2:21–40 (1943).

1940 "Linguistic factors in the terminology of Hopi architecture." *International Journal of American Linguistics,* 19:141–145 (1953).

1940 "Science and linguistics." *Technology Review (M.I.T.),* 42:229–231, 247–248 (1940).

[Reprinted in S. I. Hayakawa, *Language in action* (New York: Harcourt-Brace, 1941), pp. 302–321; T. Newcomb and E. Hartley, *Readings in social psychology* (New York: Holt, 1947), pp. 210–218; and *Collected papers on metalinguistics* (Foreign Service Institute, Department of State, Washington, D. C., 1952).]

1940 "Linguistics as an exact science." *Technology Review (M.I.T.),* 43:61–63, 80–83 (1940).

Date
of
Composition

[Reprinted in *Collected papers on metalinguistics* (Foreign Service Institute, Department of State, Washington, D. C., 1952).]

1941   "Languages and logic." *Technology Review* (M.I.T.), 43:250–252, 266, 268, 272 (1941).
[Reprinted in *Collected papers on metalinguistics* (Foreign Service Institute, Department of State, Washington, D. C., 1952).]

1941   "Language, mind, and reality." *The Theosophist* (*Madras, India*), 63:1.281–91 (January 1942); 63:2.25–37 (April 1942).
[Reprinted in *Etc., a Review of General Semantics*, 9:167–188 (1952).]

1940–41   Articles in the journal *Main Currents in Modern Thought*:
1:1.3–5 (1940): Review of *Living light*, by E. N. Harvey (Princeton University Press, 1940).

1:1.9–10 (1940): "We may end the war that is within all wars that are waged to end all war."

1:1.12–13 (1940): Digest of review in *American Anthropologist*, October–December 1940, of the *Work of the gods in Tikopia* (Polynesia), by Raymond Firth, as reviewed by E. G. Burrows.

1:1.14 (1940): Digest of "Notes on the demonstration of 'wetter' water," by C. R. Caryl in *Journal of Chemical Education*.

1:1.15 (1940): [Concerning descriptive linguistics at Yale.]

1:3.4 (1941): (with F. Kunz) [Commentary regarding logic and science.]

1:3.6 (1941): "H. G. Wells."

1:3.12–13 (1941): "Interpretations of isotopes."

1:3.15 (1941): "The Hurrians of Old Chaldea."

1:4.10–11 (1941): Review of *The ways of things*, by W. P. Montague (Prentice-Hall, 1940).

1:4.13–14 (1941): "A brotherhood of thought."

1:5.12–14 (1941): "Dr. Reiser's humanism." (Review of *The promise of scientific humanism*, by Oliver L. Reiser, New York, 1940).

1:6.16 (1941): [Note on shrinking glass.]

1:7.14–15 (1941): (with F. Kunz) "Toward a higher mental world."

Unknown   ["On psychology."]   Printed for the first time in this volume, pages 40–42.

B. UNPUBLISHED MANUSCRIPTS (SELECTED)

Date
of
Composition

c. 1928   "A contribution to the study of the Aztec language."   43 pp.   A
detailed linguistic and literary treatment of the second poem
found in D. G. Brinton's compilation (*Ancient Nahuatl
poetry*), with Appendix A, Original text of the poem, and
Appendix B, A list of the most common roots in the Aztec
language.   Manuscript 157, Franz Boas collection (See *Language Monograph* no. 22, 1945).   Another copy in family
papers.

1928   "Investigations in Aztec linguistics and Toltec history.   Part II.
The phenomenon of oligosynthesis in Nahuatl or Aztec."   13
pp.   [This paper was given before the Twenty-third International Congress of Americanists, New York, September
1928.]   Among family papers.

1928   "Notes on the oligosynthetic comparison of Nahuatl and Piman,
with special reference to Tepecano."   23 pp.   Among family
papers.   [This manuscript was submitted as a supporting document when the author applied for an SSRC Research Fellowship, December 1, 1928.]

1930   "Stem series in Maya and certain Maya hieroglyphs."   28 pp.
Among family papers.   [This is a revision, dated October 30,
1930, of a paper read before the Linguistic Society of America,
Cleveland meeting, December 1929.   It was further revised
and published as *The phonetic value of certain characters in
Maya writing*.   (1933)]

1930   "Notes on two recent findings from central Mexico."   7 pp.
MS in the library of Peabody Museum, Harvard University.
[This is the text of a paper read before the American Anthropological Association, Cleveland meeting, December 1930.   It
is a summary of material later prepared (1) in the article "A
central Mexican inscription combining Mexican and Maya
day signs" (1931), and (2) in the unpublished manuscript
listed below for the year 1931, "Pitch tone and the saltillo in
modern and ancient Nahuatl."]

1931   "The problem of American history before Columbus."   55 pp.
Among family papers.   Annotated in pencil, "Read before
Conn. Historical Society, Hartford, Conn., Apr. 7, 1931."

1931   "Pitch tone and the saltillo in modern and ancient Nahuatl."
54 pp.   Manuscript 275, Franz Boas collection (See *Language
Monograph* no. 22, 1945).

Date
of
Composition

1932–5(?) "First report on Hopi." 4 pp. MS 276, Franz Boas collection (See *Language Monograph* no. 22, 1945).

1933 "Recent determinations of phonetic characters in Maya writing." 8 pp. Among family papers. [Read before Linguistic Society of America, Washington meeting, December 1933. Amplifies and goes beyond analysis published (1933) in the Peabody Museum papers.]

1935 "The Hopi language." 59 pp. Original among family papers, with note "corrected and corrections rechecked—BLW." Carbon copy is Manuscript 192, Franz Boas collection (See *Language Monograph* no. 22, 1945).

1935(?) "First steps in the decipherment of Maya writing." 112 pp. Among family papers. [Mentioned in "Maya writing and its decipherment" (1935) as being worked on—"it may be a year before publication."]

1936 "A comparative decipherment of forty-one ancient Maya written words." 10 pp. MS among family papers. [Text of paper read before American Anthropological Association, Washington meeting, December 1936.]

1938 "The reading of Maya glyph C of the Supplementary Series and other glyphs." Abstract and pencil draft of paper. MS among family papers.

1939 "Classification of the languages of North America north of Mexico." Typewritten MS, 3 pp., dated December 1939, among papers of G. L. Trager. [Apparently the basis of a talk, "Linguistic groupings north of Mexico," before American Anthropological Association, Chicago meeting, December 1939.]

1940 "The 'parts of speech' in Hopi." 15 pp., handwritten, MS among family papers. Annotated "finished Oct. 12, 1940."

C. BOOKS AND ARTICLES
RELATING TO WHORF'S WRITINGS (SELECTED)

Andrews, E. Wyllys. "The phonetic value of Glyph C of the Maya supplementary series." *American Anthropologist*, 40:755–758 (1938).

Brown, Roger W., and Lenneberg, Eric H. "A study in language and cognition." *Journal of Abnormal and Social Psychology*, 49:454–462 (1954).

Carroll, John B. Foreword to Whorf's "Language, mind and reality." *Etc., a Review of General Semantics*, 9:167–168 (1952).

Carroll, John B. *The study of language.* Cambridge: Harvard University Press, 1953.

Chase, Stuart. "How language shapes our thoughts." *Harper's Magazine,* April 1954, pp. 76–82.

Chase, Stuart. *The power of words.* New York: Harcourt, Brace, 1954.

Doob, L. W. *Social psychology.* New York: Holt, 1952.

Feuer, Lewis S. "Sociological aspects of the relation between language and philosophy." *Philosophy of Science,* 20:85–100 (1953).

Hackett, Herbert. "Bibliography of the writings of Benjamin Lee Whorf." *Etc., a Review of General Semantics,* 9:189–191 (1952). [The present bibliography represents a revision and expansion of Hackett's bibliography.]

Hackett, Herbert. "Benjamin Lee Whorf." *Word Study,* 29:3.1–4 (1954).

Hoijer, Harry. "The relation of language to culture." Pp. 554–573 in A. L. Kroeber (editor), *Anthropology today.* Chicago: University of Chicago Press, 1953.

Hoijer, Harry (editor). *Language in culture; conference on the interrelations of language and other aspects of culture.* With papers by F. Fearing, J. H. Greenberg, C. F. Hockett, H. Hoijer, N. A. McQuown, S. Newman, C. F. Voegelin, J. F. Yegerlehner, and Florence M. Robinett. Chicago: University of Chicago Press, 1954. (Also published as Memoir 79 of the American Anthropological Association.)

Kluckhohn, Clyde, and Leighton, Dorothea. *The Navaho.* Cambridge: Harvard University Press, 1946.

Kluckhohn, Clyde. "Culture and behavior." Chapter 25, pp. 921–976 in Gardner Lindzey (editor), *Handbook of social psychology.* Cambridge: Addison-Wesley Press, 1954.

Kluckhohn, Clyde, and MacLeish, Kenneth. "Moencopi variations from Whorf's Second Mesa Hopi. *International Journal of American Linguistics,* 21:150–156 (1955).

Lenneberg, Eric H. "Cognition in ethnolinguistics." *Language,* 29:463–471 (1953).

Long, Richard C. E. "Maya and Mexican writing." *Maya Research,* 2:24–32 (1935).

Long, Richard C. E. "Maya writing and its decipherment." *Maya Research,* 3:309–315 (1936).

Mason, J. Alden. "The native languages of Middle America." Pp. 52–87 in *The Maya and their neighbors.* New York: D. Appleton-Century Co., 1940.

Murdock, George P., *et al. Outline of cultural materials.* New Haven: Institute of Human Relations, Yale University, 1938.

Osgood, Charles E., and Sebeok, Thomas A. (editors). *Psycholinguistics: a survey of theory and research problems.* Indiana University Publications in Anthropology and Linguistics, Memoir 10, 1954. (Also issued as a supplement to vol. 49, *Journal of Abnormal and Social Psychology,* 1954.)

Thompson, J. Eric S. "Pitfalls and stimuli in the interpretation of history through loan words." *Philological and Documentary Studies* (*Middle American Research Institute, Tulane University of Louisiana*), 1:2 (1943).

Thompson, J. Eric S. *Maya hieroglyphic writing: introduction.* Washington, D. C.: Carnegie Institution of Washington (Publication 589), 1950. Appendix III: "Whorf's attempts to decipher the Maya hieroglyphs."

Thompson, Laura M. *Culture in crisis.* New York: Harper, 1950. [Chapter 8, pp. 152–172, includes excerpts from Whorf's writings.]

Tozzer, Alfred M. (editor). *Landa's Relación de las cosas de Yucatan.* Cambridge, Mass., 1941 (*Papers of the Peabody Museum of American Archaeology and Ethnology, Harvard University*).

Trager, George L. "Comments on B. L. Whorf's 'Phonemic analysis of the English of eastern Massachusetts.'" *Studies in Linguistics*, 2:41–45 (1943).

THE M.I.T. PRESS PAPERBACK SERIES